AUTOBIOGRAPHY AND OTHER WRITINGS

THE
OTHER VOICE
IN
EARLY MODERN
EUROPE

A Series Edited by Margaret L. King and Albert Rabil Jr.

RECENT BOOKS IN THE SERIES

Ana de San Bartolomé

AUTOBIOGRAPHY AND
OTHER WRITINGS

ꮬ

Edited and Translated by
Darcy Donahue

THE UNIVERSITY OF CHICAGO PRESS
Chicago & London

Ana de San Bartolomé, 1549–1626

Darcy Donahue is associate professor of Spanish and women's studies at Miami University, Oxford, Ohio.

The University of Chicago Press, Chicago 60637
The University of Chicago Press, Ltd., London
© 2008 by The University of Chicago
All rights reserved. Published 2008
Printed in the United States of America

17 16 15 14 13 12 11 10 09 08   1 2 3 4 5

ISBN-13: 978-0-226-14371-2 (cloth)
ISBN-13: 978-0-226-14372-9 (paper)
ISBN-10: 0-226-14371-6 (cloth)
ISBN-10: 0-226-14372-4 (paper)

The University of Chicago Press gratefully acknowledges the generous support of James E. Rabil, in memory of Scottie W. Rabil, toward the publication of this book.

Library of Congress Cataloging-in-Publcation Data
Anne of St. Bartholomew, Mother, 1550–1626.
[Autobiografia. English]
Autobiography and other writings / Ana de San Bartolomé ;
edited and translated by Darcy Donahue.
p. cm. — (The other voice in early modern Europe)
Includes index.
ISBN-13: 978-0-226-14371-2 (cloth : alk. paper)
ISBN-13: 978-0-226-14372-9 (pbk. : alk. paper)
ISBN-10: 0-226-14371-6 (cloth : alk. paper)
ISBN-10: 0-226-14372-4 (pbk. : alk. paper)
1. Anne of St. Bartholomew, Mother, 1550–1626.
2. Nuns—Belgium—Antwerp—Biography. I. Donahue, Darcy. II. Title.
BX4705.A5695A3   2008
271.97102—dc22
[B]
2008007540

CONTENTS

ACKNOWLEDGMENTS

Many people have been of assistance in the writing and publication of this book. First, I would like to acknowledge Miami University's generous assistance in providing me with time for writing and funds to help defray publication costs. I would also like to express my appreciation of my students in both Spanish and women's studies at Miami who have read and commented on excerpts of this translations and offered helpful reactions. Randy Petilos of the University of Chicago Press has provided excellent guidance in the logistics of editing and publishing, and Sharon Brinkman, also of the University of Chicago Press, did a wonderful job of copyediting this translation of a four-hundred-year-old text. Finally, I would like to thank Al Rabil for his patience, knowledge, and valuable advice in the editing of this book and for his role in the founding and continuation of this excellent series.

Darcy Donahue

THE OTHER VOICE IN
EARLY MODERN EUROPE:
INTRODUCTION TO THE SERIES

Margaret L. King and Albert Rabil Jr.

THE OLD VOICE AND THE OTHER VOICE

In western Europe and the United States, women are nearing equality in the professions, in business, and in politics. Most enjoy access to education, reproductive rights, and autonomy in financial affairs. Issues vital to women are on the public agenda: equal pay, child care, domestic abuse, breast cancer research, and curricular revision with an eye to the inclusion of women.

These recent achievements have their origins in things women (and some male supporters) said for the first time about six hundred years ago. Theirs is the "other voice," in contradistinction to the "first voice," the voice of the educated men who created Western culture. Coincident with a general reshaping of European culture in the period 1300–1700 (called the Renaissance or early modern period), questions of female equality and opportunity were raised that still resound and are still unresolved.

The other voice emerged against the backdrop of a three-thousand-year history of the derogation of women rooted in the civilizations related to Western culture: Hebrew, Greek, Roman, and Christian. Negative attitudes toward women inherited from these traditions pervaded the intellectual, medical, legal, religious, and social systems that developed during the European Middle Ages.

The following pages describe the traditional, overwhelmingly male views of women's nature inherited by early modern Europeans and the new tradition that the "other voice" called into being to begin to challenge reigning assumptions. This review should serve as a framework for understanding the texts published in the series The Other Voice in Early Modern Europe. Introductions specific to each text and author follow this essay in all the volumes of the series.

TRADITIONAL VIEWS OF WOMEN, 500 B.C.E.–1500 C.E.

Embedded in the philosophical and medical theories of the ancient Greeks were perceptions of the female as inferior to the male in both mind and body. Similarly, the structure of civil legislation inherited from the ancient Romans was biased against women, and the views on women developed by Christian thinkers out of the Hebrew Bible and the Christian New Testament were negative and disabling. Literary works composed in the vernacular of ordinary people, and widely recited or read, conveyed these negative assumptions. The social networks within which most women lived—those of the family and the institutions of the Roman Catholic Church—were shaped by this negative tradition and sharply limited the areas in which women might act in and upon the world.

GREEK PHILOSOPHY AND FEMALE NATURE. Greek biology assumed that women were inferior to men and defined them as merely childbearers and housekeepers. This view was authoritatively expressed in the works of the philosopher Aristotle.

Aristotle thought in dualities. He considered action superior to inaction, form (the inner design or structure of any object) superior to matter, completion to incompletion, possession to deprivation. In each of these dualities, he associated the male principle with the superior quality and the female with the inferior. "The male principle in nature," he argued, "is associated with active, formative and perfected characteristics, while the female is passive, material and deprived, desiring the male in order to become complete."[1] Men are always identified with virile qualities, such as judgment, courage, and stamina, and women with their opposites—irrationality, cowardice, and weakness.

The masculine principle was considered superior even in the womb. The man's semen, Aristotle believed, created the form of a new human creature, while the female body contributed only matter. (The existence of the ovum, and with it the other facts of human embryology, was not established until the seventeenth century.) Although the later Greek physician Galen believed there was a female component in generation, contributed by "female semen," the followers of both Aristotle and Galen saw the male role in human generation as more active and more important.

In the Aristotelian view, the male principle sought always to reproduce itself. The creation of a female was always a mistake, therefore, resulting

---

1. Aristotle, *Physics* 1.9.192a20–24, in *The Complete Works of Aristotle*, ed. Jonathan Barnes, rev. Oxford trans., 2 vols. (Princeton, 1984), 1:328.

from an imperfect act of generation. Every female born was considered a "defective" or "mutilated" male (as Aristotle's terminology has variously been translated), a "monstrosity" of nature.[2]

For Greek theorists, the biology of males and females was the key to their psychology. The female was softer and more docile, more apt to be despondent, querulous, and deceitful. Being incomplete, moreover, she craved sexual fulfillment in intercourse with a male. The male was intellectual, active, and in control of his passions.

These psychological polarities derived from the theory that the universe consisted of four elements (earth, fire, air, and water), expressed in human bodies as four "humors" (black bile, yellow bile, blood, and phlegm) considered, respectively, dry, hot, damp, and cold and corresponding to mental states ("melancholic," "choleric," "sanguine," "phlegmatic"). In this scheme the male, sharing the principles of earth and fire, was dry and hot; the female, sharing the principles of air and water, was cold and damp.

Female psychology was further affected by her dominant organ, the uterus (womb), hystera in Greek. The passions generated by the womb made women lustful, deceitful, talkative, irrational, indeed—when these affects were in excess—"hysterical."

Aristotle's biology also had social and political consequences. If the male principle was superior and the female inferior, then in the household, as in the state, men should rule and women must be subordinate. That hierarchy did not rule out the companionship of husband and wife, whose cooperation was necessary for the welfare of children and the preservation of property. Such mutuality supported male preeminence.

Aristotle's teacher Plato suggested a different possibility: that men and women might possess the same virtues. The setting for this proposal is the imaginary and ideal Republic that Plato sketches in a dialogue of that name. Here, for a privileged elite capable of leading wisely, all distinctions of class and wealth dissolve, as, consequently, do those of gender. Without households or property, as Plato constructs his ideal society, there is no need for the subordination of women. Women may therefore be educated to the same level as men to assume leadership. Plato's Republic remained imaginary, however. In real societies, the subordination of women remained the norm and the prescription.

The views of women inherited from the Greek philosophical tradition became the basis for medieval thought. In the thirteenth century,

---

2. Aristotle, *Generation of Animals* 2.3.737a27–28, in *The Complete Works*, 1: 1144.

the supreme Scholastic philosopher Thomas Aquinas, among others, still echoed Aristotle's views of human reproduction, of male and female personalities, and of the preeminent male role in the social hierarchy.

ROMAN LAW AND THE FEMALE CONDITION. Roman law, like Greek philosophy, underlay medieval thought and shaped medieval society. The ancient belief that adult property-owning men should administer households and make decisions affecting the community at large is the very fulcrum of Roman law.

About 450 B.C.E., during Rome's republican era, the community's customary law was recorded (legendarily) on twelve tablets erected in the city's central forum. It was later elaborated by professional jurists whose activity increased in the imperial era, when much new legislation was passed, especially on issues affecting family and inheritance. This growing, changing body of laws was eventually codified in the Corpus of Civil Law under the direction of the emperor Justinian, generations after the empire ceased to be ruled from Rome. That Corpus, read and commented on by medieval scholars from the eleventh century on, inspired the legal systems of most of the cities and kingdoms of Europe.

Laws regarding dowries, divorce, and inheritance pertain primarily to women. Since those laws aimed to maintain and preserve property, the women concerned were those from the property-owning minority. Their subordination to male family members points to the even greater subordination of lower-class and slave women, about whom the laws speak little.

In the early republic, the paterfamilias, or "father of the family," possessed patria potestas, "paternal power." The term pater, "father," in both these cases does not necessarily mean biological father but denotes the head of a household. The father was the person who owned the household's property and, indeed, its human members. The paterfamilias had absolute power—including the power, rarely exercised, of life or death—over his wife, his children, and his slaves, as much as his cattle.

Male children could be "emancipated," an act that granted legal autonomy and the right to own property. Those over fourteen could be emancipated by a special grant from the father or automatically by their father's death. But females could never be emancipated; instead, they passed from the authority of their father to that of a husband or, if widowed or orphaned while still unmarried, to a guardian or tutor.

Marriage in its traditional form placed the woman under her husband's authority, or manus. He could divorce her on grounds of adultery, drinking wine, or stealing from the household, but she could not divorce him. She could neither possess property in her own right nor bequeath any to her children upon her death. When her husband died, the household property passed not to her but to his male heirs. And when her father died, she had no claim to any family inheritance, which was directed to her brothers or more remote male relatives. The effect of these laws was to exclude women from civil society, itself based on property ownership.

In the later republican and imperial periods, these rules were significantly modified. Women rarely married according to the traditional form. The practice of "free" marriage allowed a woman to remain under her father's authority, to possess property given her by her father (most frequently the "dowry," recoverable from the husband's household on his death), and to inherit from her father. She could also bequeath property to her own children and divorce her husband, just as he could divorce her.

Despite this greater freedom, women still suffered enormous disability under Roman law. Heirs could belong only to the father's side, never the mother's. Moreover, although she could bequeath her property to her children, she could not establish a line of succession in doing so. A woman was "the beginning and end of her own family," said the jurist Ulpian. Moreover, women could play no public role. They could not hold public office, represent anyone in a legal case, or even witness a will. Women had only a private existence and no public personality.

The dowry system, the guardian, women's limited ability to transmit wealth, and total political disability are all features of Roman law adopted by the medieval communities of western Europe, although modified according to local customary laws.

CHRISTIAN DOCTRINE AND WOMEN'S PLACE. The Hebrew Bible and the Christian New Testament authorized later writers to limit women to the realm of the family and to burden them with the guilt of original sin. The passages most fruitful for this purpose were the creation narratives in Genesis and sentences from the Epistles defining women's role within the Christian family and community.

Each of the first two chapters of Genesis contains a creation narrative. In the first "God created man in his own image, in the image of God he created him; male and female he created them" (Gn 1:27). In the second, God created Eve from Adam's rib (2:21–23). Christian theologians relied principally on Genesis 2 for their understanding of the relation between man and woman, interpreting the creation of Eve from Adam as proof of her subordination to him.

The creation story in Genesis 2 leads to that of the temptations in Genesis 3: of Eve by the wily serpent and of Adam by Eve. As read by Christian theologians from Tertullian to Thomas Aquinas, the narrative made Eve responsible for the Fall and its consequences. She instigated the act; she deceived her husband; she suffered the greater punishment. Her disobedience made it necessary for Jesus to be incarnated and to die on the cross. From the pulpit, moralists and preachers for centuries conveyed to women the guilt that they bore for original sin.

The Epistles offered advice to early Christians on building communities of the faithful. Among the matters to be regulated was the place of women. Paul offered views favorable to women in Galatians 3:28: "There is neither Jew nor Greek, there is neither slave nor free, there is neither male nor female; for you are all one in Christ Jesus." Paul also referred to women as his coworkers and placed them on a par with himself and his male coworkers (Phlm 4:2–3; Rom 16:1–3; 1 Cor 16:19). Elsewhere, Paul limited women's possibilities: "But I want you to understand that the head of every man is Christ, the head of a woman is her husband, and the head of Christ is God" (1 Cor 11:3).

Biblical passages by later writers (although attributed to Paul) enjoined women to forgo jewels, expensive clothes, and elaborate coiffures; and they forbade women to "teach or have authority over men," telling them to "learn in silence with all submissiveness" as is proper for one responsible for sin, consoling them, however, with the thought that they will be saved through childbearing (1 Tm 2:9–15). Other texts among the later Epistles defined women as the weaker sex and emphasized their subordination to their husbands (1 Pt 3:7; Col 3:18; Eph 5:22–23).

These passages from the New Testament became the arsenal employed by theologians of the early church to transmit negative attitudes toward women to medieval Christian culture—above all, Tertullian (On the Apparel of Women), Jerome (Against Jovinian), and Augustine (The Literal Meaning of Genesis).

THE IMAGE OF WOMEN IN MEDIEVAL LITERATURE. The philosophical, legal, and religious traditions born in antiquity formed the basis of the medieval intellectual synthesis wrought by trained thinkers, mostly clerics, writing in Latin and based largely in universities. The vernacular literary tradition that developed alongside the learned tradition also spoke about female nature and women's roles. Medieval stories, poems, and epics also portrayed women negatively—as lustful and deceitful—while praising good housekeepers and loyal wives as replicas of the Virgin Mary or the female saints and martyrs.

There is an exception in the movement of "courtly love" that evolved in southern France from the twelfth century. Courtly love was the erotic love between a nobleman and noblewoman, the latter usually superior in social rank. It was always adulterous. From the conventions of courtly love derive modern Western notions of romantic love. The tradition has had an impact disproportionate to its size, for it affected only a tiny elite, and very few women. The exaltation of the female lover probably does not reflect a higher evaluation of women or a step toward their sexual liberation. More likely it gives expression to the social and sexual tensions besetting the knightly class at a specific historical juncture.

The literary fashion of courtly love was on the wane by the thirteenth century, when the widely read Romance of the Rose was composed in French by two authors of significantly different dispositions. Guillaume de Lorris composed the initial four thousand verses about 1235, and Jean de Meun added about seventeen thousand verses—more than four times the original—about 1265.

The fragment composed by Guillaume de Lorris stands squarely in the tradition of courtly love. Here the poet, in a dream, is admitted into a walled garden where he finds a magic fountain in which a rosebush is reflected. He longs to pick one rose, but the thorns prevent his doing so, even as he is wounded by arrows from the god of love, whose commands he agrees to obey. The rest of this part of the poem recounts the poet's unsuccessful efforts to pluck the rose.

The longer part of the Romance by Jean de Meun also describes a dream. But here allegorical characters give long didactic speeches, providing a social satire on a variety of themes, some pertaining to women. Love is an anxious and tormented state, the poem explains: women are greedy and manipulative, marriage is miserable, beautiful women are lustful, ugly ones cease to please, and a chaste woman is as rare as a black swan.

Shortly after Jean de Meun completed The Romance of the Rose, Mathéolus penned his Lamentations, a long Latin diatribe against marriage translated into French about a century later. The Lamentations sum up medieval attitudes toward women and provoked the important response by Christine de Pizan in her Book of the City of Ladies.

In 1355, Giovanni Boccaccio wrote Il Corbaccio, another antifeminist manifesto, although ironically by an author whose other works pioneered new directions in Renaissance thought. The former husband of his lover appears to Boccaccio, condemning his unmoderated lust and detailing the defects of women. Boccaccio concedes at the end "how much men naturally surpass women in nobility" and is cured of his desires.[3]

---

3. Giovanni Boccaccio, *The Corbaccio, or The Labyrinth of Love,* trans. and ed. Anthony K. Cassell, rev. ed. (Binghamton, N.Y., 1993), 71.

WOMEN'S ROLES: THE FAMILY. The negative perceptions of women expressed in the intellectual tradition are also implicit in the actual roles that women played in European society. Assigned to subordinate positions in the household and the church, they were barred from significant participation in public life.

Medieval European households, like those in antiquity and in non-Western civilizations, were headed by males. It was the male serf (or peasant), feudal lord, town merchant, or citizen who was polled or taxed or succeeded to an inheritance or had any acknowledged public role, although his wife or widow could stand as a temporary surrogate. From about 1100, the position of property-holding males was further enhanced: inheritance was confined to the male, or agnate, line—with depressing consequences for women.

A wife never fully belonged to her husband's family, nor was she a daughter to her father's family. She left her father's house young to marry whomever her parents chose. Her dowry was managed by her husband, and at her death it normally passed to her children by him.

A married woman's life was occupied nearly constantly with cycles of pregnancy, childbearing, and lactation. Women bore children through all the years of their fertility, and many died in childbirth. They were also responsible for raising young children up to six or seven. In the propertied classes that responsibility was shared, since it was common for a wet nurse to take over breast-feeding and for servants to perform other chores.

Women trained their daughters in the household duties appropriate to their status, nearly always tasks associated with textiles: spinning, weaving, sewing, embroidering. Their sons were sent out of the house as apprentices or students, or their training was assumed by fathers in later childhood and adolescence. On the death of her husband, a woman's children became the responsibility of his family. She generally did not take "his" children with her to a new marriage or back to her father's house, except sometimes in the artisan classes.

Women also worked. Rural peasants performed farm chores, merchant wives often practiced their husbands' trades, the unmarried daughters of the urban poor worked as servants or prostitutes. All wives produced or embellished textiles and did the housekeeping, while wealthy ones managed servants. These labors were unpaid or poorly paid but often contributed substantially to family wealth.

WOMEN'S ROLES: THE CHURCH. Membership in a household, whether a father's or a husband's, meant for women a lifelong subordination to others. In western Europe, the Roman Catholic Church offered an alternative to the career of wife and mother. A woman could enter a convent, parallel in function to the monasteries for men that evolved in the early Christian centuries.

In the convent, a woman pledged herself to a celibate life, lived according to strict community rules, and worshiped daily. Often the convent offered training in Latin, allowing some women to become considerable scholars and authors as well as scribes, artists, and musicians. For women who chose the conventual life, the benefits could be enormous, but for numerous others placed in convents by paternal choice, the life could be restrictive and burdensome.

The conventual life declined as an alternative for women as the modern age approached. Reformed monastic institutions resisted responsibility for related female orders. The church increasingly restricted female institutional life by insisting on closer male supervision.

Women often sought other options. Some joined the communities of laywomen that sprang up spontaneously in the thirteenth century in the urban zones of western Europe, especially in Flanders and Italy. Some joined the heretical movements that flourished in late medieval Christendom, whose anticlerical and often antifamily positions particularly appealed to women. In these communities, some women were acclaimed as "holy women" or "saints," whereas others often were condemned as frauds or heretics.

In all, although the options offered to women by the church were sometimes less than satisfactory, they were sometimes richly rewarding. After 1520, the convent remained an option only in Roman Catholic territories. Protestantism engendered an ideal of marriage as a heroic endeavor and appeared to place husband and wife on a more equal footing. Sermons and treatises, however, still called for female subordination and obedience.

THE OTHER VOICE, 1300–1700

When the modern era opened, European culture was so firmly structured by a framework of negative attitudes toward women that to dismantle it was a monumental labor. The process began as part of a larger cultural movement that entailed the critical reexamination of ideas inherited from the ancient and medieval past. The humanists launched that critical reexamination.

THE HUMANIST FOUNDATION. Originating in Italy in the fourteenth century, humanism quickly became the dominant intellectual movement in Europe. Spreading in the sixteenth century from Italy to the rest of Europe, it fueled the literary, scientific, and philosophical movements of the era and laid the basis for the eighteenth-century Enlightenment.

Humanists regarded the Scholastic philosophy of medieval universities as out of touch with the realities of urban life. They found in the rhetorical discourse of classical Rome a language adapted to civic life and public speech. They learned to read, speak, and write classical Latin and, eventually, classical Greek. They founded schools to teach others to do so, establishing the pattern for elementary and secondary education for the next three hundred years.

In the service of complex government bureaucracies, humanists employed their skills to write eloquent letters, deliver public orations, and formulate public policy. They developed new scripts for copying manuscripts and used the new printing press to disseminate texts, for which they created methods of critical editing.

Humanism was a movement led by males who accepted the evaluation of women in ancient texts and generally shared the misogynist perceptions of their culture. (Female humanists, as we will see, did not.) Yet humanism also opened the door to a reevaluation of the nature and capacity of women. By calling authors, texts, and ideas into question, it made possible the fundamental rereading of the whole intellectual tradition that was required in order to free women from cultural prejudice and social subordination.

A DIFFERENT CITY. The other voice first appeared when, after so many centuries, the accumulation of misogynist concepts evoked a response from a capable female defender: Christine de Pizan (1365–1431). Introducing her Book of the City of Ladies (1405), she described how she was affected by reading Mathéolus's Lamentations: "Just the sight of this book . . . made me wonder how it happened that so many different men . . . are so inclined to express both in speaking and in their treatises and writings so many wicked insults about women and their behavior."[4] These statements impelled her to detest herself "and the entire feminine sex, as though we were monstrosities in nature."[5]

The rest of The Book of the City of Ladies presents a justification of the female sex and a vision of an ideal community of women. A pioneer, she has received the message of female inferiority and rejected it. From the fourteenth to the seventeenth century, a huge body of literature accumulated that responded to the dominant tradition.

4. Christine de Pizan, *The Book of the City of Ladies*, trans. Earl Jeffrey Richards, foreword by Marina Warner (New York, 1982), 1.1.1, pp. 3–4.
5. Ibid., 1.1.1–2, p. 5.

The result was a literary explosion consisting of works by both men and women, in Latin and in the vernaculars: works enumerating the achievements of notable women; works rebutting the main accusations made against women; works arguing for the equal education of men and women; works defining and redefining women's proper role in the family, at court, in public; works describing women's lives and experiences. Recent monographs and articles have begun to hint at the great range of this movement, involving probably several thousand titles. The protofeminism of these "other voices" constitutes a significant fraction of the literary product of the early modern era.

THE CATALOGS. About 1365, the same Boccaccio whose Corbaccio rehearses the usual charges against female nature wrote another work, Concerning Famous Women. A humanist treatise drawing on classical texts, it praised 106 notable women: ninety-eight of them from pagan Greek and Roman antiquity, one (Eve) from the Bible, and seven from the medieval religious and cultural tradition; his book helped make all readers aware of a sex normally condemned or forgotten. Boccaccio's outlook nevertheless was unfriendly to women, for it singled out for praise those women who possessed the traditional virtues of chastity, silence, and obedience. Women who were active in the public realm—for example, rulers and warriors—were depicted as usually being lascivious and as suffering terrible punishments for entering the masculine sphere. Women were his subject, but Boccaccio's standard remained male.

Christine de Pizan's Book of the City of Ladies contains a second catalog, one responding specifically to Boccaccio's. Whereas Boccaccio portrays female virtue as exceptional, she depicts it as universal. Many women in history were leaders, or remained chaste despite the lascivious approaches of men, or were visionaries and brave martyrs.

The work of Boccaccio inspired a series of catalogs of illustrious women of the biblical, classical, Christian, and local pasts, among them Filippo da Bergamo's Of Illustrious Women, Pierre de Brantôme's Lives of Illustrious Women, Pierre Le Moyne's Gallerie of Heroic Women, and Pietro Paolo de Ribera's Immortal Triumphs and Heroic Enterprises of 845 Women. Whatever their embedded prejudices, these works drove home to the public the possibility of female excellence.

THE DEBATE. At the same time, many questions remained: Could a woman be virtuous? Could she perform noteworthy deeds? Was she even, strictly speaking, of the same human species as men? These questions were debated over four centuries, in French, German, Italian, Spanish, and English, by authors male and female, among Catholics, Protestants, and Jews, in ponderous volumes and breezy pamphlets. The whole literary genre has been called the querelle des femmes, the "woman question."

The opening volley of this battle occurred in the first years of the fifteenth century, in a literary debate sparked by Christine de Pizan. She exchanged letters critical of Jean de Meun's contribution to The Romance of the Rose with two French royal secretaries, Jean de Montreuil and Gontier Col. When the matter became public, Jean Gerson, one of Europe's leading theologians, supported de Pizan's arguments against de Meun, for the moment silencing the opposition.

The debate resurfaced repeatedly over the next two hundred years. The Triumph of Women (1438) by Juan Rodríguez de la Camara (or Juan Rodríguez del Padron) struck a new note by presenting arguments for the superiority of women to men. The Champion of Women (1440–42) by Martin Le Franc addresses once again the negative views of women presented in The Romance of the Rose and offers counterevidence of female virtue and achievement.

A cameo of the debate on women is included in The Courtier, one of the most widely read books of the era, published by the Italian Baldassare Castiglione in 1528 and immediately translated into other European vernaculars. The Courtier depicts a series of evenings at the court of the duke of Urbino in which many men and some women of the highest social stratum amuse themselves by discussing a range of literary and social issues. The "woman question" is a pervasive theme throughout, and the third of its four books is devoted entirely to that issue.

In a verbal duel, Gasparo Pallavicino and Giuliano de' Medici present the main claims of the two traditions. Gasparo argues the innate inferiority of women and their inclination to vice. Only in bearing children do they profit the world. Giuliano counters that women share the same spiritual and mental capacities as men and may excel in wisdom and action. Men and women are of the same essence: just as no stone can be more perfectly a stone than another, so no human being can be more perfectly human than others, whether male or female. It was an astonishing assertion, boldly made to an audience as large as all Europe.

THE TREATISES. Humanism provided the materials for a positive counter-concept to the misogyny embedded in Scholastic philosophy and law and inherited from the Greek, Roman, and Christian pasts. A series of humanist treatises on marriage and family, on education and deportment, and on the nature of women helped construct these new perspectives.

The works by Francesco Barbaro and Leon Battista Alberti—On Marriage (1415) and On the Family (1434–37)—far from defending female equality, reasserted women's responsibility for rearing children and managing the housekeeping while being obedient, chaste, and silent. Nevertheless, they served the cause of reexamining the issue of women's nature by placing domestic issues at the center of scholarly concern and reopening the pertinent classical texts. In addition, Barbaro emphasized the companionate nature of marriage and the importance of a wife's spiritual and mental qualities for the well-being of the family.

These themes reappear in later humanist works on marriage and the education of women by Juan Luis Vives and Erasmus. Both were moderately sympathetic to the condition of women without reaching beyond the usual masculine prescriptions for female behavior.

An outlook more favorable to women characterizes the nearly unknown work In Praise of Women (ca. 1487) by the Italian humanist Bartolommeo Goggio. In addition to providing a catalog of illustrious women, Goggio argued that male and female are the same in essence, but that women (reworking the Adam and Eve narrative from quite a new angle) are actually superior. In the same vein, the Italian humanist Mario Equicola asserted the spiritual equality of men and women in On Women (1501). In 1525, Galeazzo Flavio Capra (or Capella) published his work On the Excellence and Dignity of Women. This humanist tradition of treatises defending the worthiness of women culminates in the work of Henricus Cornelius Agrippa On the Nobility and Preeminence of the Female Sex. No work by a male humanist more succinctly or explicitly presents the case for female dignity.

THE WITCH BOOKS. While humanists grappled with the issues pertaining to women and family, other learned men turned their attention to what they perceived as a very great problem: witches. Witch-hunting manuals, explorations of the witch phenomenon, and even defenses of witches are not at first glance pertinent to the tradition of the other voice. But they do relate in this way: most accused witches were women. The hostility aroused by supposed witch activity is comparable to the hostility aroused by women. The evil deeds the victims of the hunt were charged with were exaggerations of the vices to which, many believed, all women were prone.

The connection between the witch accusation and the hatred of women is explicit in the notorious witch-hunting manual The Hammer of Witches (1486) by two Dominican inquisitors, Heinrich Krämer and Jacob Sprenger. Here the inconstancy, deceitfulness, and lustfulness traditionally associated with women are depicted in exaggerated form as the core features of witch behavior. These traits inclined women to make a bargain with the devil—sealed by sexual intercourse—by which they acquired unholy powers. Such bizarre claims, far from being rejected by rational men, were broadcast by intellectuals. The German Ulrich Molitur, the Frenchman Nicolas Rémy, and the Italian Stefano Guazzo all coolly informed the public of sinister orgies and midnight pacts with the devil. The celebrated French jurist, historian, and political philosopher Jean Bodin argued that because women were especially prone to diabolism, regular legal procedures could properly be suspended in order to try those accused of this "exceptional crime."

A few experts such as the physician Johann Weyer, a student of Agrippa's, raised their voices in protest. In 1563, he explained the witch phenomenon thus, without discarding belief in diabolism: the devil deluded foolish old women afflicted by melancholia, causing them to believe they had magical powers. Weyer's rational skepticism, which had good credibility in the community of the learned, worked to revise the conventional views of women and witchcraft.

WOMEN'S WORKS. To the many categories of works produced on the question of women's worth must be added nearly all works written by women. A woman writing was in herself a statement of women's claim to dignity.

Only a few women wrote anything before the dawn of the modern era, for three reasons. First, they rarely received the education that would enable them to write. Second, they were not admitted to the public roles—as administrator, bureaucrat, lawyer or notary, or university professor—in which they might gain knowledge of the kinds of things the literate public thought worth writing about. Third, the culture imposed silence on women, considering speaking out a form of unchastity. Given these conditions, it is remarkable that any women wrote. Those who did before the fourteenth century were almost always nuns or religious women whose isolation made their pronouncements more acceptable.

From the fourteenth century on, the volume of women's writings rose. Women continued to write devotional literature, although not always as cloistered nuns. They also wrote diaries, often intended as keepsakes for their children; books of advice to their sons and daughters; letters to family members and friends; and family memoirs, in a few cases elaborate enough to be considered histories.

A few women wrote works directly concerning the "woman question," and some of these, such as the humanists Isotta Nogarola, Cassandra Fedele, Laura Cereta, and Olympia Morata, were highly trained. A few were professional writers, living by the income of their pens; the very first among them was Christine de Pizan, noteworthy in this context as in so many others. In addition to The Book of the City of Ladies and her critiques of The Romance of the Rose, she wrote The Treasure of the City of Ladies (a guide to social decorum for women), an advice book for her son, much courtly verse, and a full-scale history of the reign of King Charles V of France.

WOMEN PATRONS. Women who did not themselves write but encouraged others to do so boosted the development of an alternative tradition. Highly placed women patrons supported authors, artists, musicians, poets, and learned men. Such patrons, drawn mostly from the Italian elites and the courts of northern Europe, figure disproportionately as the dedicatees of the important works of early feminism.

For a start, it might be noted that the catalogs of Boccaccio and Alvaro de Luna were dedicated to the Florentine noblewoman Andrea Acciaiuoli and to Doña María, first wife of King Juan II of Castile, while the French translation of Boccaccio's work was commissioned by Anne of Brittany, wife of King Charles VIII of France. The humanist treatises of Goggio, Equicola, Vives, and Agrippa were dedicated, respectively, to Eleanora of Aragon, wife of Ercole I d'Este, duke of Ferrara; to Margherita Cantelma of Mantua; to Catherine of Aragon, wife of King Henry VIII of England; and to Margaret, Duchess of Austria and regent of the Netherlands. As late as 1696, Mary Astell's Serious Proposal to the Ladies, for the Advancement of Their True and Greatest Interest was dedicated to Princess Anne of Denmark.

These authors presumed that their efforts would be welcome to female patrons, or they may have written at the bidding of those patrons. Silent themselves, perhaps even unresponsive, these loftily placed women helped shape the tradition of the other voice.

THE ISSUES. The literary forms and patterns in which the tradition of the other voice presented itself have now been sketched. It remains to highlight the major issues around which this tradition crystallizes. In brief, there are four problems to which our authors return again and again, in plays and catalogs, in verse and letters, in treatises and dialogues, in every language: the problem of chastity, the problem of power, the problem of speech, and the problem of knowledge. Of these the greatest, preconditioning the others, is the problem of chastity.

THE PROBLEM OF CHASTITY. In traditional European culture, as in those of antiquity and others around the globe, chastity was perceived as woman's quintessential virtue—in contrast to courage, or generosity, or leadership, or rationality, seen as virtues characteristic of men. Opponents of women charged them with insatiable lust. Women themselves and their defenders—without disputing the validity of the standard—responded that women were capable of chastity.

The requirement of chastity kept women at home, silenced them, isolated them, left them in ignorance. It was the source of all other impediments. Why was it so important to the society of men, of whom chastity was not required, and who more often than not considered it their right to violate the chastity of any woman they encountered?

Female chastity ensured the continuity of the male-headed household. If a man's wife was not chaste, he could not be sure of the legitimacy of his offspring. If they were not his and they acquired his property, it was not his household, but some other man's, that had endured. If his daughter was not chaste, she could not be transferred to another man's household as his wife, and he was dishonored.

The whole system of the integrity of the household and the transmission of property was bound up in female chastity. Such a requirement pertained only to property-owning classes, of course. Poor women could not expect to maintain their chastity, least of all if they were in contact with high-status men to whom all women but those of their own household were prey.

In Catholic Europe, the requirement of chastity was further buttressed by moral and religious imperatives. Original sin was inextricably linked with the sexual act. Virginity was seen as heroic virtue, far more impressive than, say, the avoidance of idleness or greed. Monasticism, the cultural institution that dominated medieval Europe for centuries, was grounded in the renunciation of the flesh. The Catholic reform of the eleventh century imposed a similar standard on all the clergy and a heightened awareness of sexual requirements on all the laity. Although men were asked to be chaste, female unchastity was much worse: it led to the devil, as Eve had led mankind to sin.

To such requirements, women and their defenders protested their innocence. Furthermore, following the example of holy women who had escaped the requirements of family and sought the religious life, some women began to conceive of female communities as alternatives both to family and to the cloister. Christine de Pizan's city of ladies was such a community. Moderata Fonte and Mary Astell envisioned others. The luxurious salons of the French *précieuses* of the seventeenth century, or the comfortable English drawing rooms of the next, may have been born of the same impulse. Here women not only might escape, if briefly, the subordinate position that life in the family entailed but might also make claims to power, exercise their capacity for speech, and display their knowledge.

THE PROBLEM OF POWER. Women were excluded from power: the whole cultural tradition insisted on it. Only men were citizens, only men bore arms, only men could be chiefs or lords or kings. There were exceptions that did not disprove the rule, when wives or widows or mothers took the place of men, awaiting their return or the maturation of a male heir. A woman who attempted to rule in her own right was perceived as an anomaly, a monster, at once a deformed woman and an insufficient male, sexually confused and consequently unsafe.

The association of such images with women who held or sought power explains some otherwise odd features of early modern culture. Queen Elizabeth I of England, one of the few women to hold full regal authority in European history, played with such male/female images—positive ones, of course—in representing herself to her subjects. She was a prince, and manly, even though she was female. She was also (she claimed) virginal, a condition absolutely essential if she was to avoid the attacks of her opponents. Catherine de' Medici, who ruled France as widow and regent for her sons, also adopted such imagery in defining her position. She chose as one symbol the figure of Artemisia, an androgynous ancient warrior-heroine who combined a female persona with masculine powers.

Power in a woman, without such sexual imagery, seems to have been indigestible by the culture. A rare note was struck by the Englishman Sir Thomas Elyot in his Defence of Good Women (1540), justifying both women's participation in civic life and their prowess in arms. The old tune was sung by the Scots reformer John Knox in his First Blast of the Trumpet against the Monstrous Regiment of Women (1558); for him rule by women, defects in nature, was a hideous contradiction in terms.

The confused sexuality of the imagery of female potency was not reserved for rulers. Any woman who excelled was likely to be called an Amazon, recalling the self-mutilated warrior women of antiquity who repudiated all men, gave up their sons, and raised only their daughters. She was often said to have "exceeded her sex" or to have possessed "masculine virtue"—as the very fact of conspicuous excellence conferred masculinity even on the female subject. The catalogs of notable women often showed those female heroes dressed in armor, armed to the teeth, like men. Amazonian heroines romp through the epics of the age—Ariosto's Orlando Furioso (1532) and Spenser's Faerie Queene (1590–1609). Excellence in a woman was perceived as a claim for power, and power was reserved for the masculine realm. A woman who possessed either one was masculinized and lost title to her own female identity.

THE PROBLEM OF SPEECH. Just as power had a sexual dimension when it was claimed by women, so did speech. A good woman spoke little. Excessive speech was an indication of unchastity. By speech, women seduced men. Eve had lured Adam into sin by her speech. Accused witches were commonly accused of having spoken abusively, or irrationally, or simply too much. As enlightened a figure as Francesco Barbaro insisted on silence in a woman, which he linked to her perfect unanimity with her husband's will and her un-blemished virtue (her chastity). Another Italian humanist, Leonardo Bruni, in advising a noblewoman on her studies, barred her not from speech but from public speaking. That was reserved for men.

Related to the problem of speech was that of costume—another, if silent, form of self-expression. Assigned the task of pleasing men as their primary occupation, elite women often tended toward elaborate costume, hairdress-ing, and the use of cosmetics. Clergy and secular moralists alike condemned these practices. The appropriate function of costume and adornment was to announce the status of a woman's husband or father. Any further indulgence in adornment was akin to unchastity.

THE PROBLEM OF KNOWLEDGE. When the Italian noblewoman Isotta Nogarola had begun to attain a reputation as a humanist, she was accused of incest—a telling instance of the association of learning in women with unchastity. That chilling association inclined any woman who was educated to deny that she was or to make exaggerated claims of heroic chastity.

If educated women were pursued with suspicions of sexual misconduct, women seeking an education faced an even more daunting obstacle: the as-sumption that women were by nature incapable of learning, that reasoning was a particularly masculine ability. Just as they proclaimed their chastity, women and their defenders insisted on their capacity for learning. The ma-jor work by a male writer on female education—that by Juan Luis Vives, On the Education of a Christian Woman (1523)—granted female capacity for intellection but still argued that a woman's whole education was to be shaped around the requirement of chastity and a future within the house-hold. Female writers of the following generations—Marie de Gournay in France, Anna Maria van Schurman in Holland, and Mary Astell in Eng-land—began to envision other possibilities.

The pioneers of female education were the Italian women humanists who managed to attain a literacy in Latin and a knowledge of classical and Christian literature equivalent to that of prominent men. Their works im-plicitly and explicitly raise questions about women's social roles, defining problems that beset women attempting to break out of the cultural limits that had bound them. Like Christine de Pizan, who achieved an advanced education through her father's tutoring and her own devices, their bold questioning makes clear the importance of training. Only when women were educated to the same standard as male leaders would they be able to raise that other voice and insist on their dignity as human beings morally, intellectually, and legally equal to men.

THE OTHER VOICE. The other voice, a voice of protest, was mostly female, but it was also male. It spoke in the vernaculars and in Latin, in treatises and dialogues, in plays and poetry, in letters and diaries, and in pamphlets. It battered at the wall of prejudice that encircled women and raised a banner announcing its claims. The female was equal (or even superior) to the male in essential nature—moral, spiritual, and intellectual. Women were capable of higher education, of holding positions of power and influence in the public realm, and of speaking and writing persuasively. The last bastion of masculine supremacy, centered on the notions of a woman's primary domestic responsibility and the requirement of female chastity, was not as yet assaulted—although visions of productive female communities as alternatives to the family indicated an awareness of the problem.

During the period 1300–1700, the other voice remained only a voice, and one only dimly heard. It did not result—yet—in an alteration of social patterns. Indeed, to this day they have not entirely been altered. Yet the call for justice issued as long as six centuries ago by those writing in the tradition of the other voice must be recognized as the source and origin of the mature feminist tradition and of the realignment of social institutions accomplished in the modern age.

We thank the volume editors in this series, who responded with many suggestions to an earlier draft of this introduction, making it a collaborative enterprise. Many of their suggestions and criticisms have resulted in revisions of this introduction, although we remain responsible for the final product.

PROJECTED TITLES IN THE SERIES

Emilie du Châtelet, *Selected Writings*, edited with an introduction by Judith P. Zinsser, translated by Isabelle Bour and Judith P. Zinsser

Helisenne de Crenne, *Complete Works*, edited and translated by Timothy Reiss

Christine de Pizan, *Debate over the "Romance of the Rose,"* edited and translated by David F. Hult

Christine de Pizan, *Early Defense of Women Poems*, edited and translated by Thelma Fenster

Christine de Pizan, *Life of Charles V*, edited and translated by Nadia Margolis

VOLUME EDITOR'S INTRODUCTION

THE OTHER VOICE

Ana de San Bartolomé's life and writings reveal much about the situation of women religious in early modern Spain, yet her voice is also unique, the product of specific social circumstances, individual psychology, and religious fervor. Ana's participation in Saint Teresa of Avila's religious reform of the late sixteenth century became the center of her life and provided an opportunity for self-expression in words and actions normally denied women of her background. Semiliterate when she entered the Discalced Carmelite Convent of Saint Joseph of Avila in 1570, Ana became one of the most prolific writers of the order, although many of her works remained unpublished until well after her death. These works include over six hundred letters, a spiritual autobiography, detailed accounts of the Teresian reform, lectures for younger nuns, and many devotional texts that reflect her intensely lived spirituality and that are among the most valuable testimonies we have of a life fully enmeshed in the processes of religious and social transformation. Given her active participation in these processes, Ana's life acquires "a dimension worthy of greater attention than it has heretofore received."[1] Her writing, clearly inseparable from her religious vocation, expresses the tensions and conflict that often accompanied the lives of women whose relationship to the divine endowed them with an authority at odds with the temporal powers of church and state.[2] Ana's insistence upon obedience to those powers placed her in the uncomfortable position of opposing such key elements of the Discalced reform as freedom of choice in confessors at the same time that it bound her to ecclesiastical superiors who misunderstood her absolute dedication to a

1. Ana de San Bartolomé, *Autobiografía*, ed. Fortunato Antolín (Madrid: Espiritualidad, 1969), 11.
2. For an interesting collection of studies of some of these women see Mary R. Giles, ed., *Women in the Inquisition* (Baltimore: Johns Hopkins University Press, 1999).

certain vision of the Discalced Order. Despite (or perhaps because of) her continual clashes with both male and female superiors, Ana became a figure to be reckoned with in the religious politics of late-sixteenth-century Spain. As companion and nurse to Teresa of Avila, she participated in the advance of the Carmelite reform throughout Spain and later was influential in its establishment in France and the Low Countries.[3] Her influence reached the upper echelons of both church and secular power structures as she became an advisor to such figures as Cardinal Bérulle, a leader of the Catholic restoration in France, and Princess Isabel Clara Eugenia, daughter of Phillip II of Spain and regent of the Low Countries.

Although she was never an advocate for women's rights in the modern sense or a model of female leadership as we might envision such a woman today, Ana used her position as convent founder and disciple of the Mother Founder to express her unequivocal allegiance to the principles of the reform as she understood them.[4] While some students of the Carmelites have perceived her as conservative and even inflexible in her interpretation of those principles, she spoke from a position of absolute loyalty to Teresa, her model, and a strong conviction of her own moral rectitude. She was at times outspoken in her censure of male prelates who attempted to change the original constitutions written by Teresa. Her works reflect the vagaries of her career as she attempted to follow her vision of spiritual virtue and religious activism, a vision, according to Alison Weber, predicated on women's exercise of power in exceptional circumstances.[5] The voice that emerges from these works is not monolithic but rather varies according to audience, purpose, and situation of the writer. It is always infused with an unshakeable faith in God's goodness and an equally strong sense of religious mission.

WOMEN'S LITERARY AND RELIGIOUS
CULTURE IN EARLY MODERN SPAIN

The acquisition of literacy skills in early modern Spain reflected existing ideas of gendered abilities and needs. Although many upper-class Spanish

3. There are many histories of the Carmelite reform. For a succinct version, see Jodi Bilinkoff, "Teresa of Jesus and Carmelite Reform," in *Religious Orders of the Catholic Reformation: Studies in Honor of John C. Olin on His Seventy-fifth Birthday,* ed. Richard L. DeMolen (New York: Fordham University Press, 1994), 165–86. For the major twentieth-century version, which includes the Discalced movement in Europe and Latin America, see Silverio de Santa Teresa, *Historia del Carmen Descalzo* (Burgos: El Monte Carmelo, 1935–52).

4. Alison Weber has characterized Ana's position as pro-woman rather than feminist in the modern sense. See "The Partial Feminism of Ana de San Bartolomé," in *Recovering Spain's Feminist Tradition,* ed. Lisa Vollendorf (New York: Modern Language Association, 2001), 75.

5. See note 4.

women learned to read, writing was generally not considered expedient or appropriate for the traditional roles of wife and mother. Humanists of the day like Juan Luis Vives recognized women's intellectual capacity to read and assimilate content but warned that strict surveillance should be exercised in the selection of reading material in order to avoid potentially corrupting influences. All reading should be limited to materials that inculcated the primary virtues of obedience, chastity, and silence. Vives recommends saints' lives, the Bible, and other religious texts as appropriate literary vehicles for the transmission of such virtues.[6] He and many other arbiters of early modern morality fulminated against popular literature of a nonreligious nature, such as the chivalric novel. Yet, despite the injunctions by both lay and religious critics against these "immoral" works,[7] many women would have had access to this literature, and Saint Teresa of Avila, founder of the Discalced Carmelites and author of several texts, mentions the tales of chivalry as a primary influence in her youth. Access to the written word, whether in print or in oral readings, was widespread. Writing, however, remained mostly a male privilege.

In early-sixteenth-century Spain, the potential for women's education and personal growth was greater in religious than in domestic life as a result of the increasing acceptance of women as spiritual equals by theologians and writers such as Erasmus of Rotterdam. Furthermore, under leaders such as Cardinal Jiménez Cisneros, women's active participation in the church was encouraged. Cisneros promoted the expression of women's spirituality and made many devotional and mystical works available to convents. In the evangelical climate of the first half of the century, women became well-known as leaders in various religious movements, both orthodox and heterodox, and some even acquired cult followings. However, the threat posed by the ascendance of Protestantism in the rest of Europe as well as the existence within Spain of diverse heterodox movements often grouped together as "Alumbrados" created a conservative backlash that ultimately worked against women's continued activism.[8] The egalitarianism and evangelism of the early sixteenth century was viewed by many conservatives in the church as a subversive offshoot of Protestantism, which if allowed to flourish, might threaten the church's very hegemony in the peninsula.

---

6. Juan Luis Vives, *The Education of a Christian Woman*, ed. and trans. Charles Fantazzi (Chicago: University of Chicago Press, 2000), 63–77.

7. B. W. Ife studies the moralists' arguments against fictional prose in *Reading and Fiction in Golden-Age Spain* (Cambridge: Cambridge University Press, 1985), 24–35.

8. There are various studies of the Alumbrados. For an overview of the early Alumbrado movement, see Antonio Márquez, *Los alumbrados: orígenes y filosofía, 1525–1559* (Madrid: Taurus, 1980).

Similarly, the increasing prominence of women in potentially heretical movements caused both church and secular authorities to severely curtail women's intellectual development and self-expression.

As a corpus, the many arguments against overeducating young girls put forth in the literature and sermons of Counter-Reformation Spain constitute a virtual taboo against an active intellectual life for women. Saint Paul's injunction against women's public speech, invoked by so many early modern moralists, became even more firmly entrenched after the Council of Trent (1545–63), the Catholic Church's response to the growing threat of Protestant reform. In 1559, the Spanish Inquisition issued an index of prohibited books (fourteen editions of the Bible, nine of the New Testament, and sixteen works by Erasmus, among others) as a measure to protect religious orthodoxy. Literacy had become a liability, particularly for women. The activism and visionary spirituality encouraged by Cisneros was now perceived as evidence of female instability and susceptibility to erroneous doctrines. As so many scholars of the early modern period have pointed out, post-Tridentine Spain proved to be a time of increased surveillance and enclosure of women, both in the home and the convent.[9]

Not surprisingly, it was the convent that both promoted and produced women's intellectual activity in varied forms, as it had done for centuries. As Electa Arenal and Stacey Schlau have observed, much of this activity was the result of collaboration among the members of cloistered communities and thus "lay outside the male intellectual sphere." In fact, many convents provided both a physical and psychic space where women could come together and express themselves spiritually, intellectually, and artistically. "No other space replicated the women's world of the convent . . . The environment that protected them from domestic violence and death in childbirth and nurtured religious ideals and practices also became a catalyst for intellectual pursuits."[10]

Women's voices were usually the only voices in the uniquely protective space of the cloister, and they were employed both audibly and in writing. Some orders, such as the Discalced Carmelites, made active use of literacy as a primary goal for their members. In fact, the Discalced *Constitution* stipulated that all nuns in the order learn to read. Most orders actually provided instruction in basic literacy skills, and communal reading was part of the

9. Increased enclosure did not keep the convent communities from interacting with the world outside. See Elizabeth Lehfeldt, *Religious Women in Golden Age Spain: The Permeable Cloister* (Aldershot: Ashgate, 2005).

10. Electa Arenal and Stacey Schlau, "'Leyendo yo y escribiendo ella': The Convent as Intellectual Community," *Journal of Hispanic Philology* 13 (1989): 218.

daily monastic routine. The reading of edifying texts such as the lives of saints and books of hours was considered an important way to prepare for spiritual contemplation and mental prayer.[11]

Writing was also a significant component of many nuns' daily lives. Teresa of Avila became a model for other women authors. Her autobiographical text, *The Book of Her Life*, although certainly not the first such work to be written in a convent, came to be considered an archetype of the female *vida*, or spiritual autobiography, and inspired many of her followers to write their own.[12] Even though the Inquisition examined her works for possible heresy, they were widely circulated among convents and read by other nuns. Many nuns also corresponded with their families and women in other convents on a regular basis. Letters were a primary form of contact with the outside world and a way to share the news of communities, conduct business, and continue personal relationships. Ana de San Bartolomé, who supposedly learned to write in one afternoon by copying Teresa's script, went on to pen over six hundred letters.

In addition to autobiographical texts and letters, women religious documented their own experiences in varied convent writings (chronicles, biographies of spiritual sisters, poems, plays, and songs, among others). These works were authored by individuals and also collectively, often with several members of a community signing. For the most part, such writing was voluntary and revealed a desire by these authors to recognize the achievements and holiness of their communities and of certain individuals within them. However, confessors frequently ordered women of exceptional spirituality to record their experiences, and writing thus became an act of obedience. In such cases, the writers might avail themselves of certain rhetorical strategies in order to both comply with the vow of obedience and protect themselves from possible prosecution by church authorities.

Certainly not all nuns received a comprehensive education, and many did not learn to write. Those who did were usually carefully monitored by both male and female superiors. In some cases the writers chose to destroy their own writings. In other cases, censors destroyed or altered the writings. Despite her vexed relationship with church authorities, Teresa's works were

11. See Pedro Cátedra, "Lectura femenina en el claustro (España, siglos XIV–XVI)," *Des femmes et des livres: France et Espagne, XIVe–XVIIe siècle: Actes de la journée d'etude organisée par l'Ecole nationale des chartres et l'Ecole normale superieure de Fontenay/Saint-Cloud (Paris, 30 avril 1998)*, ed. Dominique de Courcelles and Carmen Val Julián (Paris: Ecole des Chartes, 1999), 7–53.

12. For an excellent analysis of this work and the climate in which it was written, see Alison Weber, *Teresa of Ávila and the Rhetoric of Femininity* (Princeton: Princeton University Press, 1989), 17–77.

published in 1588 by Fray Luis de Léon, a leading theologian and poet, and she herself was beatified in 1614. To some extent, her survival and ultimate triumph, albeit posthumous, represent the triumph of the woman writer in early modern Spain. Throughout the seventeenth century, women religious continued to use writing as a second or alternate voice through which they could communicate both the intensity of their spiritual lives and the reality of their earthly experiences.

EARLY LIFE OF ANA DE SAN BARTOLOMÉ

Born in 1549, Ana de San Bartolomé was the sixth of seven children of María Manzanas and Hernán García, landowning peasants in the Castilian town of Almendral de la Cañada. According to Julián Urkiza, Ana's family was comfortable economically. They owned vineyards, cattle, and wheat fields and kept servants and even a private teacher who taught the sons to read and write and who may have also taught the daughters to read. The family lived an extremely pious existence, with both parents providing examples of Christian charity and devotion to their children. By her own account, Ana became aware of a special inclination toward the spiritual dimension of life at an early age and was predisposed to visions of supernatural origin before she could talk. As a young girl, she formed a close friendship with a cousin, Francisca Cano, later the Discalced nun Francisca de Jesús. Both girls exhibited early signs of the religious vocation that would become their later life, at one point planning to escape together from their homes in order to live a life of asceticism in the desert. The desire for an ascetic life at an early age resembles an episode in Saint Teresa's *Vida* in which she describes a childhood aspiration to run away and become a martyr for Christ. Teresa's childhood longing for martyrdom was partly the product of her reading of the popular hagiographies or biographies of saints, which depicted sanctity in highly idealized visions of suffering and martyrdom. Children of the time played "saints and pagans" much the way children of the twentieth century played "cowboys and Indians."

Orphaned at the age of ten, Ana came under the governance of her older siblings who assigned her various farm jobs, including that of shepherd in remote areas of the countryside. This time away from human company gave the young Ana more opportunity to experience visions of the Christ Child, the saints, and the Virgin Mary, to whom she became increasingly devoted. Although her brothers and sisters planned to marry her off at the earliest possible opportunity, Ana resisted this plan successfully but not without considerable distress to herself and her siblings. It seems clear that she had developed an aversion to the idea of marriage from an early age. Her attitude toward the opposite sex was, in fact, quite negative in her youth, and some scholars have speculated that it may have resulted from an unfortunate sexual encounter,[13] although there is no textual evidence to support this idea.

Given her pious upbringing and early disposition to the spiritual, it is not surprising that despite significant opposition from family members, Ana would opt for the religious life. It was also the only alternative to the marriage that her siblings were urging upon her. The convent was for many early modern women a refuge from the prospect of a loveless marriage and the unending demands of domestic life and afforded the only real possibility for intellectual, spiritual, and artistic growth for young women from Ana's social milieu. Her decision to join the Discalced Carmelites was influenced by a prophetic dream that Ana describes in her autobiography as well as by the intercession of a local priest acquainted with the order. After many altercations (including one in which an older brother threatened her life) and much foot dragging by her siblings, in 1570 Ana entered the Convent of Saint Joseph in Avila, the first convent of the Carmelite reform. There she encountered the founder, Teresa of Avila, and her life entered a new period.

COMPANION TO TERESA

The first twelve years of Ana's career were a period of training during which she received experience and knowledge that would prove useful in her later administrative duties. As she describes them, the earliest years and, in particular, the novitiate, are marked by periods of doubt and even melancholy that appear to have been widespread among recently professed nuns.[14] The visions of Christ continued and seemed to increase as evidence of her special relationship with him. Although at one point she was near death from an undiagnosed illness and a body weakened by a regime of extreme penitence, Ana recovered and in 1577 became Teresa's personal assistant, a position that she occupied until Teresa's death in 1582. During these years, Ana accompanied Teresa in the founding of convents, serving as her confidante, nurse, and eventually her secretary. By her own testimony, she learned to write in one afternoon by copying Teresa's handwriting, and this miraculous acquisition of the skill was eventually used as evidence of Teresa's sanctity

13. Electa Arenal and Stacey Schlau, introduction to *Untold Sisters: Hispanic Nuns in Their Own Works* (Albuquerque: University of New Mexico Press, 1989), 22.
14. Saint Teresa devotes chapters 6 and 7 of the *Book of Foundations* to advising superiors on how to deal with nuns who suffer from melancholy.

in her canonization proceedings. The ability to write provided Ana with another voice, one that she would use to dissent from authority, advise colleagues and family, defend her staunch adherence to a particular vision of religious life, and document the history of the Teresian reform. Writing became a necessary element of Ana's life and an intrinsic part of her self-concept. It also elevated her to a level of literacy and knowledge that was uncommon for a woman of her humble origins. Ana began her extensive writing career by taking dictation from Teresa to assist in answering her abundant correspondence. In a letter of December 4, 1581, Teresa wrote, "Ana de San Bartolomé never stops writing; she helps me a great deal."[15]

The relationship between the two women was one of mutual dependence and great affection. There do not appear to have been any ruptures or disagreements such as those that occurred between Teresa and some of her prioresses, perhaps because Ana never occupied a position of authority during Teresa's lifetime. Despite their unequal social and religious status, each woman actively sought out the company and advice of the other, and each had much to offer the other. The Mother Founder's preference for Ana became a source of considerable pride for her. As an icon of sanctity and the most powerful female voice for religious reform, Teresa was both spiritual mentor and model of leadership for her disciple. Ana's loyalty to Teresa was absolute, and this must have been reassuring to the saint, who had suffered criticism and even opposition from some of her closest associates. Ana's strong identification with Teresa is evident throughout her writings, and Teresa refers to Ana in the *Book of Foundations* as "so great a servant of God and so discreet that she can help me more than others who are choir nuns."[16]

Ana herself recognized the degree to which Teresa relied upon her services, describing a number of occasions on which Teresa required them, even when she (Ana) was physically unable to perform them. She affirms that "truly it was heaven to serve her, so that my greatest sorrow was to see her suffer." According to her account, she was present at Teresa's death and actually held her in her arms as she died. Even after Teresa's death, the relationship continued in the form of appearances by Teresa to her spiritual daughter.[17] Indeed, she appears to Ana in visions almost as regularly as

15. *Obras completas de Ana de San Bartolomé,* 2 vols., ed. Julián Urkiza (Rome: Teresianum, 1982–85), 1: 169, n.9.

16. E. Allison Peers, *Handbook to the Life and Times of Saint Teresa and Saint John of the Cross* (Westminster, MD: Newman Press, 1954), 169.

17. Such after-death appearances were common at the time and formed part of the ideology of mortality and the afterlife. There was a widespread belief that souls who went to heaven became active agents on behalf of their loved ones who remained in the world and often

Christ does, and Ana clearly relied upon this after-death contact as much as she had relied upon the relationship with the flesh and blood Teresa. "Teresa consoles Ana, offers her advice and reveals the future to her, particularly as it pertains to the Discalced reform, reinforcing her decisions in the political struggles between various factions of the order."[18] Occasionally these visions lasted for extensive periods of time. For example, Ana describes God as replacing the problematic new prioress of the Discalced convent in Madrid with Teresa, thereby facilitating the transition to new leadership for all. For Ana, this experience was so real that she actually saw the figure of Teresa when she looked at the real prioress, María de San Jerónimo. This vision continued for several months and helped Ana adjust to the new prelate.

The impact of her extended close association with the Mother Founder upon her companion was enormous and is reflected in Ana's writings and forms of religiosity. Much of her autobiography is an account of her years with Teresa, and she also wrote a biographical text entitled *Ultimos años de la madre Teresa de Jesus* (The Last Years of Mother Teresa). Both as literary and spiritual mentor, Teresa was the most important human influence on Ana's writing and visionary experiences. Ana's emulation of Teresa extends even to the content of some of her visions, which closely parallel some that Teresa describes in the *Book of Her Life*. The intimate contact gained at Teresa's side was the source of the almost proprietorial attitude Ana demonstrated toward Teresa and the Discalced Carmelite Order. After Teresa's death, as she began to assume roles of greater authority as prioress and foundress of convents in Spain, France, and the Low Countries, this attitude became increasingly apparent.

PRIORESS, FOUNDRESS, AND DISSENTER

Her prolonged association with Teresa accorded Ana de San Bartolomé a certain measure of authority as spokeswoman for the Discalced Carmelite philosophy and regimen. During the many conflicts that arose within the order in the years following Teresa's death, she did not hesitate to present herself as the most faithful representative of the Teresian reform and was regarded by some as the true guardian of the order's original constitution

---

reappeared to them in order to assist them. Carlos Eire provides an excellent analysis of Teresa's apparitions in *From Madrid to Purgatory* (Cambridge: Cambridge University Press, 1995), chap. 5. He convincingly argues that these visions of Teresa were useful to Ana in supporting her own vision of the Discalced Rule.

18. Weber, "Partial Feminism," 74.

and rule as written by Teresa. Despite her peasant origins and lack of education, Ana's voice became one of the most widely heard among the Discalced women. However, Ana's interpretation of the Teresian legacy was highly subjective, based at times on nothing more than her recollection of conversations with Teresa in life and also in her postmortem appearances. In the 1590s conflict known as "the nuns' revolt," she refused to join the faction of nuns that opposed the increasingly stringent measures by the provincial of the Discalced Order to curtail convent self-governance, particularly in matters of confession.[19] Rather, she sided with the provincial Nicolás Doria, who wished to eliminate what he viewed as too much freedom of the prioresses in choosing confessors and too much familiarity between confessors and nuns. Ana's rationale for her decision to support Doria was, as in almost everything, her understanding of Teresa's emphasis on obedience to superiors. Her stance placed her in direct opposition to two other of Teresa's closest spiritual daughters, María de San José and Ana de Jesús, and to Teresa's supporter and confessor Jerónimo Gracián. Ultimately, the more conservative faction with which Ana had aligned herself won out, and Doria's regime was instituted.

Yet, despite the fact that like other monastic women she viewed obedience as a crucial virtue, Ana's own conformity with authority figures varied significantly on several issues, and she occasionally found herself in full-blown confrontation with them. She certainly did not agree with all the new rules that Doria attempted to institute, and she was much more flexible on certain matters than some of those who had opposed him. When Doria tried to restrict the hours of recreation in the convents as a way of restoring the order to its original regime of silence and asceticism, Ana resisted this effort by writing in defense of them.[20] Similarly, she was willing to accept as novices women who were of Protestant origin as well as women who were not from upper-class backgrounds. In one case she expressed her disagreement with Ana de Jesús, then prioress at Paris, for her reluctance to accept an ex-Calvinist as novice, stating that if she was not willing to accept converts from Protestantism there was no sense in coming to France in the first place. She even suggests that this refusal to accept converts by Ana de Jesús might just be an excuse to leave France, since, according to Ana, all the French postulants are converts. Furthermore, she characterizes acceptance

---

19. Weber, "Partial Feminism," 74.

20. For a similar defense of convent recreation by one of Ana's contemporaries, see María de San José Salazar, *Book for the Hour of Recreation*, ed. Alison Weber, trans. Amanda Powell, Other Voice in Early Modern Europe (Chicago: University of Chicago Press, 2002).

of non-Catholics as an essential element of the order's rule and constitution, as ordained by the Holy Mother.[21] Although she never alludes to it specifically, it is possible that Ana would have known of Teresa's own *converso* background, and this would have inclined her favorably toward novices of non-Catholic heritage.[22]

Her commitment to obedience was most sorely tested during the early years of the order in France. Always ambivalent about her own aptitude for carrying forth the reform in an alien culture known for its heretical sects, Ana nevertheless accepted the challenge after numerous visions and urgings from the Lord, who at one point told her, "Don't delay going; if you don't go, nothing will be done; all the others will come back once they get there." Among the difficulties that France posed for her, not the least was her decision to take the black veil and become a choir nun. As a lay, or white-veiled nun, Ana had remained in the underclass of convent culture, relegated to the chores of cleaning, nursing, and cooking, activities that she seemed to enjoy. Her resistance to the change in status may have originated in an insecurity related to her humble origins and lack of education. The black-veiled nuns had to know enough Latin to be able to read the liturgies of the hours or the Eucharist. Their literacy and the dowry they brought to their convent communities signified a socially privileged background. Although it is impossible to know exactly what level of reading skill Ana had achieved by the time she became prioress of the Paris convent, it is clear from her autobiography that literacy was a source of concern for her, which was undoubtedly exacerbated by the cultural differences between her and her French novices. In any event, she did take the black veil in 1605 after having been ordered to do so by a Jesuit superior and remembering a vision of herself wearing the veil with Teresa's encouragement. Her misgivings were apparent, however. "And, in the end, I obeyed, my spirit quite disturbed, for I was not certain of anything."[23]

---

21. She expressed this disagreement in a letter to Tomás de Jesús, her spiritual advisor and superior. It was one of many occasions on which she communicated such differences with Ana de Jesús. The two Anas held widely divergent ideas on many of the fundamental principles of the Carmelite reform. See Concha Torres, *Ana de Jesús. Cartas (1590–1621)* (Salamanca: Universidad de Salamanca, 1995), 23, for a brief summary of these differences. Also Ildefonso Moriones, *Ana de Jesús y la herencia teresiana* (Rome: Teresianum, 1968), 20.

22. Teresa's Jewish ancestry has been the subject of much study. See, for example, Márquez Villanueva, "Santa Teresa y el linaje," in *Espiritualidad y literatura en el siglo XVI* (Madrid: Alfaguara, 1968), 141–205.

23. For a brief discussion of the role of literacy in the distinction between white and black veiled nuns, see Jane Ackerman, "Teresa and Her Sisters," in *The Mystical Gesture: Essays on Medieval and Early Modern Spiritual Culture in Honor of Mary E. Giles*, ed. Robert Boenig (Burlington, VT: Ashgate, 2000), 130–32.

Ana's greatest clashes with authority occurred as a result of her confrontation with Cardinal Pierre Bérulle, her confessor and immediate superior in France. An entire section of her autobiography is dedicated to describing what she perceived as his persecution of her and she also writes negatively of him in *Defensa de la herencia teresiana* (Defense of the Teresian Legacy) and other works. While it is very possible that many of her complaints were well-founded, at least some of her resentment of Bérulle stemmed from personality and cultural differences.[24] She vehemently opposed his efforts to install French confessors in the new Discalced convents in France. Ana also believed that he was reneging on a promise to bring Spanish male Carmelites to France and was unhappy that he was reluctant to found male Discalced monasteries in France. Bérulle may well have seen such an importation of Spanish priests as threatening his own control over the Discalced nuns, a control that he certainly attempted to exercise over Ana. While she was prioress in Paris, the cardinal succeeded in alienating the young French novices from her, telling them that she possessed an evil spirit and hatred toward the French. The situation was particularly difficult, given that he was Ana's confessor, a duty that he refused to assign to another priest.

Although Bérulle had initially been one of Ana's strongest supporters, he regarded the Spanish nuns as his subordinates. This proved a bitter pill to swallow, not only for Ana, but also for other members of the founding group in France. These women had known and worked closely with Saint Teresa, and this was one of the primary criteria in their selection for this mission. It was also a source of pride and confidence in their knowledge of the reformed order and its rule. As mentioned previously, Ana was particularly proud of her close personal relationship with Teresa and the special understanding of the order that accrued from it. Her conviction that she was the living heir to a soon to be canonized saint gave the uneducated Spanish peasant the courage to defy an extremely powerful church prelate. She viewed her lived experience of the reform as vastly superior to Bérulle's intellectualized concept of it, which was gained almost entirely from reading. Yet, although Ana describes herself as outspokenly opposed to the cardinal's high-handed administration of the Discalced Carmelite community, her letters to him reveal that she acknowledged his authority and attempted to remediate the

---

24. Raymond Deville, *The French School of Spirituality: An Introduction and Reader,* trans. Agnes Cunningham (Pittsburgh: Duquesne University Press, 1993), chap. 3, provides a detailed analysis of the vexed relationship between Bérulle and the Carmelites. See also William M. Thompson, ed., *Bérulle and the French School: Selected Writings* (New York: Paulist Press, 1989).

problems that had arisen between them.[25] The relationship remained a difficult one, aggravated by linguistic and cultural differences. Although she does not name him, Bérulle is the adversarial confessor to whom Ana refers in *Prayer in Abandonment*.

Much of the tension between the Spanish founders and French prelates and postulants was class based. Saint Teresa had quite deliberately democratized the order's entry requirements, seeking women of any background who were dedicated to the regime of austerity that the reform instituted. As a consequence, many of the Spanish postulants came from the middle levels of Spanish society. The French, from the beginning, had drawn upon the highest levels of the aristocracy for prelates and postulants. Complicated by her seeming lack of ability to assimilate the French language, the class difference was clearly one source of Ana's difficulties with Bérulle. As she describes it, the period of almost seven years that she spent in France was one of extreme stress and humiliation, yet throughout the constant discord and frustration, she is supported and comforted by numerous visions of God, Christ, and Teresa. With this supernatural support and confidence in her own correctness, Mother Ana managed to successfully found and administer convents in Pontoise and Tours, in addition to the problem-ridden convent in Paris. Dependent upon her interior life as the only alternative to the exterior world of intrigue and skullduggery, she never lost sight of human motives and interests. When Bérulle and the French prelates attempted to convince her to stay with them in France, she saw through their seeming cordiality. "They didn't like me or want me for anything except vanity, to tell the world that Saint Teresa's companion found their governance good and wanted to stay with them." She left France for Flanders in October 1611.

Although it was always the spiritual that most concerned Mother Ana, in Flanders as in her other assignments she was unable to avoid the intrusion of the outside world. Given the inseparability of religion and politics in this period, and the Discalced Order's commitment to battling "heresy," it was inevitable that international power struggles would affect the lives of the Spanish nuns in France and the Low Countries.[26] Although she does

25. For a discussion of the correspondence between Ana and Bérulle, see María Pilar Manero Sorolla, "Cartas de Ana de San Bartolomé a Monseñor Pierre de Bérulle," *Criticón* 51 (1991): 125–40.

26. According to Torres, one goal of the Discalced foundations in the Low Countries was decidedly political. She suggests that the Spanish regents, Archduke Alberto and Princess Isabel Clara Eugenia, actively used the Discalced Carmelites' expansion into France and Flanders to cultivate loyalty among the local aristocracy by attracting their daughters to a Spanish order. The Discalced foundations were essential in the final establishment of post-Tridentine

not provide details about events in the world outside the convent, it is clear from the autobiography that they did affect Ana, often quite directly. As Fortunato Antolín observes, "We see pass through the *Autobiography* of Mother Ana, although fleetingly and on tip toe, the essential Spain of her time: the King, the Empress, Antonio Pérez, the Invincible Armada, the wars in Flanders."[27] While still in France, Ana was visited by the infamous secretary of Phillip II, Antonio Pérez, who had escaped to France, after being condemned to death. She alludes to this visit only briefly, describing Pérez as "desperate about his salvation, in his view, because of the evil deeds he had done." It is significant that a figure of Pérez's notoriety visited Ana, and his visit reveals the extent of her influence as a woman of sanctity. In Antwerp, Princess Isabel Clara Eugenia, Phillip II's daughter and coregent of the Low Countries, consulted Ana concerning the possibility of maintaining the Twelve Year Treaty or renewing war with the Protestants of Flanders.[28] Although Ana refers to this consultation only in passing, it is part of a long-term relationship of mutual respect between these two deeply religious women. The princess regent had invited Ana to Flanders to establish the Teresian reform. In her own country, Ana was deeply affected by the catastrophic defeat of the Spanish Armada in 1588, attributing it to the misplaced faith of Spanish rulers in the fraudulent Nun of Lisbon.

Ana's years in Antwerp were the culmination of her long experience as administrator and reformer. Respected as a "living saint" for her mystical life and her capacity as prioress of the Antwerp convent, she came to be regarded by many as a protectress of the city. On two occasions her prayers and those of her nuns in the Antwerp convent were credited with destroying the fleet of the Protestant forces in storms, earning Ana the title of "Liberator of Antwerp."[29] In addition to acquiring a reputation as guardian of the Catholics in the Low Countries, as prioress in Flanders, Ana assisted English nuns fleeing from persecution in founding an English Discalced convent in

---

Catholicism in "a region as conflictive as Flanders." See her discussion of the relationship between the reformed Carmelites and Flemish society, 35–38.

27. *Autobiografía*, 19.

28. The Spanish Archduke Alberto and Princess Isabel Clara Eugenia were pacifists. The treaty, which was in effect from 1609 to 1621, was much debated in the Spanish Court.

29. Ana's "intervention" in the defeat of the Protestants is described in an excerpt from the *Chronicles of the Carmel of Antwerp* in *Autobiography of the Blessed Mother Anne of Saint Bartholomew*, translated from the French by a Religious of the Carmel of St. Louis, Missouri (St. Louis: H. S. Collins, 1916), 106–8. For a study of the idea of "living saint," see Gabriella Zarri, "Living Saints: A Typology of Female Sanctity in the Early Sixteenth Century," in *Women and Religion in Medieval and Renaissance Italy*, ed. Daniel Bornstein and Roberto Rusconi (Chicago: University of Chicago Press, 1996), 219–303.

Antwerp. She was a mentor and supporter of this convent and its prioress, Anne of the Ascension, until it separated from the jurisdiction of the male Carmelites in 1624.[30]

By the time she died of apoplexy at the age of seventy-seven, Ana de San Bartolomé had achieved great renown throughout her order and beyond. She was widely recognized as one of the most legitimate successors of Teresa of Avila, and many revered her merely for her closeness to the saint. Ana certainly continued the tradition of mystical contemplation and religious activism that had marked her mentor's career. Although her vision of governance and her concept of obedience did not follow Teresa's as closely as she may have believed, she was nevertheless extremely influential in extending the Discalced Order throughout Spain and Europe. For a woman of modest social background and very limited education, Ana was able to create a voice of great impact and authority, undoubtedly amplified by her writings. Always inspired by her model Teresa, she became a leader in her own right. She was beatified in 1917.

ANA DE SAN BARTOLOMÉ'S WRITTEN VOICE

Ana de San Bartolomé wrote copiously, and not all of her writings have been found. As one Teresian scholar observes, she appears not to have suffered from the "anxiety of authorship" that afflicted so many women writers of the day, perhaps because of "her conviction that she was the vehicle through whom Teresa's spiritual and historical legacy would be transmitted."[31] Although she occasionally wrote because she was ordered to do so by superiors, Ana may have enjoyed putting pen to paper, and never mentions any reticence about it. Given the many hours of solitary activities in the Discalced routine, it is quite possible that she perceived writing as her real voice, through which she could express experiences and sentiments otherwise silenced. Indeed, writing may well have been absolutely necessary as a form of cathartic release as well as a connection to the world outside the convent walls. It was also an activity learned and initially practiced under the guidance of the Holy Mother, and one Teresa herself practiced. This in itself would have increased its appeal

---

30. Ana de San Bartolomé had engaged in voluminous correspondence with Anne of the Ascension and regarded her decision to place the English convent under the Bishop of Antwerp rather than Carmelite male superiors as a kind of betrayal. The issue of restricting nuns' choice of confessors was, again, central in this conflict. See Anne Hardman, *English Carmelites in Penal Times* (London: Burns, Oates and Washbourne, 1936), 1–18, for a history of this convent and Ana's relationship to it.

31. Weber, "Partial Feminism," 71.

for Teresa's faithful companion. Although it is not always possible to date the composition of many texts, it is likely that for at least the last twenty years of her life Ana wrote on a daily basis, producing varied works in a style and language that reflect her social origins as well as the influence of the cultures in which she lived.[32] The works that appear here in translation communicate some of the diversity of her experience and writing.

Lives (Vidas)

There are actually two autobiographies, or *Vidas*. The first and longer of the two, which is the version translated here, is most likely a composite of various texts composed between the years 1607 and 1624 with a final paragraph added in 1625.[33] The second version is much shorter and was probably written over a period of six months in 1622. The two narratives share many anecdotes and reminiscences from her youth, with the later version providing somewhat more detail on her family life. The longer version is of much greater interest with regard to her interactions with prelates and her visionary experience. In addition to these two works, there is much writing of self in other compositions, such as her letters and chronicles of the Carmelite reform.

The *Vida*, or *Life*, translated here is typical in many ways of the spiritual autobiography that had become a common form of writing in early modern convents in Spain and throughout Europe.[34] Like its model, Saint Teresa's *Book of Her Life*, it is a record of intense religious experiences, characterized by highly personal contact with Christ, the Virgin Mary, and various saints. It is the interior or spiritual life of the writer/narrator that is the subject of the narrative, rather than the earthly, material existence. It is impossible, however, to completely disentangle the spiritual from the material, and Ana goes into great detail about convent culture, the politics of the cloister, and the Discalced Order. As was often the case, Ana's *Vida* is written in obedience to an order from a superior, although it is not clear precisely who this was. In most cases, a confessor ordered his penitent daughters to record the

32. According to Urkiza, most of the writing was done while Ana was in Antwerp between the years 1611 and 1626 (*Obras completas*, 1: 77). Yet she had written *The Last Years of Mother Teresa* as early as 1584 and also corresponded regularly with many members of the order prior to leaving Spain.

33. Urkiza, *Obras completas*, 1: 280.

34. For a brief overview of this genre as well as several examples from Spain and colonial Latin America, including excerpts of Ana's *Autobiography*, see Arenal and Schlau, *Untold Sisters*. For a longer, more detailed study of autobiographical writing by women religious, see Isabelle Poutrin, *Le voile et la plume: Autobiographie et saintete feminine dan l'Espagne moderne* (Madrid: Velasquez, 1995).

nature of their spirituality and forms of religiosity, often as a way of over-
seeing their orthodoxy. Ana begins her narrative by stating simply, "Jesus,
Mary, Joseph, and our Holy Mother Teresa of Jesus, in whose name I do this
which holy obedience orders me." The reference to Saint Teresa in juxta-
position with the names of the members of the Holy Family is significant
because it reveals the powerful influence that Teresa still exercised over her
companion and disciple more than forty years after her death.

Like other such narratives, Ana's *Vida* is a hybrid of several genres—
pious memoir, biography, hagiography, and even some poetic forms. Her
own story is inextricably intertwined with that of Teresa, whom she portrays as performing miracles and other acts that reveal her sanctity. Indeed,
Teresa looms almost as large in this text as Christ and God the Father. "In
Ana's eyes, Teresa was a saint with power to heal, protect, intercede, and
prophesy the future, in vita and in morte."[35] However, Ana's story is also the
story of the Discalced Order after Teresa's death, and she provides an eye-
witness account of successes and failures in the continuation and expansion
of religious reform. Her accounts are particularly valuable for what they
reveal of the adaptation of the Spanish woman-centered movement to the
foreign cultures of France and the Low Countries. While the focus is on her
own experience, we understand that it is always inseparable from the order,
which at one point she refers to as her "center."

Ana's representation of self in the autobiography reveals a contradictory mix of humility, confidence, hope, and doubt. At the same time that
she engages in the mystical rhetoric of self-negation and total subjection to
the divine beloved, Ana emerges as a strong-willed individualist, more than
a little self-righteous in her claim to the legacy of the Mother Founder.
Although we cannot doubt her sincerity, at times her visionary discourse
may seem almost contrived in its fervor and self-recrimination, particularly considering her confidence in matters of order governance. Given
that the *Song of Songs* was a probable source for some of her visions, it is not
surprising that these should be erotic in nature. Following the metaphor
of a relationship between lovers, the writer frequently describes God as a
tender yet demanding spouse and her soul as his yearning bride. She does
not possess the elegance of style or educated imagination of other writers
but rather communicates her experiences in a more direct language, which
nonetheless expresses their physical and spiritual intensity. Her reactions
to God's presence in her life are varied but always passionate. Ana describes
herself on different occasions as "drunk" or "inflamed" with love of God,

35. Weber, "Partial Feminism," 73.

"completely transformed" by him, and a number of times as unable to bear
the ardor of her reaction to the divine presence. On one occasion, for example, she describes the Lord as "he came so softly and from behind like
a man in love about to play a joke on his wife. Coming closer, he put his
hand over my heart, and it seemed to me that he had torn it out."

Ana's contact with the supernatural occurs most frequently during "recollections" or states of deep meditation, during which the physical world
seemingly vanishes from consciousness. In these trance-like states she hears
the voice of God, Teresa, and other otherworldly beings. Visions, however,
could also be the work of the devil, and women were considered particularly
vulnerable to his wiles.[36] Although Ana refers to the presence of demons
in her world, on at least one occasion she describes herself as largely unaf-
fected by them. Like her mentor Teresa, she occasionally expresses doubts
concerning the possibly demonic origins of her visions, and she certainly
recognizes the presence of the diabolic in human affairs. In some cases, the
devil and his minions are permitted by God to torment the faithful as a test.
Often the devil appears in some form as a warning of future problems. For
example, Ana recounts a vision in which she sees certain members of her
order turn into black crows as they engage in conversation with laypeople
and religious of other orders. Within a year, the order experienced the 1590
"revolt of the nuns" referred to above.

Her visions are experienced with such intensity and often last for so
short a time that Ana is unable to communicate them adequately in words,
and she is honest in admitting this, frequently stating that these occurrences
are beyond her comprehension or capacity to describe.[37] However, she attempts to make her spiritual life accessible by positing images from nature as
analogous to her situation. In describing the presence of Christ in her soul,
for example, she uses the following imagery: "The vision that I carry at other
times in my soul is like a little silkworm, and how it is cared for and fed, and
when it is properly grown, it begins to spin through its mouth a thin thread
of silk and make its cocoon, and with the pleasure and sweetness that there

36. In *Tratado de la verdadera y falsa prophecia* (Segovia, 1588), Juan de Horozco warns of apparitions staged by the devil and the susceptibility of women to such counterfeit visions. Even
Gracián, sympathetic to the visionary experiences of Saint Teresa, cautioned against unques-
tioning acceptance of women's visions. See, for example, Jerónimo Gracián, "Dilucidario del
verdadero espíritu," in *Obras*, ed. Silverio de Santa Teresa (Burgos: El Monte Carmelo, 1933),
1: 187–94.

37. The inability to communicate adequately the mystical experience is not unique to Ana. It
is a topos of writing by both male and female mystics. In the case of women, however, it may
also have been part of a discourse of self-effacement seemingly in accord with existing notions
of female intellectual inferiority.

is in that, it doesn't feel that it's dying until in giving the goodness that it has, it closes itself in its cocoon and dies. In this way did I see my soul, or was shown it. . . ."[38]

Many of the visions involve dialogue with the divinity or a saint, often in very colloquial language. God appears to her at times as though speaking to a friend or family member, while on other occasions he seems to be more remote, the biblical God of splendor and majesty. Ana asks her Lord for assistance in times of crisis and receives answers that frequently affirm her righteousness and exceptionality. In such visions, even her ignorance or lack of education can become a manifestation of God's grace. "Another time, thinking of my little worth and how I was nothing, the Lord spoke to me and told me, 'That's how I want you, without being or knowing anything, in order to do through you what I want to do. The wise men of the world with their human prudence don't listen to me, for they think that they know everything.'" Despite her seeming humility, statements such as this imply spiritual privilege and also testify to her keen awareness of her educational inferiority.

Ana's accounts of convent life provide a realistic, if not very detailed, portrayal of the varied communities in which she lived. She knows that her readers, male and female, are familiar with convent culture and takes for granted that such readers will immediately understand her references to the locutory, the refectory, and the routine of prayer, meals, and work.[39] Although the emphasis is on her own activities, in relating her duties as nurse and as Mother Superior she communicates a sense of the collective enterprise of the cloister as well as her individual experience of it. This is particularly true of her depiction of situations of danger such as the flooding that almost destroyed the Discalced house at Burgos. Describing such emergencies, she often switches from the self-focused first person singular that predominates in her narration to the "we" of the shared experience.

Similarly, although she frequently portrays the workload as overwhelming, a sense of shared effort and communal identity also emerges in her description of daily activities. Activities and chores benefit others, both the community at large and occasionally individual nuns. At times her descriptions are quite graphic, as in the case of nursing a leprous nun in Flanders. Ana

---

38. *Autobiografía*, 98–99. This is a clear example of the influence of Saint Teresa's spirituality on her companion. In *Las moradas* Teresa develops this same metaphor of worm/soul at some length. See Mujica, "Ana de San Bartolomé: Hacía Paris y Flandes," 25–27.

39. The exact schedule of daily activities and the guiding principles of Discalced routine are laid out in the *Constitutions*. See *Complete Works of St. Teresa*, ed. Allison Peers (London: Sheed and Ward, 1944), 3: 219–38.

represents herself as willing to undergo the most arduous tasks on behalf of her spiritual sisters knowing that she is doing the bidding of her conscience and God and also because, in her own words, she was "loving by nature."

It appears that after Teresa's death Ana did not form any close personal relationships but rather, following the founder's advice, attempted to remain detached while serving the community at large.[40] It is clear, however, that she had favorites in the various convents in which she lived, and she does not hesitate to express disapproval for some nuns and their actions. When Isabel de la Cruz at the Madrid convent tried to convince Ana to accompany her in establishing an ultra ascetic community in the remote countryside outside of Alcalá de Henares, Ana referred to the plan as "craziness" and steadfastly refused, stating that she could not presume "to do something of more perfection than what the Saint had done." Nuns who disagreed with Teresa or showed her any disrespect are always subject to Ana's criticism, although they are not usually identified by name.

If the *Vida* seems somewhat vague with regard to exact dates, and even at times with regard to the places where certain events occurred, this may well be due to the extensive period of time over which the longer autobiography was written. Time is frequently marked by such imprecise expressions as "one day" or "one Christmas" without any more concrete information. There is often no way of knowing how much time elapsed between one incident and another, creating the effect of fragmentation, a chain of individual episodes that may or may not be causally related. People are not always referred to by name, perhaps because they were still alive at the time of writing and Ana was unwilling to affect their public image, or perhaps because she really did not remember their names. It is quite possible that Ana was occasionally narrating events that had transpired over forty years earlier, so it is not surprising that chronology and other specific information are unclear or absent. The sequencing of the action, while for the most part linear, is at times interrupted by the insertion of events or action unrelated to the narration at hand. Ana herself was aware of these disruptions of the narrative, but apparently felt compelled by obedience to include everything she could remember, on one occasion stating, "What I'm going to say and something of what's been said is off the subject of which I was speaking, but it is so I do not forget to say anything as I have been ordered." Awareness of the act of narrating is common in the writing of nuns. These women wrote in a self-conscious manner, revealing the conflict between adherence to the

---

40. Teresa warns against affective relationships between individual nuns in *Way of Perfection*. See Peers, *Complete Works of St. Teresa*, 2: 15–17.

obedience imposed upon them and their own need to be selective in narrating their experiences.[41]

While details of time and place are sparse, the dialogues and visions are documented vividly in language that is simple and concise, creating an almost theatrical effect in the narration. The conversations between Ana and God, Ana and Jesus, and Ana and Teresa all are short but effective examples of the frequent exchanges between the writer and these primary influences in her life. The language throughout the autobiography is colloquial[42] and creates the impression of a sustained oral monologue in which a woman of rustic origin and strong convictions attempts to recreate her religious commitment. "Her writings exemplify the speech of peasant women of Castile, although form and formulas were undoubtedly modified by the association with women of more privileged classes in the convent and increasingly, by the daily use of spoken French during the last twenty-two years of her life."[43]

Ana's grammar and vocabulary reflect the still fluctuating forms of the rural Spanish of Castile in the late sixteenth century.[44] Her spelling is erratic and exhibits numerous characteristics of the spoken language such as metathesis or switching of sounds within a word. Many of these characteristics reflect archaic or antiquated forms still in use among the Castilian peasants. Her syntax also reveals aspects of the spoken language. For example, Ana frequently engages in abrupt changes of subject within a sentence, making it difficult to follow the original thought, or occasionally interrupts one idea before it is complete by including a clause that introduces a completely different thought. As mentioned previously, it is as though the writer is engaged in spontaneous recounting of her experience, remembering certain events as they occur to her. The final effect of these interruptions in the flow of thought is to shift the reader's attention rapidly from one subject or idea to another, resulting in a considerable lack of clarity. While in some writers such changes might constitute a strategy aimed at creating a deliberate literary effect, it is

41. See Weber, *Teresa of Ávila and the Rhetoric of Femininity* (Princeton: Princeton University Press, 1990), 42–48, for an analysis of the "double bind" in which women writers found themselves vis-à-vis their male censors and religious superiors.

42. I agree with Weber's caveat that "writing is seldom a transparent transcription of speech and does not preclude rhetorical strategies, whether these have been absorbed through written or oral sources" ("Partial Feminism," 84, n.1). The seeming orality of Ana's speech may be a rhetorical strategy aimed at projecting an image of honesty and directness.

43. Arenal and Schlau, *Untold Sisters*, 30.

44. Urkiza considers her language of great interest for what it reveals of the evolution of Castilian Spanish. He provides a detailed analysis of her discourse in the "Introducción general" to *Obras completas*.

quite likely that in Ana's case they are part of an unsophisticated and untutored style that differentiates little, if at all, between spoken and written language. Some of this informal and occasionally chaotic discourse may be the result of the limited time she had for writing. She wrote, quite literally, whenever she could and seemingly without any preoccupation about style, creating an effect of plainspoken unpretentiousness. Another possible explanation is her lack of familiarity with a broad range of written texts as models.

It is unclear exactly how many literary sources Ana may have drawn upon. If at times she cites the Bible, particularly the *Song of Songs*, these citations are the only sign of literary knowledge other than some brief references to Teresa's works and John of the Cross's *Cántico espiritual*. Ana certainly would have read some books and heard many sermons and oral readings, and all of these may have influenced her writing, albeit at an unconscious level. However, the primary source of her narrative appears to be her own lived experience, both worldly and mystical.

In sum, the *Autobiography* provides material for study from a variety of perspectives: religious, literary, cultural, and linguistic. From the perspective of feminist cultural analysis, it supplies unique insights into the vocation of a key figure in the creation of a religious regimen that was, in its origins, woman centered. It also reveals much about women's autobiographical discourse at the time. There is an ambivalence between disclosure and reticence which characterized the texts of other women religious. As in much writing of the self, memory is selective and frequently self-justifying, so that some of the narrative seems to be little more than a record of the persecutions and problems that the writer claims to have suffered as a result of adherence to her vision of the reform. On the other hand, the voice that emerges from this text testifies to self-actualization in a communal enterprise of dedicated and energetic women and particularly to the inspiration that one strong woman can provide to another.

OTHER WRITINGS

An Account of the Foundation at Burgos

In the *Autobiography*, Ana refers to the numerous trials and tribulations that Saint Teresa experienced, stating, "If I had to tell the troubles she suffered during the years that I was with her, I would never finish, for what is told in her books is nothing. Of what happened in Burgos, which was the last foundation she made, what's told in the books is nothing." Ana's account rectifies these omissions by detailing the many obstacles encountered in the last of the truly Teresian foundations. It is the second part of a text entitled *Ultimos años de la Madre Santa Teresa* (The Last Years of Mother Saint

Teresa), probably written at the end of 1585, at the order of a superior, more than likely Nicolás Doria. Ostensibly this account was ordered as part of the effort by Discalced superiors to gather information about Teresa prior to initiating her beatification proceedings. It begins with the particulars of the trip from Avila to Burgos. In her description of the flooded roads and dangerous bridges, Ana highlights the heroic conduct of Teresa, who offers to lead the way through such perils despite her ill health. The writer also focuses on the politics of the Burgos foundation, in particular the resistance of the archbishop, a distant relative of Teresa. Although she is careful to advise her readers of his sanctity, Ana's attitude toward this prelate is far from favorable. Repeated references to him by the title of respect "His Lordship" are juxtaposed with her depiction of his lack of cooperation and unresponsiveness to the situation of the nuns who anxiously awaited his permission to found the convent. Throughout all of these difficulties, Saint Teresa is a model of optimism and faith for her daughters; she is finally rewarded with the license for the convent, and the house gains the esteem of the populace in the area. Her influence is such, according to Ana, that when a flood hits Burgos, the townsfolk, including the once recalcitrant archbishop, believe that they have been saved because of her presence in the town.

In addition to the foundation itself, Ana narrates the circumstances of Teresa's death and the preparations for the transferal of her body from Alba to Avila. She describes the death of her mentor simply and without excessive emotion, despite its enormous impact on her life. Insinuating that "notable things" occurred at the moment of Teresa's passing, she does not elaborate on them, leaving them for the prelates to reveal, "if they want." While her reticence may seem surprising given her important presence at the saint's deathbed, it is the presence of others with more authority at the death scene that inhibits her on this occasion.[45] The condition of the body and its removal to Avila may seem like gratuitous and even gruesome detail to a modern reader, but they were standard elements in the narrative of a saintly life, which, after all, did not cease at physical death. Rather, the fresh and fragrant state of Teresa's body after two and a half years is a sign of the sanctity of the deceased and the favor she has achieved from God for her long sufferings and trials in the world, as Ana is careful to inform us.[46]

45. Eire mentions that other versions of Teresa's death differ somewhat in their accounts of her final moments. Neither Francisco de Ribera, author of the first biography of Teresa, nor Diego de Yepes, the presumed author of a biography published in 1599, alludes to Teresa's summoning of Ana prior to her death. See *From Madrid to Purgatory*, 410. See also pages 413–15 for an analysis of the signs and portents described by some at Teresa's death.

46. For an excellent study of the miraculous state of the saint's cadaver as well as the disputes surrounding its final resting place, see Eire, *From Madrid to Purgatory*, chap. 3.

Prayer in Abandonment (1607)

As the date indicates, the writer was in Paris when she composed this heart-felt plea for divine assistance. She undoubtedly wrote it during the worst moments of her disagreement with Pierre Bérulle. According to Urkiza, the tribulation to which she refers at the outset is the lack of a confessor in whom she can truly confide. Although she never actually identifies Bérulle, it is evident from her references to the "Father who is confessing me" that he is the unnamed priest who is the source of her anguish. In fact, the entire prayer is an indictment of this confessor whom, it is clear, she does not believe has been sent by God. She asks God for a minister "who will help me in your name, and who I can be sure is from you." Her distrust of the people around her is so great that at one point she expresses doubt about the authenticity of their Catholicism. "But this is just the opposite and all is anguish. Among such people you scarcely know if those with whom you speak are completely Catholic." At the end she describes a vision that is also in her autobiography. She sees many little crosses, which doubtless symbolize her anguished situation. The prayer ends with a reference to the difficulty of experiencing such visions without the guidance of a confessor. The importance of writing should not be underestimated here. Writing down these strongly felt emotions of anguish, resentment, and self-pity would certainly have been cathartic. Although Ana had communicated her dissatisfaction to Bérulle on a number of occasions, she was obviously limited as to what she could say to him. The confessor-penitent relationship, fraught with issues of gender, class, and, in this case, culture constrained the communication between them. It is clear that this is one of the many times when her written voice could express what she could not say aloud.

Spiritual Lecture (Pontoise, July 1605)

This lecture is most likely the first of several composed by Ana in her role as Mother Superior at the convents in France. She rewrote these lectures several times, adding or deleting fragments. This particular text ends in the middle of a sentence, suggesting that Ana was interrupted by other duties. Using it as a base text, she later expands it into other, longer lectures. Written to be delivered orally, it is directed to the convent community, and most probably to the novices in particular. As Urkiza suggests, it may well also have been directed to Pierre Bérulle as an account of her conscience and her doctrine for educating novices.[47] The ostensible purpose is to reawaken in her audience

47. *Obras completas,* 1: 525.

the dedication and self-abnegation that are central to the religious vocation. Ana occasionally speaks directly to her audience, addressing them as "dearest ones," and uses the first person plural throughout the lecture, reiterating her membership in the convent community. She speaks not so much from a position of superiority as one of counselor among equals. Only once does she remind her listeners of her position as prioress by asking them to advise her of any physical or spiritual concerns they might have. The lecture covers the responsibility of the nuns to follow their vows of poverty, obedience, and humility. In addition, Ana stresses the importance of adhering to an inner or spiritual rule, which is an intrinsic part of the religious life. This rule must subjugate the passions of self-interest that threaten to destroy the commitment of the religious to a loving and paternal God.

In the section of the lecture that is dedicated to obedience, she expresses her ideas on the qualities of a good prelate. The date of this lecture and the comments indicate that she may well have had Bérulle in mind, particularly in the final words of this section in which she admonishes the superior who does not demonstrate adequate concern for the needs of his spiritual charges but rather alienates them. Her words predict dire consequences for such an unworthy prelate. "Woe to him who proceeds in this manner, for it were better that he not have a name in this life!" Given the centrality of the confessor/penitent relationship in the lives of nuns, this admonishment is particularly significant. Under the guise of generalization, Ana actually charges her own confessor with professional incompetence and even lack of religion in meeting the needs of those who depend upon him for guidance. The power differential between female penitent and male confessor does not permit her to name her inadequate and unsympathetic confessor, and Bérulle himself may never have read this lecture, but, again, the written expression of her dissatisfaction affords Ana another opportunity for emotional release that she would not have had otherwise.

VOLUME EDITOR'S
BIBLIOGRAPHY

WORKS BY ANA DE SAN BARTOLOMÉ

Obras completas de Ana de San Bartolomé. 2 vols. Edited by Julián Urkiza. Rome: Teresianum, 1982–85.

Autobiografía. Edited by Fortunato Antolín. Madrid: Espiritualidad, 1969.

Autobiography of the Blessed Mother Anne of Saint Bartholomew. Translated from the French by a Religious of the Carmel of St. Louis, Missouri. St. Louis: H. S. Collins, 1916.

STUDIES OF ANA DE SAN BARTOLOMÉ'S LIFE AND WORKS

Arenal, Electa and Stacey Schlau, eds. "Ana de San Bartolomé: the Making of a Carmelite Oral History." In *Untold Sisters: Hispanic Nuns in Their Own Works.* Translated by Amanda Powell. Albuquerque: University of New Mexico Press, 1989.

Manero Sorolla, María Pilar. "Cartas de Ana de San Bartolomé a Monseñor Pierre de Bérulle." *Criticon* 51 (1991): 125–40.

Mujica, Barbara. "Ana de San Bartolomé: Hacía Paris y Flandes." In *Women Writers of Early Modern Spain: Sophia's Daughters.* Edited by Barbara Mujica. New Haven: Yale University Press, 2004.

Sánchez Diaz, María Milagros. "Las recreaciones en el Carmelo: Ana de San Bartolomé (Análisis de una 'Conferencia espiritual')." In *Estado actual de los estudios sobre el Siglo de Oro.* Edited by Manuel García Martín et al. 2 vols. Salamanca: Universidad de Salamanca, 1993(2):931–39.

Urkiza, Julian. "Introducción general." In *Obras completas de Ana de San Bartolome.* vol. 1: 53–205.

———. "La beata Ana de San Bartolomé y la transmisión del espíritu teresiano." In *Monte Carmelo* 84 (1976): 237–45.

Weber, Alison. "The Partial Feminism of Ana de San Bartolomé." In *Recovering Spain's Feminist Tradition.* Edited by Lisa Vollendorf, 69–85. New York: Modern Language Association, 2001.

Wilson, Christopher. "A Heroic Successor to St. Teresa of Avila: Painted Miniatures of Ana de San Bartolomé." *Carmelus* 50 (2003): 129–47.

EDITIONS AND ANTHOLOGIES OF WORKS BY
DISCALCED CARMELITE WOMEN IN EARLY MODERN SPAIN

Ana de Jesús. *Escritos y documentos.* Burgos: Monte Carmelo, 1996.

Arenal, Electa, and Stacey Schlau, eds. *Untold Sisters: Hispanic Nuns in Their Own Works.* A bilingual anthology, with translations by Amanda Powell. Albuquerque: University of New Mexico Press, 1989. Many of the writers were members of the Discalced Carmelite Order.

García de la Concha, Víctor, and Ana María Pellitero, eds. *Libro de romances y coplas del Carmelo de Valladolid.* Salamanca: Consejo de Castilla y Leon, 1982.

Cecilia de Nacimiento. *Obras completas.* Edited by Jose M. Díaz Cerón, S.J. Madrid: Editorial de Espiritualidad, 1971.

María de San Alberto. *Viva al siglo, muerta al mundo. Selected Works/Obras Escogidas.* A bilingual anthology edited with introduction by Stacey Schlau. New Orleans: University Press of the South, 1998.

María de San José Salazar. *Book for the Hour of Recreation.* Introduction and notes by Alison Weber. Translated by Amanda Powell. Chicago: University of Chicago Press, 2002.

———. *Avisos para el gobierno de las religiosas.* Edited by Juan Luis Astigárraga. Rome: Instituto Histórico Teresiano, 1977.

———. *Escritos espirituales.* Edited by Simeón de la Sagrada Familia. Rome: Postulación General O.C.D., 1979.

Simeón de la Sagrada Familia et al., eds. *Humor y espiritualidad en la escuela teresiana.* Burgos: Monte Carmelo, 1966. Humorous writings by Teresa de Jesús, Jeronimo Gracián, Ana de Jesús, and María de San José.

Teresa de Jesús (de Avila). *Collected Works.* Edited by Kieran Kavanaugh, O.C.D., and Otilio Rodriguez, O.C.D. 3 vols. Washington, D.C.: Institute of Carmelite Studies, 1980–87.

———. *Collected Letters: 1546–1577.* Edited by Kieran Kavanaugh, O.C.D. Vol. 1. Washington, D.C.: Institute of Carmelite Studies, 2001.

———. *Obras completas.* Décima edición. Edited by Tomás Alvarez. Burgos: Monte Carmelo, 1998.

Torres, Concepción, ed. *Cartas de Ana de Jesús (1590–1621). Religiosidad y vida cotidiana en la clausura del siglo de oro.* Salamanca: Universidad de Salamanca, 1995.

STUDIES IN TERESIAN REFORM AND ITS EXPANSION

Ahlgren, Gillian T. W. *Teresa of Avila and the Politics of Sanctity.* Ithaca, NY: Cornell University Press, 1996.

Bilinkoff, Jodi. *The Avila of Saint Teresa: Religious Reform in a Sixteenth-Century City.* Ithaca, NY: Cornell University Press, 1989.

———. "Teresa of Jesus and Carmelite Reform." In *Religious orders of the Catholic Reformation. Studies in Honor of John C. Olin on His Seventy-Fifth Birthday.* Edited by Richard L. De Molen, 165–86. New York: Fordham University Press, 1994.

Deville, Raymond. Chapter 3 in *The French School of Spirituality: An Introduction and Reader.* Translated by Agnes Cunningham. Pittsburgh: Duquesne University Press, 1993.

Diefendorf, Barbara. *From Penitence to Charity: Pious Women and the Catholic Reformation in Paris.* New York: Oxford University Press, 2004.

Egido, Teofanes. *Perfil histórico de Santa Teresa.* Madrid: Editorial de Espiritualidad, 1981.

Giles, Mary, ed. *Women in the Inquisition.* Baltimore: Johns Hopkins University Press, 1999.

Gracián, Jerónimo. *Obras.* Edited by Silverio de Santa Teresa. Burgos: El Monte Carmelo, 1933.

Hardman, Anne. *English Carmelites in Penal Times.* London: Burns, Oates and Washbourne, 1936.

Llamas Martínez, Enrique. *Santa Teresa de Jesús y la Inquisicion Española.* Madrid: CSIC, 1972.

Márquez Villanueva, Francisco. *Espiritualidad y literatura en el siglo XVI.* Madrid: Alfaguara, 1968.

Moriones de la Visitación, Ildefonso. *Ana de Jesús y la herencia teresiana.* Rome: Edizioni del Teresianum, 1968.

Peers, E. Allison. *Handbook to the Life and Times of Saint Teresa and Saint John of the Cross.* Westminster: Newman Press, 1954.

———. *Studies of the Spanish Mystics.* 3 vols. Reprint. London: Society for Promoting Christian Knowledge, 1960.

Serouet, Pierre. *Jean de Bretigny (1556–1634): aux origines du Carmel de France, de Belgique et du Congo.* Louvain: Publications Universitaires de Louvain, 1974.

Thompson, William M., ed. *Bérulle and the French School: Selected Writings.* New York: Paulist Press, 1989.

Weber, Alison. "Spiritual Administration: Gender and Discernment in the Carmelite Reform." *Sixteenth Century Journal* 31, no. 1 (2000): 123–46.

STUDIES OF CONVENT CULTURE IN EARLY MODERN SPAIN

Ackerman, Jane. "Teresa and Her Sisters." In *The Mystical Gesture. Essays on Medieval and Early Modern Spiritual Culture in Honor of Mary E. Giles.* Edited by Robert Boenig. Burlington, VT: Ashgate, 2001.

Arenal, Electa. "'Leyendo yo y escribiendo ella:' the Convent as Intellectual Community." *Journal of Hispanic Philology* 13 (1989): 214–29.

———. "The Convent as Catalyst for Autonomy: Two Hispanic Nuns of the Seventeenth Century." In *Women in Hispanic Literature.* Edited by Beth Miller, 147–83. Los Angeles: University of California Press, 1983.

Arenal, Electa, and Stacey Schlau, "Introduction." In *Untold Sisters: Hispanic Nuns in Their Own Works.* Albuquerque: University of New Mexico Press, 1989.

Cátedra, Pedro. "Lectura femenina en el claustro (España, siglos XIV–XVI)." Pp. 7–53 in *Des femmes et des livres: France et Espagne, XIVe–XVIIe siecle: Actes de la Journee d'etude organisee par l'Ecole nationale des charters et l'Ecole Normale superieure de Fontenay/Saint-Cloud (Paris, 30 avril 1998).* Edited by Dominique de Courcelles and Carmen Val Julián. Paris: Ecole des Chartes, 1999.

Eire, Carlos. *From Madrid to Purgatory. The Art and Craft of Dying in Sixteenth-Century Spain.* Cambridge: Cambridge University Press, 1995.

Gracián, Jerónimo. *Obras.* Edited by Silverio de Santa Teresa. Burgos: El Monte Carmelo, 1933.

Imirizaldu, Jesús. *Monjas y beatas embaucadoras.* Madrid: Editora Nacional, 1977.

Lehfeldt, Elizabeth A., "Discipline, Vocation and Patronage: Spanish Religious
Women in a Tridentine Microclimate." *Sixteenth Century Journal* 30, no. 4 (1999):
1009–30.

———. *Religious Women in Golden Age Spain: The Permeable Cloister.* Burlington, VT: Ashgate, 2005.

Perry, Mary Elizabeth. *Gender and Disorder in Early Modern Seville.* Princeton, NJ: Princeton University Press, 1990.

Sánchez Lora, José L. *Mujeres, conventos y formas de la religiosidad barroca.* Fundación Uni-
versitaria Española, 1988.

Santa Teresa, Silverio, de. *Historia del Carmen Descalzo.* Burgos: El Monte Carmelo,
1935–52.

Torres, Concepción. *La clausura imposible: Conventualismo femenino y expansion contrarre-
formista.* Madrid: Al-Mudayna, 2001.

Vigil, Mariló. *La vida de las mujeres en los siglos XVI y XVII.* Madrid: Siglo veintiuno,
1986.

STUDIES OF WRITINGS BY WOMEN
RELIGIOUS IN EARLY MODERN SPAIN

Arenal, Electa, and Stacey Schlau. "Stratagems of the Strong, Stratagems of the
Weak: Autobiographical Prose of the Seventeenth-Century Hispanic Convent."
Tulsa Studies in Women's Literature 9 (1990): 25–42.

Colahan, Clark. "Maria de Jesus de Agreda: The Sweetheart of the Holy Office." In
Women in the Inquisition. Spain and the New World. Edited by Mary E. Giles, 155–70.
Baltimore: Johns Hopkins Press, 1999.

Donahue, Darcy. "Writing Lives: Nuns and Confessors as Auto/biographers in Early
Modern Spain." *Journal of Hispanic Philology* 13 (1989): 23–39.

Herpoel, Sonja. *A la zaga de Santa Teresa: autobiografías por mandato.* Amsterdam: Rodopi,
1999.

Howe, Elizabeth Teresa. *The Visionary Life of Madre Ana de San Agustín.* Rochester, NY:
Tamesis, 2004.

Manero Sorolla, Maria Pilar. "Visionarias reales en la España aurea." In *Images de la
femme en Espagne aux XVIe et XVII siecle.* Edited by Augustín Redondo, 305–20. Paris:
Publications de la Sorbonne, 1994.

Myers, Kathleen A. "The Addressee Determines the Discourse: The Role of the
Confessor in the Spiritual Autobiography of Madre María de San Joseph (1656–
1719)." *Bulletin of Hispanic Studies* 69 (1992): 39–47.

Peers, Allison, ed. *The Complete Works of St. Teresa.* London: Sheed and Ward, 1944.

Poutrin, Isabelle. *Le voile et la plume: Autobiographie et saintete feminine dans l'Espagne moderne.*
Madrid: Casa de Velasquez, 1995.

Rhodes, Elizabeth. "Y yo dije, 'Si, señor.' Ana Domenge and the Barcelona Inquisition." In *Women in the Inquisition. Spain and the New World.* Edited by Mary E. Giles,
134–54. Baltimore: Johns Hopkins University Press, 1999.

Rossi, Rosa. *Teresa de Avila: Biografía de una escritora*. Translated by Marieta Gargatagli. Barcelona: ICARIA, 1984.

Sampson, Elisa Vera Tudela. *Colonial Angels: Narratives of Gender and Spirituality in Mexico, 1580–1750*. Austin: University of Texas Press, 2000.

Schlau, Stacey, ed. "Introduction." In Maria de San Alberto, *Viva al siglo, muerta al mundo: Selected Works*. New Orleans: University Press of the South, 1998.

Slade, Carole. *Teresa of Avila: Author of a Heroic Life*. Berkeley: University of California Press, 1995.

Surtz, Ronald E. *Writing Women in Late Medieval and Early Modern Spain: The Mothers of Saint Teresa of Avila*. Philadelphia: University of Pennsylvania Press, 1995.

Velasco, Sherry. *Demons, Nausea and Resistance in the Autobiography of Isabel de Jesús, 1611–1682*. Albuquerque: University of New Mexico Press, 1996.

Weber, Alison. "On the Margins of Ecstasy: María de San José as (Auto)biographer." *Journal of the Institute of Romance Studies* 4 (1996): 251–68.

———. *Teresa of Avila and the Rhetoric of Femininity*. Princeton, NJ: Princeton University Press, 1990.

RELATED TEXTS

Bornstein, Daniel, and Roberto Rusconi, eds. *Women and Religion in Medieval and Renaissance Italy*. Chicago: University of Chicago Press, 1996.

De Horozco, Juan. *Tratado de la verdadera y falsa prophecia*. Segovia, 1588.

Ife, B. W. *Reading and Fiction in Golden Age Spain*. Cambridge, UK: Cambridge University Press, 1985.

Márquez Antonio. *Los alumbrados: orígenes y filosofía, 1525–1559*. Madrid: Taurus, 1980.

Vives, Juan Luis. *The Education of a Christian Woman*. Edited and translated by Charles Fantazzi. Chicago: University of Chicago Press, 2000.

NOTE ON TRANSLATION

There are two principal sources for these translations. One is the monumental anthology of Ana de San Bartolomé's *Obras completas*, edited by Father Julián Urkiza. In this work, Father Urkiza has transcribed Ana's works in their original form, electing not to modernize or correct the original texts except in footnotes. The translations of the "Foundation at Burgos," "Prayer in Abandonment," and "Spiritual Lecture" are all based on the transcriptions in the Urkiza anthology. In the case of the *Autobiography*, I have also made use of the version edited by Father Fortunato Antolín. This was actually the first modern version of the text, published in 1969. Father Antolín modernized the orthography and in some cases the grammar of the original and also, in one instance, eliminated a small portion of the text that he apparently did not consider appropriate for publication. Since Urkiza does include this brief account of a nun's seeming sex change in his version, I include it in this translation. Although I consulted Urkiza's version regularly and used it to check for possible elisions and differences in Antolín's version, I have used the latter as the base text for my own translation. In so doing, I have retained Antolín's headings for the different sections of the text, headings that Ana herself did not use.

In addition to the two principal sources, I consulted an English translation of the *Autobiografía* by an anonymous member of the Carmelites in St. Louis from an also anonymous French translation of the Spanish original. This is actually a reworking as well as a translation and combines parts of both of Ana's autobiographies.

In all cases I have tried to create readable versions of Ana's writings, not always an easy task given the distance in time of four centuries and the even greater distance between the intensely religious milieu in which she lived and wrote and our own much more secular world.

Despite these important differences, her texts are still of great interest for a number of reasons, some of which have little to do with religion. As stated earlier, her voice was widely heard and recognized as influential, largely through her writing. These writings represent Ana's effort to express ideals and ideologies that were both cultural and personal. Many of them reflect the struggle, or difficulty, of accommodating the personal to the cultural. Throughout the four examples of her writing that appear here, that tension is often apparent. Her discourse is frequently one of self-excoriation, even the self-rejection typical of the mystics, yet, paradoxically, there is throughout a very strong assertion of self. As mentioned previously, her language is often colloquial and unsophisticated, and it is also inseparable from her literary self-representation as simple and unworthy.

In attempting to create a readable and comprehensible translation, I have not been concerned with reproducing her multiple spelling and grammatical errors, which, in any case, would be difficult, if not impossible, to translate, but rather with communicating the voice that is empowered through writing, despite its frequent assertions of powerlessness. In so doing, I have made no effort to embellish her style but have tried to communicate its relative directness. At times, owing to its almost stream-of-consciousness quality and the complex syntactical structures of the day, Ana's own syntax becomes convoluted and unwieldy, difficult to understand in the original, and equally difficult in English. For the most part I have not attempted to rewrite these long and awkward structures. Some of the locutions are fragmentary, partial thoughts, and again, I have left them so, except in a few cases where comprehension would be impossible without attachment to another syntactic structure. Ana's most frequent construction is an explanatory clause beginning with *que* (translated as "for," "because," or occasionally, "and"), which usually finalizes a thought (for example, "Quedó mi alma muy recogida, inflamada de Dios, que el camino que faltaba de andar siempre me duró esta asistencia de Dios" [My soul became very recollected, inflamed by God, and on the road yet to travel this assistance from God continued for me]). Many of her sentences begin with "and," creating an impression of spontaneity and, again, oral language.

Occasionally it has been necessary to alter the original for the sake of clarity. I have taken the liberty of making some grammatical adjustments, such as subject-verb agreement, or inserting a logical subject where it might be missing. Similarly, there are occasions when Ana shifts the gender of the original subject in a sentence without indicating any other change of subject (for example, she may shift from the masculine *ellos* referring to men or a mixed male and female subject to the feminine *ellas*, yet seem to be referring to the same subject). In such cases, it is impossible to know her intent, if in fact there was one, so I have generally not indicated the gender change in the text. While it is possible that some of these grammatical inconsistencies and elisions are deliberate on her part, it seems equally likely that they are the result of the speed with which she wrote and her lack of attention to these details.

Ana's vocabulary has not proved difficult to render in English. Her repertoire is typical of that used in daily conversation at the time, and although some of it was archaic even in Ana's own day, it is readily comprehensible for a contemporary reader. Whenever possible, I have opted for older forms in English (for example, "weeping" instead of "crying"). As always, there are a number of terms and expressions for which there is no truly adequate translation, particularly in the case of colloquialisms, and in such cases I have attempted to paraphrase in such a way as not to lose entirely the original meaning. Ana spent the last twenty years of her life in French-speaking cultures. In her later writings, the influence of the French language appears in her use of certain French words (for example, *fille* instead of *hija*). In such cases, I have simply translated the word into English. I have left all proper names in the original Spanish.

Ana alludes frequently to people and issues that were well-known and widely discussed at the time but would have little relevance for today's reading public. Most of these context-specific allusions are explained in the volume editor's introduction and in the footnotes. One term that is essential to understanding her spirituality and visionary experiences is the verb *recoger* (literally, "to withdraw oneself"), which I have translated as "to recollect." The state of *recogimiento* or "recollection" involved a mental and spiritual withdrawal from the physical world in order to better participate in the sanctity of the divine. It could take a variety of forms, but in the case of Ana seems to signify a kind of total immersion in meditation or interior contemplation, at times approaching what might be considered a trance-like state. It was during her frequent "recollections" that Ana often experienced visions and engaged in active communication with God, Jesus, and Teresa.

Most important are the personae that emerge in Ana's writings. I have chosen four works that reflect diverse aspects of her experience, both mystical and worldly. Like other writers, Ana used writing as an opportunity to engage in self-reinvention and often self-justification. Each of the following translations reflects this self-fashioning in a slightly different tenor.

AUTOBIOGRAPHY OF
ANA DE SAN BARTOLOMÉ

[MEMORIES OF CHILDHOOD]

Jesus, Mary, Joseph, and our Holy Mother Teresa of Jesus, in whose name I do this which holy obedience orders me.

As a little girl who didn't yet know how to speak, they stood me on my feet with my sisters who were working in a room, and as my mother was passing by she told them, "What are you looking at? Don't let that girl fall, she'll kill herself." One of them said, "God would do her a favor if she died now, she'd go straight to heaven." And the other said, "Don't let her die. If she lives, she could be a holy woman." The other repeated, "This is doubtful, and right now she is in no danger, but when children reach seven years of age, they start sinning." I understood all this, and as she spoke of sinning, I raised my eyes to heaven without really knowing, it seems to me, what I was doing.

It seemed to me that I saw heaven open; the Lord showed himself to me there with great majesty, and since this was something completely new, it caused great fear and reverence in my heart at the time. Because I knew it was God and that it was he who would judge me, there remained with me the fear that I would sin, as my sisters had said, and offend him.

One day when I was seven years old, I remembered that I would sin, and I cried. When one of my sisters asked me, "Why are you weeping?" I told her, "Because I am afraid of sinning, and I would like to die."

With this fear I became a devout follower of some of the saints, above all the angels and with them Saint Joseph, who was so simple that I considered him an angel, and above all the Holiest Virgin. I had great faith in her and the 11,000 virgins,[1] as well as Saint John the Baptist and other saints. Every

---

1. A reference to the 11,000 virgins who, according to a medieval Gallic legend, accompanied Saint Ursula on a sea voyage and were slain with her by the Huns upon their arrival in Cologne at the beginning of the fourth century.

day I asked them to keep me from sinning, and in particular, I asked them for chastity. With these advocates I was consoled and devoted to the good Jesus; I found myself greatly moved by his love, and the only thing that I desired was that he see me and watch over me and be happy with me.

These were my usual wishes and thoughts. When I was alone, in my innocence I looked out the windows at the fields to see if I could see him, but since I was a little girl, when I got together with others of my age and they were playing, I also wanted to play. One day I was comforted at prayer, it must have been the comfort of children, and I said to the Lord, "Lord, give me permission, and I'll go play with the other girls and then I'll come back." It seemed to me that the Lord was pleased, although when I stopped praying to my saints on some days I feared that they would be angry, and then I would apologize again and continue on.

This went on for ten years, when my parents died, and I was quite bereft.[2] I still had brothers and sisters who took the place of parents, and they were very good. But at this age they sent me to take charge of the cattle out in the field, although it was near the village. I resented it greatly at first, but then the Lord comforted me; the fields were a delight, and the birds entranced me with their song, so that when they began to sing I would be recollected[3] for hours. Many times the Child Jesus came and sat on my lap, and I would find him there when I came to myself.

I don't know how to tell here the gloriousness of what I felt in my spirit, that I found myself in a glorious heaven; I wanted to live there forever and not see any more people; I wanted to go some place very far away.

Once I said to the Child Jesus, "Lord, since you are keeping me company, let's not go where there are people, but rather let's go alone to the mountains. With your company, I will need nothing else." But he just laughed and without speaking he showed me that that was not what he wanted of me. With such company [as Jesus], I loved solitude so much that to see other people was like death to me. Sometimes night would overtake me half a league from the village without my noticing it, and, terrified, my brothers would look for me and scold me. But I was not surprised, since they didn't know the company I was keeping and I never told them; they could have thought something else.

2. 1558–59. These years coincided with a widespread epidemic and also very scarce grain harvests.

3. Most frequently, Ana's contact with the supernatural occurs during "recollections" or states of deep meditation, during which the physical world seemingly vanishes from consciousness. In these trance-like states she hears the voice of God, Teresa, and other otherworldly beings.

My prayer was such that, without knowing exactly what it was, I usually found myself afire with the love of Jesus. I thought about what I must do to go where no one would know I was a woman and where all would scorn me. I planned to dress like a man and leave and in that way give them reason to think poorly of me. It seemed that I didn't fear anything that could befall me. I didn't tell anyone about these things except a kinswoman of my age who had been baptized with me.[4] She was very good and had very good desires; when we went to Mass or could get together, our hearts seemed to be on fire with the love of God. I said to her one day, "Sister, why don't the two of us go to a desert dressed like men and do penance, like the Magdalen?" She was more prudent than I and told me, "Sister, this is not the time for that; there are a thousand hazards and dangers." Even so, I pressed her about this many times until I won her over and told her we would make cloaks like those of the pilgrims and one night we would go.

And we did. We arranged to leave one night when everyone was sleeping, and we thought we could do it. But the Lord didn't want it; we both worked at it all night and couldn't get out. Although it seemed easy to open the doors, it wasn't possible. In the morning we met at church and asked each other, "Why didn't you go?" and we laughed at how the Lord had tricked us. We had agreed to dye our faces so that we didn't look like women. We did this so authentically and with such a good heart that if the Lord had given the word, it seemed that nothing else was lacking. It was quite a secret between the two of us, who were like one person, except that she was much better than I.

STRUGGLES FOR THE VOCATION

My brothers and sisters, seeing that I had grown up, tried to marry me off. I had no such ideas. I called upon the Virgin, whom I had taken as my mother, and all my saints, and I increased my devotion and penitence. I went to church and hid in a chapel of the Conception of Our Lady the Virgin, and with bare feet and my bare knees on the ground, I called upon her to help me. A thousand terrible temptations against my wishes tormented and afflicted me. The trickery of the devil was never lacking on these occasions. But I took scourges and lay down naked on the ground in a cave, even though it was damp, until the fury of the temptation died down. I slept on

4. Francisca Cano, daughter of Ana's godfather, Alfonso Sánchez. She entered the Carmelite convent at Medina del Campo as Francisca de Jesús in 1578 and died in February 1626. She wrote an account of the childhood and youth of her friend, Ana.

brambles and other rough things instead of wearing a shift, which I gave to the poor so they wouldn't know at home that I went about without it. At other times I put on a hair shirt of pig's bristles.

One day they told me to sleep with a sister who was afraid. I hadn't prayed the rosary, and so as not to fall asleep I took with me a big, sharp rock; after putting out the light I got into bed with it, since I had used it many times as a pillow. This time I put it beneath my naked body so as not to sleep, but it was not enough because before I finished the rosary I fell asleep. In dreams I saw the Mother of God enter the room in great splendor; she carried the Child Jesus in her arms and sat down on the bed with him. The Child began to pull on the rosary, as though wanting to play. He pulled so hard that he woke me up, and the Mother [of God] told me, "Don't be afraid or worried. I will take you where you'll be a nun and wear my habit." With this she disappeared. I was very comforted, with greater desires to serve God.

Another day, since my family was after me, I was wondering if there were a man nearby who hadn't sinned and was very intelligent and handsome; because I didn't think I had seen such a one as I was imagining—for they were all ugly; if only there were this man who didn't sin and didn't have any other involvement and if they [i.e., her family] would let me alone [I would marry him], but if he were not like that, I wouldn't want him for anything in the world. One day Jesus appeared to me all grown up, about my age, very beautiful and completely lovely, because ever since I was a little girl out in the fields and he had appeared to me, it seemed to me that he was growing up with me. This time, coming to me as I have said, he told me, "I am the one you want and whom you will wed" and then disappeared.

But my soul remained on fire and inflamed with his love; from then on I went about ordinarily with such impulses that they took away my natural strength. Day and night I had no other thoughts than what I would do for the Beloved. I wanted to suffer trials and dishonors and be taken for crazy.

Once my sister, who was married,[5] sent for me to come to her house, and I asked the maid who was there with her [i.e., Ana's sister], and she told me, "A brother of her husband who is unmarried." I knew that they wanted to marry me to him and were making great efforts. I dressed myself in a completely disheveled way with some kitchen rags and went there dressed that way. My sister, when she saw me come in, was extremely angry and said, "What are you doing? Are you crazy? Get out of here." I returned home completely happy.

5. Probably her older sister, Maria.

I avoided talking with men or giving them occasion to speak to me; and if my brothers' friends came into the house I would go outside, or I would make a face at them as though they were a bad vision. I used this type of caution because I saw myself, as I have said, often [as a person] with great willfulness, and on the other hand, [as a person] with great obligations to God, which required perfect purity and faithfulness. The one and the other fought in my spirit with violence.

Sometimes they sent me a quarter league from the village to the wheat fields and pastures, with my sisters and people from the house. I went, keeping quiet the whole way, and when we got there, I withdrew among the trees and told them to leave me alone and began to pray. And the good Jesus came with me and sat on my lap, as I have said. I said to him, "Let's go, Lord, alone," and although he seemed to be pleased, it wasn't convenient. He gave me to understand this without speaking, smiling at me. I wanted to go to some very high ground near there, and this time he gave me to understand that it wasn't advisable; and asking him again to take me there, I slept a little, and he showed me the monastery of Avila, which is the first that our Holy Mother[6] and the nuns with that habit had founded.[7] I asked them to give me something to drink, because I was thirsty. All this was in dreams. And they gave it to me. The glass in which they gave it to me I recognized later when I went to the monastery.

With this, I abandoned the desires I had to be a hermitess in the desert and began to want to be a nun.

[EARLY RELATIONSHIP WITH THE CARMELITES]

At this time God brought to this place a priest to be the pastor of that church, a doctor and great servant of God, and we two companions[8] confessed with him. Without my saying anything about the desires that I had to be a nun in Avila, he told me, "A new monastery has just been founded; if you want me to try to ask them for a place for you, I will." I saw the heavens open and said yes, that it would make me very content. He did it with great love, since I had only confessed with him a short time. When he told them at the convent of my desires, they told him that I should go there, that they wanted to see me first.

6. Holy Mother is a reference to Saint Teresa of Avila, not to the Virgin Mary.

7. Monastery can refer to the living quarters of male or female religious and is used interchangeably with convent in this translation.

8. Ana and her close friend, Francisca Cano.

With this, I revealed my desire to be a nun to my brothers and sisters. I told them that I had already contacted this monastery and that they wanted to see me. They took it very badly, but since they were fearful of God, they didn't refuse and went with me; it pleased God that the nuns accepted me right away with pleasure. I was also happy with them, and I recognized those I had seen in the dream. But that was only a first look, and it was arranged that they would notify my family and me when we should come.

My family said, "Why do you want to go with these nuns, who seemed very strict to us?" I told them, "To me they seem like saints and that I've been with them and known them all my life."

On the way back, people sat down to rest next to a fountain. I went to one side and placed my eyes on God, praising him for the favor he was doing me. But since the evil spirit saw me return to the world and didn't know the secrets of God, a great many demons came together in front of me in the air and danced with a great show of happiness as though now they had me. They were like very little men, and all feet and heads, fierce things and so many that they made a shadow like flocks of birds. And although God didn't let them get away with what they were planning, he let them wage quite a war against me, with family and friends, as well as the interior and exterior temptations of the devil, which, if they had bothered me before, now did so even more. But God didn't permit it, for if he doubled the temptations, he also doubled my spirit and strength to resist them.

My brothers and sisters threatened me with tests of strength, and they put me to the work of laborers and burdened me with things that required the strength of men; house servants said that two of them together couldn't do what I was doing. I laughed because the weight that they were ordering me to lift was like a straw to me. My fervor became very strong and would have been overwhelming without these activities to distract me. And they made me carry them all by myself and take them to the threshing floor; those who were reaping made the sheaves two times bigger than those they made for the men, thinking that I couldn't lift them onto the carts. I lifted them with great ease, so that the men stopped reaping to watch me, and they were amazed and didn't know if it was the strength of God or the devil.

After the wheat was on the threshing floor, they gave me two or three teams of oxen to thresh it. They ordered me to yoke them to the thresher. The oxen were fierce, and God did me such a favor that as I called to them they lowered their heads and came to the yoke as though they were lambs.

I did this and other exertions all through one summer in the great sun and heat that there is in that area. Once they sent me to the pasture for these oxen, and I couldn't find one that had gotten into some bushes. Just as I was about to look for them a rabid dog came toward me. I didn't think it was rabid, and as it approached it rushed forward to bite me. I threw myself face down on the ground so as not to take in its breath. It was on me and tore all my clothes, although they were new that day, and the ox that I hadn't found was hidden nearby. When it saw that the dog was attacking me it came out and confronted the dog, and at this the dog left and the ox came up to me as though it were a person, licked me with its tongue, and got on the road and made signs to me that I should hold on to it. I did so, and it took me to the village, so that those who saw it were amazed.

Another time I was with my companion in the mountains with the cattle. We were on a rock that was at the bottom of the mountains when we saw a shepherd far away walking toward us. We were afraid and got under the rock; there were tall grasses next to it with which we covered ourselves, and also there was God, who wanted to keep us safe. The man arrived and got up on the rock where he had seen us and said, "Where have they gone? May the devil take them!" We hid there until it was late, at which time we saw that he was gone. Our fear had left us drenched in sweat. When I came home they told me I was crazy and that I had to drop all the prayer and desire to be a nun, that if I went to the monastery I wouldn't be able to take it, and I would come back home and dishonor them, that it was better to drop it before I went.

My family was doing these things, sometimes with severity, while at other times they showed me favor and said they did it for my own good, because I wouldn't have the strength to withstand all that rigor. They brought me other people to talk to me and give me the same advice, saying that I should look out because I wasn't doing the right thing, that I should take another road.

One night when the moon was very beautiful, a kinswoman asked my brothers' permission for me to go to her flax field, because she had an inherited property next to the village houses. When we arrived we heard a great noise, so that I was very afraid. They were dragging chains and making loud groans. Seeing me upset, my kinswoman said, "It's nothing, it's some animal passing on the road." Then there appeared near us a very black vision like a statue with the height of two men, so big, so thin, and approaching us. I fainted and fell to the ground saying, "Help me, Holiest Trinity!" and my kinswoman fell over me to take away the fear. But when I came to, she took my hand and brought me home. From the space between the flax field and my house I saw in front of us, somewhat apart, three people dressed in white, and I said, "Who are those people?" They told me, "They must be shepherds who are coming in from the flocks." But when they got to the houses, they disappeared.

I knew it was the Holiest Trinity, whom I had called upon. This fear and weakness of heart stayed with me, so that upon entering a room alone at night I was afraid; I carried a dark shadow about with me. I told this to my brothers and sisters around Saint Bartholomew's Day, and they made me say masses, but it didn't go away. There was a shrine to this blessed apostle about five leagues away, and in that region they're very devoted to him. They took me there to make a novena to him, and three leagues before arriving I asked my brothers' permission to go on foot, so that God would do me the favor of healing me, and they gave it to me. Since I was tired, before entering the shrine I sat down and could not move, so that they had to carry me. When I entered the shrine, it all went away; I was completely cured and felt a certainty that my desires would be realized.

[AT LAST A CARMELITE]

When we got home, they sent for me from the monastery, but my family was not inclined to go. Every day for a whole year I had a Mass said for the souls in purgatory asking for their intercession and for the Virgin's help in softening my relatives' hearts, and they [i.e., her relatives] just kept delaying from one day to the next, thinking that my desire would go away.

Some nuns who were going to make a foundation in Talavera came to the village, and they [i.e., her family] brought them to our house. My sisters asked them for the love of God to persuade me to go with them, since it was nearby. They [i.e., her sisters] would feel better having me there. The nuns gave their counsel and were closeted with me a whole afternoon, preaching to me, and they came forth with all the inducements and favors that could be imagined. They were Hieronymites.[9] But the more they persuaded, the stronger and firmer I was not to be remiss in what the Lord had shown me, and without a doubt it was His Majesty who gave me the strength, because naturally one would desire the honor that these servants of God were promising me; and being near the family, which others might have desired, I detested.[10] In the end, God helped me, and I didn't change one thought, even though they were putting pressure on us from the monastery in Avila.

9. Members of the Order of Saint Jerome.

10. Separation from family and friends was a necessary part of the process of entering the religious life. Ana's vehemence is doubtless intended to communicate the sincerity of her commitment.

My brothers wrote that they would take me there at All Saints Day. One day before the eve of this holiday, they were in a bad humor and didn't say anything to me. We were having dinner at the table, three sisters and two brothers. I asked them, "Aren't we going to make the trip?" This infuriated my oldest brother so that he got up from the table and drew his sword to kill me.[11] One of my sisters got up and held back his hand, or I think it might have been an angel of God, because I saw the naked sword descend on my head, and God came to me in that brief instant with a resignation to die for his love as great as that which I hope to have at the hour of death. I said to the Lord in my heart, "Lord, I will die very comforted for the sake of justice." The sister who held back his hand told me, "Get out of here; we don't want to see you, you upset the house." I hid in a cellar and left them quite upset, so much so that in the whole night they didn't think to look for me; it seemed that many evil spirits were about the house.

In the morning I went out without them seeing me; I went to church and my confessor, when he saw me, said, "What's this? Aren't you going to the monastery?" I told him what had happened, that I had just come to confess. I wasn't angry with them and could see very well that they weren't to blame, but rather the devil was, and my confessor ordered me to take Communion. I said I had qualms about taking Communion without apologizing to them. He told me there was no reason to apologize, and finally he let me go. I got on my knees and asked them to forgive me, and they responded rudely, "Get out of here! So you're back after having upset us?" Without answering I went back and took Communion. After taking Communion, I recollected a little; between sorrow and contentment, I gave thanks to God for everything.

And as I was in that state, the brother who had tried to kill me came to the church looking for me, his face like that of a dead man. He said that everything was ready, to come with him. I was sorry to see him so afflicted; he was like an angel, and the one I loved the most. He and the sister who had defended me and some other people went with me. They were weeping the whole way and almost didn't speak to me. I was very happy but at the same time so assailed by evil temptations that it seemed that all hell had gotten together to wage war against me. I didn't dare say a word and rightly so, for if I had they would have said I was crazy to enter the monastery that way. The blessed souls took me there in the morning on their own day.[12] Upon

11. Fernán, born in 1538.

12. November 2, 1570. The term blessed souls refers to the souls of the dead, whose official day of recognition is November 2 in the church calendar.

entering, all that turmoil disappeared, just as if they had taken a hat off my head, and I was in a heaven of contentment, so that it seemed to me that I had been raised all my life among those saintly women.

FIRST STEPS IN THE CARMELITE LIFE

After a few days there the Lord hid from me, and I remained in darkness. I was quite disconsolate and said, "O Lord, what is this? Why have you abandoned me? If I didn't know you, I would think that you had deceived me, and if I thought that you were going to leave me, I would not have come to the convent." This lasted the whole year of the novitiate.[13] One day at the end of the year, upon entering a shrine to Christ of the Column, sinking down upon my knees, a recollection came over me, and the Lord appeared to me crucified upon the cross. The first thing he told me responded to my desire to know if the thirst he had on the cross was bodily thirst, and he told me, "My thirst was only for souls; now it's necessary for you to look at this and take a different road from the one you have been taking until now." It was as though he had said, "Don't look for me anymore as a child." He showed me all the virtues in perfection, very beautiful, which amazed me, for I was very far from his beauty and perfection. With this the Lord disappeared, leaving my heart greatly wounded with his love at seeing him so injured on the cross from his love of souls. This favor remained so alive in my soul that it never left me day or night; rather, my heart was usually with him, and His Majesty was in my heart everywhere that I went; I had a zeal for the souls and the virtues that he showed me in the vision I have spoken of. And then he told me that they would have to be won on the road of the cross.

Another day I entered the shrine of San Francisco to pray. There was a very soft fragrance of flowers, and I began to recollect. The Lord entered, looking as when he was in the world, very handsome, but showed himself to be very distressed. He came to me and put his holy hand on my left shoulder; it was the right hand of the Lord, and with a weight I can never describe. It unburdened the sorrow it carried in my heart, and he told me, "Look at the souls that are being lost, help me." He showed me France as though I were there and the millions of souls that were lost in heresies.[14] This lasted no more than a moment; if it had lasted longer, I would have felt my life was ending.

13. November 1570–November 1571.

14. Calvinism had made great inroads in France. Saint Teresa also refers to the need to battle "heretics" there.

I don't know what this sorrow was like; it's not something I can say. With this vision and favor I was so on fire with the love of God and souls that I couldn't live with the desire I had for them. Neither sleeping nor eating was of pleasure to me, nor could I put this desire aside. For penance during the time that this urge and fervor lasted—at least fifteen years as a laywoman and a nun—if they had given me permission, I would have done foolish things according to my desires. Anyway, I did what I could to get permission, and when they didn't give it to me for scourges, I asked them to pinch me; I had arms that were black and blue from bruises. At meals I put ground-up bitter incense on my food, taking care that the others would not see it.

The confessor, since he knew my soul, made many tests to see if my spirit was true.

Once I was sorry for some men they were taking to hang who were passing by the monastery, and I said, "If I thought that this man was not willing to die, I would wish them to put me in his place." And the confessor said, "Your charity is not for that." I said yes it was, that they should test it. He told me, "Go to the fire and put a finger in the middle of the live coals for the space of a creed and come tell me what you feel." I trusted in obedience and did as he ordered me. I came back to the confessor, and I don't know how I prayed the creed while I held the finger there, but I didn't feel it, nor did it bother me at all. Had I done it on my own, I might fear that the evil spirit wanted to deceive me. But in matters of obedience I haven't feared, rather I have been confident it is God. Going back, as I have said, to tell the confessor, he told me, "Get out of here, you're a stupid fool."

After these years I have spoken of, although my prayer was not always of one kind, but now of one kind, now of another, I always found myself assisted by God to do the mortifications for which they gave me permission, sometimes in the refectory and others as the occasion arose. Many times I threw myself naked on thorns, others on stinging nettles, but this needn't be held in high esteem when the spirit orders the flesh. I did many things to make myself a fool, as though I were in truth wise, but since I really am foolish no artifice was necessary. Once on a Good Friday, in imitation of the Lord and his Passion, I had a desire that the sacristan slap me soundly. He, since I was the portress, considered me to be a good woman; I wanted to undeceive him. I said to him one day, "Who do you think I am? Know that I am a great sinner and I've been around in the world," wanting to give him the impression that I was a wicked woman. He believed it, and I told him, "For this reason, I pray you that from now on you believe it and when the men come with the wood (the convent was under construction) that you tell one of them to strike the nun who opens the door, over her veil. You'll give me great pleasure. I'll give you something for it." The boy did it, and upon opening the door the man struck me. Later I thought about what I had done and that it wasn't good or useful for the house. Since I had scruples I told the confessor, and he scolded me soundly. He told our saint [Teresa, here and throughout.—Ed.] who was there as prioress, and she was silent. She didn't say anything to me but ordered that the door never be opened without two nuns present; since it was still the beginning and we were few, this order had not been given until then.[15]

My soul was so on fire with the Passion of Jesus Christ (since I was a little girl I had felt this fire) that if I went to church and saw the paintings of the Passion of the Lord, I cried and wanted to be poor and mistreated for his love, and when I left the house, I took off my shoes and walked over rocks and little stones so that they would hurt me. What I could give away of my clothes without being seen, I did. I remained only with what I was wearing that could be seen, and I gave the rest to the poor. Anything I could take for them I took, and I hid the food.

One day my sister said to me, "You didn't eat what they gave you?" I said yes [that I did eat it], and what I meant was that if the body didn't eat it, the soul did. One day I told the confessor that I was deceiving my brothers and sisters, telling them that I was eating but with this meaning [of giving the food away to feed my soul]; if it was a lie, then I didn't want to say it for all the world; but I thought it was true. And he said, "Who taught you that this is a lie, since your intent is to give it to the soul?" This I did for the Passion of Jesus Christ.

What I'm going to say and something of what's been said is off the subject of which I was speaking, but it is so I do not forget to say anything as I have been ordered.

Another Good Friday, when I was quite little, a great preacher came there. My brothers and sisters and I went to the sermon. I went with the great desire that he say things of the love with which Christ had suffered, but the good man said almost nothing to my liking. I was greatly distressed at seeing him so lukewarm during the whole sermon, and upon leaving the sermon I began to cry, and my sisters said to me, "Why are you weeping, girl?" I said, "I'm weeping because this father has not preached well." And

15. According to Teresa's constitution of 1568 there must be two nuns present when the clois-ter door is opened. "When the doctor or barber or other necessary persons and the confessor enter, two mediators should bring them in." *Constituciones de la Orden Carmelita Descalza* (Ed. De 1581), 4.1 (Madrid: Biblioteca de autores cristianos, 1972). The translation is mine.

they said, "What do you know about it?" If I could preach, I would have said it better, that's what I think.

SICK WITH THE LOVE OF GOD

Returning to what I was saying about my inclination to have strong impulses on behalf of the souls the Lord had shown me, anything I could do did but little to satisfy my desires. As my confessor saw that the zeal and love of souls had lasted so long, he told me one day, "Look, daughter, this is the devil's charity and he is trying to deceive you." I went to our saint for her to tell me if that's what it was and told her all that had happened. She told me not to worry, that it wasn't the devil, that she had gone through the same kind of prayer with confessors who didn't understand her. I was comforted by this and believed that what the saint told me was from God.

I couldn't stop the love of God and zeal for souls that burned in my heart without leaving me, and because I didn't sleep, the saint told me one day, "Daughter, when the bedtime bell rings, stop the prayer, and sleep." I wanted to do as they ordered and said to the Lord when I went to bed, "Lord, I don't have permission to be with you, you have to let me sleep." It's marvelous how the Lord wants us to obey; for he let me sleep the same amount of time as the others and upon waking I found him in my soul; it seemed he was watching over me in my sleep. My body was as light as if it were not real, so much so that I feared it was a trick, and as I walked around it lifted up like a straw, and wherever I rested I was full of this love.

One day while seated, doing some work at the turnstile (because they gave me many chores to distract me), my soul began to burn with the love of the beloved more than usual, and in this instant the Lord came to me as when he was in the world. He came so softly and from behind like a man in love about to play a joke on his wife. Coming closer, he put his hand over my heart, and it seemed to me that he had torn it out; I was in such pain at this moment that without noticing it, I groaned. It was beautiful that he stole my heart and left it in such a way that it seemed to want to leave my body in exquisite pain. These visits kept me from being able to turn my attention away from him

Another day I was in prayer at the shrine and a recollection overcame me. In it I was shown a view of eternity and the Holiest Trinity, and although I saw it, I don't know how to say what it was like. It happened in a blink of the eye and was something beyond my understanding. As I was thus recollected, they rang the bell for the meal at the refectory, and without feeling it, like someone sleepwalking, I got up at the bell and came to the refectory.

I didn't come back to myself until I sat down at the board and a little water fell on my hands. It all seemed to have been a dream.

My body and strength were worn down so greatly by these impulses that they said I was dying. They called the doctors, and they didn't know what I had. Some said it was consumption. They gave me a lot of cures and made me even worse; I became so weak I couldn't lift my feet off the ground. My whole body was an open sore and they poulticed it. But none of this did me any good.[16]

At this time our saint went to Seville and couldn't take me with her. Since I had desired hardships, I told the Lord, "Lord, I've asked you for hardships, but now that I see that you give them to the whole community I would like you to give them to me alone and in such a way that I can serve the sisters and not make work for them. I want them just for me." And the Lord said to me, "I'll do what you ask; you will have something to suffer in the company of my friend Teresa. The two of you will go through it on the road." And with that I was there until our saint came back from Seville.

IDEAL NURSE

This lasted a year, and then the saint came back from Seville.[17] She found me in such a state that I seemed to have completely fallen apart. The saint told me the night she arrived, "Daughter, come to my cell, although at present you are ill." And it seemed I was not in any condition to serve her. There were five who were sick in bed with fever, and one in very bad condition with such discomfort that she couldn't eat anything, whose name was Isabel Bautista.[18] The saint told me the morning after arriving from Seville, "Daughter, although you are not well, I want you to be the nurse for these sick ones, since there is no one else to care for them." I kept quiet so as not to go against obedience, but I thought to myself, "How will I do it when I can't lift my feet from the ground?" As best I could I went to the kitchen to prepare something for the one who was most ill. In front of her cell there was a stairway of fourteen steps. At the bottom of the stairs I stopped and said to the Lord, "Help me, my Lord, for I can't take one step up." At the top the Lord appeared to me, very beautiful as all the other times, as when he was in the world and told me, "Come up." And when he said this, I found myself lifted up to his

---

16. Ana was ill from 1575 to 1577, although she refers to this period as a year.

17. July 1577.

18. Isabel del Águila, who professed at the Convent of Saint Joseph in Avila in 1570 at twenty years of age and died in July 1626.

feet without any effort, and he went with me to the sick woman's cell. Upon entering he knelt at the head of the bed like a nurse who wants to take good care of his patients and told me, "Put down here what you have brought and go give some to the others. I shall feed this one."

I went as though nothing were wrong with me at all, very healthy and very quick, wanting to go back and see my Lord. But although I hurried, when I got back I couldn't find him. The sister was so pleased and told me, "Sister, what is this you've brought? In my whole life I've never tasted anything so good." I didn't tell her anything about what I had seen, although we were very fond of each other. But later I asked her if someone else had been with her and she said no. With that I kept silent. But she told me she had never felt her soul to be so content and comforted, that she seemed to have nothing wrong with her.

And then all my sisters got better, and the saint told me, "Be their prioress and don't ask my permission; give them whatever you see they need."

The fervor came back to me as before, so that exercise was necessary to resist it. I was like a hungry man with many dishes placed before him; he's dying for them, but he sees that if he eats them as his appetite dictates he will die. They stop him, and the more they hold him back, the greater his hunger.

I exercised myself in charity in everything that presented itself, thanks to the Lord who had given me health and occasion to use it, which I didn't deserve, but His Majesty made me deserve it through his love. The sisters were amazed when the saint ordered me to be a nurse when I was so ill. God permitted it so that the strength he gives to his prelates could be seen; the Holy Mother also had it, for she knew what she was ordering, and everyone marveled at it, I, most of all, because I did not deserve such goodness.

In this time that I was a nurse, one day I had a sick [patient] in very bad condition, and leaving her resting I went for a bit to a cave to hide and pray; as I was recollected, they told me in a loving voice, "Come out." I said, "Master, what are you ordering, Lord?" For I knew his sweet voice, but he didn't respond. I went out to see what they wanted of me. They were looking for me all over the house because the sick woman was calling me. When I went there, I found her very anguished from the weakness that had come upon her. I attended to all the work of the house as the saint had ordered me. I also attended to the Holy Mother in her loving company with great pleasure and quickness, as can be believed, for it was the Lord who was doing it all.

Another sister became very ill from a carbuncle on one eye, which is a very bad illness in that land, and the doctors gave up hope for her. One day, the surgeon had to leave the place to go to another patient and told me, "Don't go near the wound till I come back, which will be soon." I was so diligent about everything this patient needed that I seemed not to have a body that held me back. She was a great servant of God. Her name was Petronila Baptista.[19] At night I fell asleep next to her, and in dreams I saw that two religious men from our order were coming in, who I think were Elijah and Elisha.[20] They came up to the sick one and took the cloths off the wound on her eye and cured her. The smaller one, who was Elisha, came and went for things with such diligence that I was amazed. When they finished curing her, they told me, "That is how the ill must be cured, not with the negligence with which you do it."

I thought about this—that our acts are different in the eyes of God than in the eyes of men—because they gave me to understand this. I thought I was doing well, and this made me understand that what was very good for me was really very imperfect.

The Lord didn't do me these favors because I was good but so that his goodness could be seen. Since I am so unworthy of favor, he seeks me without my knowing it, so that I am not lost and his goodness is seen. In these external tasks, which I did with great contentment when obedience ordered it, I deserved nothing, for I didn't take notice of the wickedness that must have been in me. Although I had so many faults, I comforted myself in these works, and it seemed to me that it was all for the love of God. Since the Lord saw and loved my soul, he brought me some situations in an untoward fashion, so that I would recognize my self-love and the fervor would be mitigated.

AT TERESA'S SIDE

At this time our Holy Mother broke an arm on her way to the choir for compline one night.[21] It was dark and there was a stairway in front of the entrance; the evil spirit threw her down there, so that the bone was broken in half and the pain was very great, from which we all suffered—I most of all, because I loved her dearly and felt all her troubles and sorrows. Along with these trials the Lord was giving me, I had other sick ones, and I was also cellaress and kitchen-sister, so that it was necessary to do things at night in

19. Petronila Orejón, who professed at Saint Joseph of Avila in 1568 and died at eighty-eight years of age in 1619.

20. Two Old Testament prophets whom the Carmelites claimed as founders of the order. The Carmelite Order was actually founded by hermits in Palestine in the twelfth century.

21. December 24, 1577.

order to attend to the saint and the others by day. She saw me going about very tired, so she took on a sister[22] who seemed very good and desirous of serving God. This sister later became unhappy with the convent life but pretended she was happy and that she was prayerful, though she was not. She deceived the prioress and the confessor, and they were very fond of her. She was tempted against the saint and me and told the confessor that I was confessing with Mother Teresa, that he should look out because she was deceiving him and I was too, that it was a case for the Inquisition. I told him the truth, but he didn't believe me. I told him that that sister was unhappy and he said it wasn't so, that she was very good and a real Saint Catherine of Siena, that I was the bad one and walking in sin. This went on for some days without the poor girl knowing about it.

Our saint, although she kept silent, knew about it but was hopeful (because the sister was the niece of a friend who had brought her to the saint, and wanted her to straighten out), and she was really sorry about the trouble that this sister was giving me, for she was using bad words with me, which were not appropriate for a nun. But the confessor and prioress were on her side. After a few days the saint had to leave to found new convents and was happy to take me out of there because of the grief that this sister was causing me. Since the prioress and confessor had such confidence in her, she found a way to leave the monastery, and she married very miserably.

With this and other things that had been said, the inquisitors came one day for the saint and investigated, but seeing that [the charges] weren't true, they dropped [the case]. And since the saint was free and clear of that of which they accused her, she was happy that this affront had occurred. Because of this situation and others I asked the prioress[23] to take me away from the turnstile, inasmuch as there was always someone who believed these things and was tempted because the saint had put me there, but although I asked her two or three times she refused. One day at Mass I was troubled, and I recollected in prayer; as I was in this state, the Lord appeared to me in the manner of "ecce homo," as when Pilate took him out to the town crowned in thorns, hands tied, and a rope at his throat and completely wounded, and all the shouting of the Jews entered my head saying, "Crucify him!"[24] And the Lord came up to me and with loving speech told me, "Daughter, look at me, the way that I am; do you think your troubles are like mine?"

---

22. This was a novice whose exact identity remains unknown.
23. María de San Jerónimo (Dávila), a cousin of Saint Teresa.
24. Mk 15:1–15.

These words entered my heart like arrows and left me so inflamed that I was very encouraged to suffer much more than what had already befallen me. This vision then disappeared and I remembered what the Lord had told me before, that I would suffer greatly. I was beyond my own weakness, and I complained about little, remembering the vision and the troubles that I would undergo in the company of the saint. With her so ill and on the road, she suffered more than I, but I felt it more than I can say, because there were few amenities at the roadside inns with which to attend to her.

Another time in this convent at Avila on Wednesday of Holy Week, thinking about the troubles that were about to come to Christ, I recollected a little. And the Lord appeared to me like a man who is fleeing because they want to arrest him and he comes through a friend's doorway. That's how the Lord came into me; he was so different, like a man who turns to look at those who are coming for him, and he said nothing to me. I felt so afflicted that I said to him, "Lord, what do you want? Here is my heart; enter it." But without saying anything, he went back out and left me penetrated by his affliction.

When our saint was doing the chapters,[25] many times the Lord comforted us; it seemed we were in heaven and at times the saint was resplendent.

Returning to other troubles on the road, one day in the foundation of Villanueva de la Jara,[26] there was a very deep well but no water, and the saint put in a crank to take out the water more easily. She went to see how it was going, and while she was looking at it, the official was careless. Before he could tie the crank, it came loose. Since God loved her, he wanted to give her ways to be deserving of his love, and he let loose the crank over her bad arm, which hurt it again so that in a few days she had an abscess on that side. It would have been fatal if God had not done us the favor of letting her stay with us a bit longer; awaiting death, the abscess burst. This affliction of the saint was like death for us, her daughters, and for me in particular.

If I had to tell the troubles she suffered during the years that I was with her, I would never finish, for what is told in her books is nothing. Of what happened in Burgos, which was the last foundation she made, what's told in the books is nothing.[27] Sometimes it was poverty: we lacked food and other necessary things. I remember that one day when the saint was very weak I had nothing to give her except a little bread soaked in water, because the river had risen so that those in the village couldn't help us or send us

25. Chapters were assemblies or general meetings of the convent community as a whole.

26. The Convent at Villanueva de la Jara was founded on February 21, 1580.

27. See Saint Teresa of Ávila, *The Book of Foundations*, ed. and trans. E. A. Peers (London: Sheed and Ward, 1973), chap. 31.

anything (the house was outside the village, right on the riverbank); the river rose so high that water came into the house. The house was old, and with each wave from the river it shook as though it would fall. Our saint's room was so poor that you could see the sky through the ceiling; the walls were all cracked and it was very cold, for that city is cold. The river came into the house up to the first floor, and since we were in danger we took the Holiest Sacrament up to the high part of the house. Every hour we expected to be flooded. We were saying litanies, and from six in the morning until midnight we were in this danger without eating or resting, for everything we owned had been flooded.

Our saint was the most distressed person in the world, for the house had just been founded. And the Lord left her so alone that she didn't know if we should stay there or leave as other nuns were doing. At this time we were all so upset that we didn't remember to give our saint anything to eat. Very late at night she told me, "Daughter, go see if there's a little bread left; give me a piece, I feel very weak." This broke my heart, so we made a novice who was strong go in and take some bread from under the water, which was up to her waist, and we gave the saint some of that, for there was nothing else; if some swimmers hadn't come in, we would have perished. It seemed that they were angels of God; we didn't know how they had come, and they went under water and broke down the doors of the house, so that the water began to leave the rooms. But the rooms were so flooded and full of stones that they took out more than eight wagons full of what the water had brought in, and our saint's room was shaking as though it would fall, as I have said. It was in such poor condition that even the evening dew was damaging it.

I had two quilts on my bed; I put one over her at night and the other on the side of the bed so that she couldn't tell that I was taking it off, for she wouldn't have allowed it. Once she had fallen asleep I came up quietly to sit next to her side of the bed, and when she called me I pretended that I was coming from my bed. The saint would ask me, "How can you come so fast, daughter?" Other times I left her sleeping and went to wash her bandages, for, as she was ill, I was happy to give her clean ones. Cleanliness was very pleasing to her. I went many nights without sleeping, and I didn't need the sleep if I could make her happy. I was very happy to do this until her death, and the day she died and couldn't speak, I dressed her all in clean robes and sleeves. She saw how clean she was; looking at me she smiled and thanked me by making signs. She was so pure and such a friend of purity that she showed it in everything.

Returning to what I was saying, I was as healthy and my spirit as comforted as if I had slept all night and eaten royally. The Lord did this for the comfort of the saint, for if she had felt that the work was bad for me, she would have regretted it greatly. God ordinarily did this wonderful thing and others for his friend through this miserable sinner, who didn't deserve to serve her.

Because of these things, I live with much fear of my fault of not taking advantage of this goodness, and I certainly should be very fearful, because ever since I was a girl I have had an inclination to enjoy and delight in child-ish things. I told the Lord when I felt scruples, "Lord, if I were with a saint, I would be better; I would want to be what I saw in her." With these thoughts I used to recollect when I played.

The Lord did me this favor not because of my desires, although it could be thought that they were not really mine but rather his, who with his wis-dom and mercy had everything planned and ordered and made me desire this, but so that later, seeing that I was in this holy company and not doing my duty, I would be distressed by my own vanity and pride at wanting what I didn't deserve, and not taking advantage of it as another in my place would have done.

LAST TRIP WITH MOTHER TERESA

Returning to the troubles that the saint suffered on the road after those that she had undergone at the convent in Burgos, the Lord told her that she should go ahead: she had gone through many troubles and there were others to come. On the road from Burgos she came to Valladolid, where another trouble befell her concerning her brother's[28] will, who had ordered that his estate go to the monastery at Avila after his days on earth if his children had no inheritors. His family didn't want to recognize the will as valid and were planning to win it from the saint; she was not easy in things that were not entirely of God, and since she didn't agree to what they were asking, one of the lawyers was so discourteous that he came to the monastery and spoke badly to her, saying that it seemed as though she was not so good, that many laypeople were greater examples of virtue than she. She told him with her great patience, "May God grant you a favor for the one you are doing me."

The prioress[29] of this monastery was quite won over by these people, and although she was a person that the saint was very fond of, she did not

---

28. Lorenzo de Cepeda

29. María Bautista (de Ocampo). She was the daughter of Diego de Cepeda, Saint Teresa's first cousin, and Beatriz de la Cruz. Born in 1543, she professed at Saint Joseph of Avila in 1564 and died in Valladolid in 1603.

show her respect on this occasion. She told us to leave the house and go with God, and upon our leaving, she pushed me to the door and said, "Go now, and don't come back here," which the saint felt very deeply, because she was one of her daughters. It seemed to her that she should have had more respect for her than for laypeople, and she didn't.

From there the saint went to Medina del Campo, which was on the road to her monastery at Avila, where she was prioress. The night we arrived at Medina, she had something to advise the prioress[30] of, which did not go well. The prioress took it badly, and the saint, upon seeing that the devil was unsettling her daughters who had been so obedient to her, was very distressed and withdrew to a room, and the prioress withdrew to another. The saint was so afflicted by this turn of events that she didn't eat or sleep the whole night.

In the morning we left[31] without taking anything for the road. The saint was now ill with the sickness from which she died, and this whole day I could find nothing to give her to eat. One night in a poor little place where there was nothing to eat, she told me, "Daughter, give me something, if you have it, I am about to faint." She had a fever, and I had nothing except some dried figs. I gave four reales for them to find two eggs, whatever they might cost. When I saw that even for money nothing could be found, that they were returning it to me, I couldn't look at the saint without crying; her face was half dead. The affliction that I felt on this occasion I cannot exaggerate. It seemed my heart was breaking, and I did nothing but weep in this urgent situation, for I was watching her die and could do nothing to help her. She told me with the patience of an angel, "Don't cry, daughter, God wants this now."

As the hour of her blessed transit was approaching, the Lord was testing her in all ways, but she took it as always, like a saint. I suffered more, with less mortification, so that it was necessary for the saint to comfort me. She told me there was nothing to worry about, that she was content with the fig she had eaten. The next day we arrived at Alba with such a deterioration of her body that right away the doctors abandoned her as hopeless, a very difficult thing for me, and even more so because I was in Alba and thinking that I would have to stay in this world. Aside from the love that I had for her and that she had for me, I had another great consolation in her, that I ordinarily saw Christ in her soul, as though he were united with her soul in heaven, so that I felt great respect as should be felt in the presence of God.

30. Alberta Bautista (Mencia Ponce) professed at Medina del Campo in 1569 and died there in August 1583.

31. September 19, 1582.

Truly it was heaven to serve her, so that my greatest sorrow was to see her suffer. I served her for more or less fourteen years, because from the time I entered [the convent] to put on the habit, she took me with her. I was always with her except when she went to Seville when, as has been said, I was sick. All this time did not even seem like one whole day to me. The saint was so accustomed to my poor, rude service that she was never without me, so much so that one day I had a great fever and the next day she had to leave to visit her monasteries. I was not in any condition to travel, it seemed, and she told me, "Don't worry, daughter, I will leave an order for them to send you to me as soon as the fever goes away." At midnight she called to me and asked how I was; I checked and had no fever. She got out of her bed and came to see me and said, "It's true, daughter, you don't have a fever; we can go ahead and travel, for I was wishing for it and commended it to God." And that's how it was; we left in the morning.

The five days I was in Alba before she died I was more dead than alive, and two days before she died she told me when we were alone, "Daughter, the hour of my death has arrived." That pierced my heart. I didn't leave her side for one moment. I asked the nuns to bring me whatever was necessary, and I gave it to her, because my presence there comforted her. The day she died, she was unable to speak from the morning on, and in the afternoon the father who was with her (Friar Antonio de Jesús, one of the first two Discalced Carmelites), told me to go eat something, and as I was leaving, the saint didn't lie still, but rather looked from one side to the other. The father asked her if she wanted me, and she answered yes by signs and they called me. Upon returning, she saw me and laughed and showed such grace and love that she took my hands and placed her head in my arms, and I held her there in my arms until she passed away; I was more dead than the saint herself. She was so on fire with the love of her spouse [i.e., Christ] that it seemed she would never see the hour in which she would leave her body to be with him.

Since the Lord is so good and saw my scarce patience to bear this cross, he appeared to me at the foot of her bed in all his majesty in the company of the blessed souls who were coming for her soul. This very glorious vision lasted the time of a creed, so that I had time to change my sorrow and anguish into a great resignation and ask the Lord for forgiveness and tell him, "Lord, if Your Majesty had wanted to leave her here with me for my consolation I would ask you, now that I have seen your glory, not to leave her here one more minute." With this, she died, and this blessed soul went to be with God, like a dove.[32]

---

32. She died at nine o'clock in the evening on October 4, 1582.

AT SAINT JOSEPH'S CONVENT IN AVILA AGAIN

Since the saint loved me so, I had asked her to comfort me and ask the Lord to free me from attachments to anyone. By nature I was loving, and I loved her more than anyone can love; I was also very fond of other nuns whom I thought had perfect saintliness and whom the saint loved. Sometimes the saint would tell me that this attachment to friends wasn't good for my soul, that I should stop it for my soul's sake. But up until the hour that God took her with him I hadn't stopped this kind of bond; she did it for me, because since then I've been free and unattached, and it seems that I have even more love for those I love, without the defect of self-love. In all the rest it's as though I'm alone in the world, for I love all in God and for God. I was left with a strong spirit to take care of her holy body, which I did as though her death had not touched me.

I wanted to stay in that convent, but the prelate and nuns at Avila, which was my convent, didn't want it; they sent for me right away. I was a little perplexed until the saint appeared to me and said, "Obey, daughter, what they are ordering you and go." After I was in the convent at Avila, I prayed to the saint and commended myself to her and told this to the confessor. He told me that it was bad to commend myself to the saint, that she wasn't canonized and ordered me not to do it. That night, as I slept, the saint appeared to me very glorious and resplendent and in great glory and told me, "Daughter, ask me for all that you want; I'll get it for you." I awoke saying, "I ask you that the spirit of God be always in my soul," and she disappeared, leaving me assured in my opinion of her sanctity. I was troubled by what the confessor had ordered me, but with this vision all the worry left, for although I didn't doubt her sanctity, since the confessor had ordered it, it was a worry because he told me not to pray to her as a saint.

But I, not only because of the outstanding favors that God had granted her and that gave testimony of how much he loved her, but even more because of the love with which she had suffered many hardships for him, from what I could see and the part of the hardships in which I was involved, was witness that she was really a true saint and that what the Lord had told me about suffering many troubles in her company was true. And these were only the visible ones; the troubles that she suffered without being seen were infinite.

I remember one Christmas Eve, which was at the time of her great troubles and persecutions, for the nuncio had given a patent so that the Mitigated would take control of all the Discalced Carmelites and arrest them.[33] That

---

33. The year is 1578. Felipe Sego, the papal nuncio, submitted the Discalced friars to the jurisdiction of the mitigated Calced Order. He also removed Father Jerónimo Gracián, confessor

night a bundle of letters arrived that said that all her sons would be thrown out and that the nuncio wanted to disband their houses; and before going to matins I asked her to go have a bite to eat. While she was in the refectory, so afflicted, the Lord came to her and broke the bread and put a piece in her mouth, and told her, "Eat, daughter, I see that you are suffering a great deal, take heart, for it can't be otherwise." That night, in matins, her eyes were fountains of tears, and those of us who saw it were no less sorrowful; her troubles were deeply felt and a good part of all of them were also mine, as I loved her so. And since part of her troubles were also mine, so were her contentment and blessedness after she appeared to me in the glorious fashion I have said.

I wanted her holy body to come back to Avila, and one day, I wondered if they would take her holy body out, and they were afraid to because they didn't know its condition. I wanted to know this, and I commended it to God and fell asleep. The angels took me to her tomb and showed me how the body was whole, and the fragrance and color in such a condition that later they did take it out. These angels showed me two sleeves I had put on her arms, untorn, just as I had put them on, and they said to me, "Are you happy? Do you want more? Anything else?" I said, yes, that I would be happier if I saw her in the convent at Avila, but the duke would not consent to it. They told me, "Pay no attention to the duke, as long as the king wants it; that is what does or doesn't do it."[34] But then the dukes died and the king didn't do it, so as to please their survivors.

Before this happened the order wanted to bring the holy body to Avila.[35] With the distress I was experiencing I commended it to God and the Lord told me, "Don't worry, the body will come to this house." I importuned God. I wanted to know when it would be, and they answered me that it would be around the Presentation of the Virgin, but that was still almost a year away. And that's how it was that on that day they took her out of the house at Alba and brought her to Avila, where she was received with great rejoicing and illuminations.[36] The whole house seemed to be a heaven with all of the lights,

---

and great friend of Saint Teresa from his position as commissary of the order and placed him under house arrest at the monastery at Pastrana, and finally, in December of that year, sent him to house arrest at the Discalced school at Alcalá de Henares. These are the troubles and persecutions to which Ana refers.

34. King Phillip II (1527–1598) and the Duke of Alba, Fernando Alvarez de Toledo (1502–1582) and his successor, the Duke Fadrique Alvarez de Toledo (d. 1585).

35. The order had arranged with Álvaro de Mendoza, Archbishop of Avila, for Saint Teresa's body to be buried at the Convent of Saint Joseph in Avila, no matter where she died.

36. The saint's body actually arrived a few days later. It was exhumed on November 24, 1585, not November 21, the Day of the Presentation.

and the saint so favored her daughters that they couldn't go to any part of the convent where she did not appear to them and comfort them.

One day I told the confessor a matter concerning my soul, but he didn't take it well and said, "That seems like an idea of Mother Teresa's. Come now, don't be like her, drop all that." It seemed to me he said this with little respect for the saint. It bothered me, and I withdrew to a corner of the garden. With this concern that I had, I began to pray, seeing that he didn't esteem the saint as he should. As I was recollected the Lord came to me as when he was in the world, dressed in a pontifical cape, all of glory. Coming close to me he raised one side of the cape, the side that the heart is on, and showed me the glorious saint whom he carried under his arm, as though one with him, and the Lord said, "See? I bring her to you here, don't worry about anything; let them say what they want." Then he disappeared, leaving my soul all recollected and in more fervor with that same love that God had shown to the saint.

Another time I asked her to find out for me from God which of the virtues was most pleasing to him, so that I could better practice it; one day she spoke to me and told me it was humility.

Another time, in matins, on the eve of Saint Sebastian and as the prioress was about to say the Office, I saw the saint above her chair with such splendor, saying the same words as the prelate, and I felt my whole soul so inflamed with the love of God, and during all the matins I felt so grateful to see the saint's glory that I didn't cease to give thanks to the Lord. I was zealous to suffer something for such a good God who repays his followers in such a fashion.

At many other times she comforted me with a love and a fragrance as though her holy body were next to me, and although she didn't show herself, I felt her fragrance and favor near me.

I will tell of one time in particular that was notable. I was quite tired, for the whole house was sick; almost no one could get up to serve themselves, except myself and another sister. I went to the holy tomb of the saint and told her, "Mother, help me, my whole body is in such a state that I cannot be any more tired. Give me strength, I want it to serve all the others." I felt in my spirit that she would do it, and she told me, "I will do what you ask." I went to the kitchen and opened the ashes, and it was as though I saw that she was there; the fragrance of her holy body in the ashes was so great that it gave me great strength of spirit and none of my fatigue remained. My body was as though it were all spirit, and I was comforted this way until the others were healthy.

Many times the frying pans and everything in the kitchen smelled of the relics of her holy body, which was a marvelous thing, as though she had made them with her own hands.

Another time there was some misunderstanding between the prioress of that house and another one at another monastery because each one wanted the Holy Mother's niece, the daughter of one of her brothers,[37] who was a professed nun at Avila, and the Mother Prioress sent me to the holy tomb to ask the saint what was of most service to God and the good of that sister. The saint told me, "Teresa [de Jesús] will never leave here." And that's how it was. Although they tried to take her away on other occasions, they couldn't do it, and she died there quite young, a death that the fathers who were present said could only be that of a saint. It really seemed that the saint was with her. At this time I was in France, quite unaware that she was dying, and as I was a little recollected, I saw the saint pass before me, leading her by the hand. I felt it and was really envious. But I wondered if I was mistaken. A little later they wrote me how she had died at the very hour I'd seen her.

IN THE CARMEL AT COURT

Going ahead some time, ten years after the death of our saint, she appeared to me, the saint I mean, and she was crying, her face covered with a black veil, but it didn't keep me from seeing her and knowing it was the saint. She was weeping bitterly. I said to her, "Mother, why are you crying, since you are where there is no sorrow?" And she told me, "Look, daughter, the nuns who are leaving the order." She showed me many, together in a locutory, who were speaking with laypeople. Those from the outside were religious people and laypeople, and clerics from other orders, and while speaking with them the nuns turned black like crows, and the outsiders had horns. The nuns had beaks as though they really were crows. This vision terrified me, and I told it to the confessor who said, "Don't believe that this is about our order, daughter. If it were true, it would be a miserable thing."[38]

A year after this vision there occurred a great uproar; they wanted to take all the nuns out of the order and give them a separate vicar.[39] This

---

37. Teresa de Jesús, daughter of Saint Teresa's brother, Lorenzo, and Juana Fuentes. She professed at the convent of Saint Joseph in Avila in 1582 and died there on September 10, 1610.

38. This vision probably occurred in 1589, one year before the "revolt of the nuns" mentioned in the volume editor's introduction.

39. Ana misstates the causes of the disturbance. Nuns who did not agree with Nicolás Doria's proposals to restrict the prioresses' authority and freedom to select confessors applied to the Holy See for approval of the 1582 constitutions, and in 1590 Pope Sixtus V granted their petition. Ana herself opposed this rebellion against Doria, as is evident in this passage. The desire of those who participated in this "revolt" was never to leave the order but rather to preserve what they believed was the truly Teresian rule.

subsided, but before it did, there was much scandal, and everyone had something to say about it. This happened ten years after our saint's death. And on this occasion the prelates took out the prelate who was in Madrid[40] and brought in the prioress of our convent at Avila, who in this house had not yielded to the turbulence, nor had she broken with any of the things established by the saint.

This mother's name was María de San Jerónimo, a cousin of our saint,[41] and she asked the prelates for me to go with her to Madrid. Against the wishes of those in Madrid, they took us there. The reason they didn't want us was because the tempest had started there; with the help of the king's sister, the empress, they had gotten a brief for this vicar, thinking that they were right. It was a mistake and a scandal, for even if some monasteries had tried to leave the order, the rest didn't want to because it was contrary to the spirit of the saint, who had worked to leave her nuns in obedience to the Discalced friars.

We embraced the cross, this mother and I, for the love of God and for the sake of obedience, which is no small thing. And although we suffered, the cross was more moderate in some things that the Lord worked through us. For the first three months, the Lord did the prioress such a favor that the saint was put in her place and governed for her; I could see her as clearly as when she was alive. She gained such respect from me that I couldn't even look at her. Whenever I took messages to the prioress, I saw not her, but the saint. The others weren't aware of this, and said, "What prioress is this, whom we imagined was harsh and seems more like an angel than a human? Why have we been so opposed to bringing her here?" They were all so surprised that they didn't know what to say, they and the house were as though in heaven. I felt it most but didn't say a thing to anyone. After three months, the saint was seen no longer, but rather the prioress, who, like a good disciple, governed for her three years with much prudence and wisdom, which was great, and she had great talent in everything. But even so, the peace was not like before, because sometimes the past situations would recur, and the nuns didn't have the same freedom they had had before. They

40. María del Nacimiento (Ortiz), daughter of Cristóbal Ortiz and Inés de la Fuente, professed at Toledo in 1572 and died at Consuegra in 1597. She accompanied Ana de Jesús in the foundation at Madrid, where she was elected first subprioress and then prioress.

41. María Davila professed as María de San Jerónimo at Saint Joseph's in Avila in 1565 and died there at sixty-two years of age in 1602. As mistress of novices at Saint Joseph's, she played an important part in Ana's training and spiritual education. She left a written account of the life of her cousin, Saint Teresa, and also of her student and friend, Ana. She was prioress at Madrid 1591–94 and again at Saint Joseph's after she left Madrid.

felt their troubles, and the prioress was not lacking in them either, because she couldn't predict, I mean permit, the things that they wanted, and that's why the prelates had brought her.

I went about with a great desire for peace and served and attended to the nuns with much love and happiness, so that they trusted me, without my losing the obligation that I owed to my prelate. When they came to me tempted against her, I would tell them, "Our mother loves you greatly, don't think otherwise of her, and if not, test it, go to her openly; I know that she wants to serve you in all that she can." And I would say to the prioress, without complaining about the nuns, but rather looking toward God and charity, "Mother, the nuns are very fond of you; comfort them when they come to you, for they really are good, but they are disheartened. Show them your good graces."

I had this trial for all those three years,[42] accepting whatever worries presented themselves, for since it was all for the sake of the good Jesus they didn't seem like worries but rather like soft music. Sometimes on these occasions my soul felt that the prayer was so intimate, that it was like when a man falls asleep in a fortress and there's a great wind outside, and the sound makes one who is safe on the ground floor sleep very sweetly. Other times it seemed to me that the Lord carried me over the water like a stick of cork, which doesn't sink no matter what tempests might come.

In this way I carried the Lord with such familiarity in my soul that it seemed he never left my side, and I wouldn't know how to tell truthfully all the favors and delights the Lord did for me and how he repaid this sinner for that small hardship she was suffering. I will tell some things that I remember in particular.

One was while I was feeding a sick nun after the refectory [had closed], one of the downhearted against whose wishes the prioress had come.[43] Because of this and the affliction she had she spoke some sharp words to me. I didn't say a word or give the slightest acknowledgment of the affront to me, because I had God in my heart, and it seemed to me she didn't offend me, but rather our Lord. After I had served her I went to the garden. I went to my cell and felt so full of God that upon kneeling a great recollection came over me; and while I was in this state, I felt that Jesus Christ was next to me, as a gardener, and he put his arm under my head and I leaned over his holiest arm, and the Lord said to me, "Here you will see what it is to live without complaint and what charity is." I understood as though they had told me, "Whoever is in charity is in God and God is in them." He showed me that he had liked very much what

42. 1591–94.

43. The identity of this patient remains unknown.

I had done on that occasion. What my soul felt during this cannot be told nor believed, nor could it be endured if God had not increased the strength of love that inflamed my spirit. It was in that grace that the bride says in the Song of Songs, "The Bride has entered the garden, she rests in the arms and pleasure of her Beloved, her neck reclining over the sweet arms of the Beloved."[44]

On another occasion at this same time, there was a great lack of water, so that the grains were being destroyed in this region; there were many processions, and the sky was like bronze, not a sign of rain. My father confessor came to the turnstile and told me (I was the portress), "Aren't you asking God for rain?" I told him, "No, father, there are many good people asking for it." And he ordered me in obedience to go pray and ask the Lord for rain. At this moment some important people came to speak with their sister, and the prioress ordered me to be their mediator; I didn't tell her what the confessor had ordered me to do, with the intent to be there praying, and that's what I did. We were in the confessional for about half an hour, and when we came out there was so much rain that it seemed the sky had opened. I had recollected with the intent of obeying the confessor; and that's how it was, there had been no sign at all of rain, but God in his mercy showed us the strength of my soul with its simple obedience.

Another day, Saint Joseph's Eve, it was my week in the kitchen and I had permission to get up upon waking. Desiring on this day to hear Mass and the sermon with tranquility, I went to the kitchen very early in the morning and cooked all of the food with such prayer and presence of God that it seemed I had no body but only a spirit that commanded me. Everything went as I had planned and desired, almost without feeling the work, and I felt happiness and sweetness toward all those who needed me. The hour of Mass arrived, and I was completely free; while going to hear the Mass and as it began, the spirit grew within me, and more recollection. At the moment of Communion, the reverence in my soul for the Holiest Sacrament was so great that, finding myself to be nothing before God, it seemed to me that all that I had within myself was like tongues of reverence. After Communion this impulse subsided, and I was left with peace and recollection. In this recollection I saw on both sides of me four white animals like lambs, their mouths pressed against the ground; they were adoring God, whom I had received. I heard a voice telling me, "Similar to these is your reverence." And I understood that they were saying, "These are the four animals of the prophet Ezekiel, of the Apocalypse."

44. Antolin states that this is a verse from Saint John of the Cross's *Cántico espiritual*, but that it is not entirely correctly cited (n.83).

Although my soul was always recollected in the presence of the Lord, in all of these favors he did for me, it was more so, with the great weight and feeling of my nothingness. This brings me into a truly interior silence that cannot be described. Later, when I was reading what Saint Paul says to Saint Timothy,[45] I found myself in that same silence, which is a great and wondrous thing, which, although it is felt, cannot be understood but is a splendid thing.

I had this experience wherever I was, without anyone getting in the way anymore than if I were alone in the house. I found myself in this state another time, without going to prayer, but I had entered a room carelessly, and such a sudden suspension of feeling came over me that I don't know how it happened. I found myself taken to a vision before all of eternity and a vision of the essence of God that had no name or figure that can be named or even meditated upon. This was like a dark fog over everything, [which is the way] that it can be understood here on earth. Neither before nor after have I ever seen anything like it in my soul, although other similar favors [I have seen] a little bit, but they were far from that plenitude and majesty that are so obscure to our understanding. This was in the blink of an eye. It seems incredible to see such a thing in such a short space of time.

Once, while meditating upon a lesson of Saint Bonaventure, my spirit rose up, and I found myself with a vision almost like this last one, but it didn't have the same plenitude, rather it showed me part of that essence as if from the door, but it was not the same as the one I have described. Although on these occasions adversities presented themselves, in my soul they were as soft as the music of many birds singing sweetly is to the ear.

While I was in this convent at Madrid, there was a nun who was very devout and inclined to penitence; they gave her special permission to do it in order to satisfy her desires, and she went mad and was very demented for seven months. We had her tied with chains, but she broke them. We took weekly turns caring for her, and at the end of those seven months, one day during my week, she was so wild that the prelate ordered that she be punished. After they whipped her soundly, we left her locked up as we used to do. At dawn, as I was sleeping, it seemed that they were calling me, and I woke up. I saw our saint at the door of the cell as though she were alive; she beckoned me with her hand without speaking.

45. Antolín states that "it is not exactly clear what Ana is referring to in this phrase. Nothing similar is found in the canonical Epistles. It is possible she is referring to some letter of Pseudo-Dionysius in which he has Saint Paul telling Timothy the doctrine about interior silence in contemplation" (86). The translation is mine.

I got up and followed her; she took me to the door of the one who was mad and then disappeared. I didn't dare open it. But since she sensed my presence, she told me, "Open it. Don't be afraid; I'm sane." I opened it, for I had the key, and I found her sane and very happy. She told me, "The Mother of God has been here, and our Holy Mother, and they have cured me." Never again did she have that illness.

After this, while I was in a foundation and sick, I had been almost three days without a mouthful of food, from Holy Thursday to Saturday after the offices, because this indisposition began in a sensation that I had had in the Passion on Holy Thursday. When they enclosed the Holiest Sacrament, I had a fainting spell. At the end of these three days I didn't feel like eating anything but some sweet oranges; in that region they are not grown but come from far away. I didn't say that I wanted them so as not to bother them. But while I was eating, a pauper came to the turnstile, calling out and asking for alms and told the portress, "Take these three oranges and give them to a sick one that you have there." When I saw them, I praised the Lord, not so much to eat them, although I'd never seen prettier ones, as at seeing the goodness of the Lord, who cares so for those who hope in him. It is a great thing to abandon something for his love, for he knows how to repay you well.

Another time, which was a day of purging, I was very distressed and told the nurse that I felt weak and that she should give me something to eat. The house was so poor that she could find nothing to give me. While the nurse was in this worry and bother, they called at the turnstile, and the portress went to answer and didn't find anyone there. But at the turnstile she came upon a pot full of sweetmeats very suitable for my needs. The person who brought it was not seen, but God moved someone to bring it there.

IN OCAÑA AND MADRID

While at this foundation I have just spoken of in Ocaña, Christmas night after matins,[46] I recollected, and in dreams I was shown my arrival in France that was to occur. They put me on a very dark sea that frightened me, and they sent me with some companions who were not acquaintances of mine, except one I knew later in this recollection. I found my spirit in this vision forced into an intense desire to be a martyr. And although sometimes these desires have pressured me, never as perfectly as this time, so that I found myself in harmony and with pleasure, taking it to be for the sake of God,

---

46. December 24, 1595.

and I was inflamed with the most love that I have ever had of this kind, because at the other times I'd always felt some fear along with the desires.

After this, I communicated it to a friend who was there as subprioress.[47]
She was very fervent and said, "I want us to go together to France and distant lands; if what you have seen is true, we two will go." We went about for
some days not resisting hardships or fearing death in order to please God.

They took this nun to Madrid as subprioress. Since she had the desire
and fervor, she began to want to go to the desert with very solitary nuns
who would live in extreme rigor. Knowing her intent from her letters, I saw
that she was mistaken, that it was not what we two had talked about. Commending it to God, I feared it would not go well and that she wanted me
with her in that foundation. I did not think it was right, and I asked the Lord
to free me from that mistake that she was making.

One Saint Martin the Martyr's Day, I asked him to help me and show
what God wanted of me; he gave me to understand without speaking that
he would help me. This mother asked the prelates to bring me where she
was. On the road there was a river that, although wide, seemed not to have
much water, and they entered it with the coach; in the middle of the river
a sudden wave of water grew so big that it flooded the coach and everyone
was afraid. God gave me such faith and certainty that my soul in this faith
seemed as safe as in heaven. So it turned out as well for me as if God had
held the coach in his hands. Before arriving at Madrid where the mother
was, while resting at a shrine on Saint Phillip and Saint James's Day, I commended myself to the Holy Apostles, and suddenly I found myself recollected in a great clarity of spirit.

They told me, I don't know whether it was God or the apostles, "Don't
fear, for what she wants is not to be," as though all that she was doing was
nothing. My soul was very recollected, inflamed with God, and on the road
yet to be walked this assistance from God always continued for me; I was as
safe as though I were in a paradise.

When I got to Madrid, this mother told me that I had to go with her to
the desert. I told her that I was not moved to do it nor would I stray one inch
from the orders of our Holy Mother, that she should see that it was a devil's
trick that she was attempting. They didn't want to believe me. But the prelate, observing me and what I was saying, ordered me not to go. This mother
took out her writings about that desert, and to me it seemed to be craziness,

---

47. Isabel de la Cruz (de Córdoba y Figueroa). Widowed after eleven years of marriage, she took
her vows at Madrid in 1591. She was subprioress and mistress of novices at Ocana. Later she was
at Guadalajara. She was also prioress at Villanueva de la Jara and died at Alcalá in 1613.

that it wasn't possible that women could maintain it, and finally she went to do it after all.[48] After three months I, along with everyone else, was watching to see who was right. The court, the courtiers, and the empress[49] supported it, since they didn't have to experience it. But I felt strongly that her writings and ceremonies went against the orders of the Holy Mother Teresa. I felt in my spirit that I would sin by presuming to do something of more perfection than what the saint had done. So I let them talk, and all those who knew about it murmured a great deal about it to me. It seemed to them that I was lax, and that's what one lady countess came and told me, "I am little edified by you. I wouldn't have thought it."[50]

I went through this for the love of God who had shown me what I have said [that it would be folly to go in to the desert.—Ed.]. After three months in these exercises, God showed that it was not his will. The monastery was completely undone by the judgment of God, as was evident and could not be hidden; because a great plague came and entered that convent, and the prelate contracted it and two others who died. And they took out the prelate, the founder, to cure her, and when the doctors went to cure her, they found she had become a man.[51] When they told the prelate, he was disturbed and said she should be kept outside the convent until he gave an account to His Holiness. His Holiness was also upset and asked what woman this was and how she had lived. They told him she was a very high-ranking lady, a widow who had become a nun. And His Holiness said, "If she hadn't been married, I would think she was a man and I could disband this convent, thinking that they knew she was a man; but since God has ordered things this way, don't let her live with the others; make her a little hut in a garden near the church with a little window where she can hear Mass and take Communion." That's what was done, and in that solitude she set a good example for others. The monastery was completely undone by its practices, and the prelates ordered that it become like all the others of our saint in everything.

48. Isabel de la Cruz founded the Convent of Saint Mary of Corpus Christi in Alcalá de Henares on May 11, 1599.

49. María, the daughter of Carlos V and Isabel of Portugal. Born in 1528, she married the Emperor Maximilian II on September 13, 1548, in Valladolid. As a widow she entered the Franciscan Convent of the Descalzas Reales in Madrid. She died in 1603.

50. Possibly the Countess of Castellar, Beatriz de Mendoza, who was one of the patrons of the convent at Jerónimo.

51. Isabel de la Cruz had to leave the Convent at Jerónimo after three months because of the plague. Ana de Jesús María came from Villanueva de la Jara to Jerónimo in November of the same year, 1599, to reorder the life of the community in accord with the Teresian model. Antolín eliminates this episode of Isabel de la Cruz's apparent sex change entirely from his edition of the *Autobiography*.

VISIONS AND REVELATIONS

Once while sleeping in our saint's cell, in dreams I found myself before our Lord Jesus Christ who came as a judge to judge. I found myself in purgatory. It was like the bed of a very big river, and instead of water, everything was fire, narrow. I found myself in it up to my waist. Many other souls were completely submerged, others not so much. As I was in this condition, a beautiful and resplendent angel came and said to me, "Do you feel the fire much?" "Yes," I said, "but with the hope of seeing the Lord soon, it doesn't distress me." The bad angels were on the shore with hooks and seemed to be threatening me, but they did not do anything to me. But when the good angel that I've told of arrived, everything disappeared and I found myself awake and my gown all wet, as though I had been in water, but quite sad at seeing myself alive, for I thought I had expired.

This vision occurred after I had been in the monastery for a few days. The saint and sisters, looking at me, asked what was the matter, that I looked like I had been disinterred. I told the saint my dream, and she told me laughing, "Go to, daughter, you won't go to purgatory." But I took this as graciousness, and I think the saint never said it for any other reason. Rather, I think I will have a lot of purgatory and that God will do me a favor by sending me there and not someplace worse, according to how I have lived.

Another time in dreams I saw another vision in this same monastery, while the house was quite upset and afflicted by the business of the order, which has been spoken of, because the evil spirit was into everything and the devils were quite adept. Once, over the wall, I saw them like a flock of birds, a very great multitude, and on this occasion I saw in dreams what I am going to say: that Saint John the Evangelist, Saint Joseph, Saint James, and Saint Bartholomew came in and were all richly dressed as priests. Saint John the Evangelist had a golden staff and was sprinkling holy water around the house, and he told me, "This one we're guarding." And that's how it was. In that adversity, all the others suffered some harm, and this house stayed whole without changing anything, although there was much conflict..

At the time of the Nun of Portugal,[52] when it seemed that everyone considered her a saint, I saw another time in a vision that a wind arose from

52. María de la Visitación, the Nun of Portugal or Lisbon, a Dominican nun who claimed to have received, among other divine favors, the stigmata and who acquired a cult following in Spain and throughout Europe. Her followers included the theologian and mystic, Fray Luis de Granada, Pope Gregory, and Phillip II, who invited her to bless the Armada before it set off to its disastrous encounter with the English navy in 1588. She was investigated by the Inquisition and pronounced a religious fraud in October 1588, admitting that she had painted on the holy

that place where she was, so strong that it knocked over everything in its path, and the dust that arose from the earth blinded people in such a way that only those in the fields who got under trees could remain standing. The others fell to the ground. Those close to the trees were the ones who didn't fall. I understood this: that these were the ones who did not believe in her and left it to God, without any affinity for that kind of sanctity.

The king and grandees were blinded by that dust, and on the counsel of this woman sent a fleet to England, which was very unfortunate. As though she were a saint, all of the armada went for this woman's blessing. She gave it to them, and they expected to achieve victory with it. But since her blessing was not really good, the armada was lost. The devil had snared many souls, and when they were not together they communicated through his astuteness as though they could see each other and knew about each other. Since the armada had entered the sea, the evil spirit as inventor appeared and spoke to one of these comrades and told her there had been a victory; and she, as though in a rapture, began to shout in the church. There were many people at Mass, and then it became known, and she was shouting "Victory, victory!"

A father who used to confess me told me that although it was twenty leagues away, it became known through the people's desire for victory. I feared it might not be true, because I had seen a fearful vision during prayer. Christ Our Lord appeared to me in the sky, very angry. He had in his hands a chalice of mourning covered with a black veil, and hanging from the ends of the veil there were branches, like scourges, all bloody. I was very distressed and in great anguish, my hands lifted in prayer calling to God to assuage his anger. I felt another Carmelite next to me and didn't recognize her, but she was making the same exclamation, and I think it was our saint. The Holiest Virgin, Mother of Jesus Christ, was at our Lord's side, begging him to calm his anger against sinners. And after a while in this agony, the Virgin turned to us and said, "The Lord has heard you and calmed his anger," and this vision disappeared.

And since they were saying there was victory, I went this very day to pray for this business. The Lord appeared to me very wounded; he was on the cross and they were taking his hands off the cross, very injured, and he called to me and told me, "Look what is happening." Showing me the sea, he put his right arm in the water and began taking out many of the dead,

---

wounds in order to appear truly saintly. Her sentence was relatively light owing to her seemingly sincere repentance and cooperation with the investigation. Some have suspected her of possible collaboration with the Portuguese separatist movement.

and he said to me, "Do you see victory here? All have drowned." I was so
upset that for many days the sorrow and worry didn't leave my heart, and I
saw very clearly how God was offended that such a serious thing had been
undertaken through the belief that the king and other grandees had placed
in that woman, and that everyone had been blinded.

Many prayers had been made throughout Spain, and the Holiest Sacrament was in the churches every day for this reason, and this was not completely right. I wondered when I saw the mourning chalice whether it was
because of the indecency that all of this was most praised in the churches, as
can be seen in the misfortune of this expedition that was lost.

After this that I have told about that mother in the desert, before the
events of the armada, having returned to Avila with the Mother Prioress,
the Lord showed me there with a special light what would happen in that
foundation and how it was not in the spirit of God nor our Holy Mother as I
have said, which was true; and in other things like these, although in different matters, the Lord has granted that it happen as he showed me.

One of these was that while I was commending the matter of returning
our Holy Mother's body to Avila and the case was in Madrid, they told me,
"It's been decided against justice; but don't worry, let them do their will for
now, and in due time I will do mine." This they told me. I didn't know if it
was true, and then came the news of how it had been decided against the
monastery. This was true. The hope of the transferal that they gave me has
not yet been fulfilled. I don't know if it's true, but it's been more than twenty
years since this happened. Perhaps the Lord doesn't want it to happen in
my lifetime, but if it was the Lord who spoke to me, he will not go back on
his word, even if it's late. Later on, here (in Antwerp) the saint appeared to
me and told me, "Daughter, I will go to Avila." But it hasn't happened. I live
always in hope.

At the time I have just spoken about, while I was in prayer commending this business about our saint to God, our Lord showed me a vision that
amazed me. A great personage told me that he had written a message to
Rome from the king so that the holy body would come to Avila; they were
doing it to please me and the desire that I had. While I was commending
it to God, sure that he would tend to it, they showed me in a vision an old
trunk and told me, "Open it." I went to open it, and it was empty, full of
spider webs. I was frightened for I didn't know what this meant. And they
told me, "This is like what they tell you they will do in this matter. They are
words with which they deceive you."

I was very distressed, and then I saw a very venerable woman on her
knees at the other end of the trunk; she wore white robes like a widow, and

I didn't know her. But they told me, "Through this woman what you want will be done; the holy body will return to Avila." Up to now I am ignorant about this, I don't know what it means. After the high lady-in-waiting, the Duchess of Gandia left, I wondered if she might be the one to finish this business and said this to Don Iñigo, may he rest in heaven.[53] He made many efforts, all that he could, with his mother [the Duchess of Gandia] before he died, so that she would do it, but up to now, she hasn't done anything.

Another time there was a holiday in Avila, and the day that they earned it, upon taking Communion, I stayed after for a bit commending it to God, asking him for all to earn it and be in his grace. While I was like that, the Lord showed me most of the city, and their souls were white like doves, from which I received great comfort in my soul. It was the reason that an impulse of love of God and thanksgiving was inflamed in me, as though I were the only one to receive it.

LOVE OF OTHERS

Another time there was, in a convent where I was, a nun who was plagued by temptations; she didn't understand herself, and the confessors didn't understand her. The prelate came and ordered me to care for her and comfort and attend to her. While I was commending her to God, they appeared to me and told me, "Ask her if she has confessed such and such matters." When I asked her she said no. Commending her to God again, I saw that her soul was black and dark. I went back to her and told her, "Confess very clearly all that has to do with what I have asked you." She did so and must have been truly contrite, for when she finished confessing the Lord showed me her soul as clear as glass. There were just a few little veins that went from one side to the other like fine silk threads. I didn't understand what they were. Asking the confessor, he told me, "They are the inclinations and passions of which we are made." I was very comforted by the favor that the Lord had done for this good sister, and she was so grateful to God and what they had ordered me to do that she continues to be grateful to this day, and I expect she will be a saint.

At this time I was burdened with responsibilities, and I desired that obedience would let me be alone with the Lord. Having just finished Communion, I recollected and the Lord told me, "Get up, my will is that you

---

53. Iñigo de Borja, one of Ana's greatest supporters in Antwerp. He donated money for the foundation at Antwerp. A counselor to the Spanish regents in the Low Countries, at the end of his life, he was a captain of the Spanish artillery. He died in November 1622. His mother was the Duchess of Gandia, to whom Ana refers.

do the will of all in whatever they order you." This gave me great comfort, seeing that the Lord wanted it, because it satisfied me to act with more freedom, since by nature I was inclined to please others. I wondered many times if it was the spirit or self-love, and in this way the Lord removed this doubt that I had.

Another time I sat down next to the turnstile; I was the portress, and I was troubled, for it seemed to me that it bothered the older nuns that the prioress had placed me, a young woman, at the turnstile; and it seemed to be true on this occasion. I recollected, and while in that state I saw in my spirit that the Lord was showing me a dry thorn bush on the patio with many white and red roses. Since it was dry and not the time for roses, the Lord told me, "These roses may not be taken without going through the thorns." He wanted me to understand that in suffering and adversities, virtue is acquired.

I will say for the glory of the Lord that he always gave me the comfort of doing good for others and their needs on the occasions that presented themselves. Although I was inconvenienced on these occasions, I didn't find it to be inconvenience, but rather a joy. I owe this to the Lord up to the present day. May his name be praised. Amen

In our convent at Avila there was a nun so afflicted with temptations and interior troubles that they couldn't imagine what it was, and no remedies worked.[54] The confessors didn't know what to make of it. One day she told me for the love of God to commend her to our Holy Mother and ask for light for her and for those who were dealing with her so that they would understand her troubles. A few days after I asked the saint for this, one day, commending it to our Lord, they showed me how a big black dog came out of her that had only a white neck, and the saint said to me while I was looking at that evil vision, "This one will not bother her any longer." I saw that next to the nun was her beautiful guardian angel who made these interior problems leave her. That very nun told me after a few days that they had gone away. I saw that she was like a different person after I had commended it to our saint, but I didn't tell her anything of what had happened, for it was not to tell. Later they made her prelate in that convent, and it pleased the Lord to give her a sickness that kept her almost always in bed. At this time I was in Madrid with the one who had gone there to be prioress of that house, as has been said; and when we came back, she [the nun in Avila] was sick,

54. Mariana de Jesús (de Lara). She professed on January 9, 1576, and died in Avila at the age of fifty-three in 1603. She was elected prioress at Saint Joseph's Convent in Avila in 1591 and again in 1602.

and they made me her nurse. But since we human beings change, she liked others more than she liked me. I pretended that I didn't notice and served her with a good heart, as though it were God who was sick. She showed great displeasure whenever I fed her and served her. I wasn't surprised; I attributed it to her illness and with the love with which I served her it was a pleasure for me to find this mortification. One day I took her food that I had cooked with a great desire that she could eat it; and upon seeing me she said many unpleasant things, among them, "Get out of here, don't bring me anything to eat." I said, "Mother, try it, Your Reverence, it's good." She became angrier. "I don't want you to give it to me. Get away from me." I left her and went to the chapter with great delight because of the love that I harbored because this humiliation had presented itself to me. I had such great joy at the love of God that it seemed it could not be greater if the Lord had spoken to me. Entering the chapter on my knees, I recollected, and the Lord came to me and said, "Do you think I repay you like those in the world?" leaving my soul full of spiritual joy, as though in paradise. Of these words, of the comings and goings of the Lord in my soul, I would not know how to say with words the richness that the Lord left in my soul, and the wondrous effects.

Once our holy mother was in one of her convents, speaking about some business with the prioress, who was a little abrupt with our saint. I got angry at her, and although I went to confess that very day, I went to Communion. Coming to the little window, the Lord showed himself to be angry with me and said, "This one who offended you has pleased me greatly in many other things, and you do not please me in being angry with her. Your slightest fault offends me more than the evils of the world could offend you because you do not feel anything except what touches you; I feel all the sins of the world." This generated a great effect of love and charity in my soul for that nun, which lasted for a long time, and later I held her in high esteem.

Another time one who had great temptations was working with me, and one day she told me not to speak to her, that she didn't believe a thing I told her. I told her to make an effort and to believe that all matters of faith were true. She told me, "I can't anymore, although I try." I went to Communion and prayed for her. The Lord told me, "Tell her she certainly can, that what she says is not true; I have given you free will, and my grace has more strength than evil; she certainly can believe, if she wants."

Another time a nun in our convents who had always had some temptations regarding her prioress died. Three months after she died, she appeared one day to me and I saw how she was leaving purgatory and that she had spent all this time under her prelate's bed.

One day of the Octave of the Holiest Sacrament, the Lord showed me much grace as I was on my knees praying; he was inviting me to ask favors of him, and it seemed that he wanted me to, that he had many favors to bestow upon me. Recollected in this vision, I saw three people: one was my sister, and the others were a cousin and another man, and all were quite far away. I asked for salvation for those three people, and the Lord showed that it pleased him. Shortly thereafter letters came telling how my sister had died that very day and my cousin too: he of a great fever and my sister, an unfortunate death, drowned. The other was Antonio Pérez,[55] who had done some wicked things in Spain and was sentenced to death but escaped and went to England, where there were other worse evils for his soul. While I was in France, he came to see me and seemed desperate about his salvation, in his view, because of the evil deeds he had done. While he spoke, I began to feel love for him and a desire for his salvation. They tell me that the Lord touched him, and although I wasn't there, they wrote to me that he died with very sure signs of salvation, receiving the sacraments frequently, with his confessor always at his side. The day he died, he got on his knees in a great impulse of the love of God; and he remained like that, as I say, with great signs of his salvation.

PERSECUTIONS OF THE DEVIL AND FAVORS FROM HEAVEN

On one occasion the prelate ordered me, because I had asked her for it, to have a little solitude, for I was tired and with desires for some repose for my spirit, which I wanted in order to enjoy the Lord as my teacher alone for a bit. While praying on this occasion, a devil came in front of me, doing stupid things and saying, "Woe unto him who does such good for you." And then I could hear a voice saying, "Leave her alone, she really needs these comforts."

These evil spirits have appeared to me on different occasions, but I don't fear them anymore than I fear flies. Once I was in bed during the day and fell asleep, and in a dream I heard a noise like someone in the room. I awoke and saw a pack of demons. As I raised my head, they began to leave and went into a hole in the cell; it made me want to laugh, because they were fleeing from me. They stuffed their heads in like people, and they left so many feet outside the hole kicking like someone running away; each one wanted to be the first one to get out, and they stuck their heads in first, with their feet outside.

55. Antonio Pérez (1540–1611) was Phillip II's Secretary, imprisoned and condemned to death for his part in the murder of Escobedo, secretary of Juan of Austria, and also for his possible sexual liaison with the Princess of Eboli. He escaped from jail in 1590 and fled to France and England, where he offered his services to the French and English governments as an informer against Phillip II. He died in poverty in Paris in 1611.

Another time I was going to do something at night, because our saint was sick, and I was carrying a little lamp in my hands. A cat came—the devil came in this figure that time—and got up on the lamp and put it out. I was far away from our saint. I was angry, and if I hadn't been in the dark I would have thrown the thing in my hands at it. When I came back to our saint, I found her laughing and she said, "What happened to you, daughter?" I told her what had happened and that I had gotten angry with the evil spirit. She said, "That's not good. I didn't want you to be angry." I thought that she had seen it, although she didn't say anything else.

Another time the saint sent me for a light if I was not afraid, because everyone was in bed. I said, "Since your reverence orders it, I am not afraid." I went to the fireplace and lit the fire, and as I got the flame going I saw a black mastiff going up the chimney, and then it was gone. This was in Burgos. There were bad things in that house, for it had belonged to a rich man who was damned. He never wanted to confess, and right after he died so many flies came that they took his body and soul to hell. Thus, no one had wanted to live in this house for years. Since our saint could not find a house, some of his relatives invited her to this one and gave it to her for almost nothing; and until the Holiest Sacrament was placed in it, we were bothered by things that disquieted us day and night. Sometimes it seemed that glasses were breaking over us. Our saint sent me once to see what had broken, and there was nothing except the evil spirit that bothered us. Our saint went through all kinds of things there.

Another time, in Paris, we were at matins, and a sister was very gay and laughing, not mindful of what she was saying. I didn't know what this was, and in these thoughts I saw a little devil at the foot of the candlestick playing, which was distracting her in this manner.

One day on Christmas night after Communion I recollected, and the Child Jesus who had been born in my heart appeared to me. After the offices I went to do my obligatory activities, and as I was doing them I found myself upset, so much so that everything I took in my hands I dropped. All of this being upset lasted so long that I became so impatient and angry with myself that I almost assured myself that what I had had was an illusion; I was so distrustful and dark-humored that it seemed there was no God, so I was completely deceived. The next night, having spent the whole day in great affliction, I told it to the confessor as well as the worry I had of being in mortal sin. Although he comforted me, it did not satisfy me, so upset was I by the evil spirit. The following night, as I said, I went to sleep with that worry. In dreams I saw a white dove come flying around and around the altar; it made so much noise with its wings that it seemed to want me to hear it. Listening carefully, it seemed my heart was expanding. Then came a very venerable priest, dressed to say Mass, and two deacons, and all were pontifical; and they said their Mass. The priest came to Communion with the host, and Our Lord must have been the priest, who told me, "Take Communion again." I was afraid, because I thought I had taken Communion in mortal sin, and all the restlessness I had was from this fear. As a result of this vision, I was as calm as if I had really taken Communion, and my soul had great certainty and joy.

Another time between matins and compline I went to a cross on the patio, which had a little stone chapel where the nuns went to pray. I found myself so full of the love of God that I sank down on my knees over the stones. It was very icy, and without noticing the time, I recollected; when they rang for matins, I went to get up, and my habit was stuck to the ice. I was amazed that I hadn't felt the cold anymore than if it had been heat. The Lord is powerful when he puts his grace over souls, and I felt it so greatly and was so favored that for all I knew there were only God and I.

THE ROAD TO FRANCE

Coming back to what I had started to say about that dream I had in Ocaña, I was always aware in what he had shown me that God wanted me to bear a cross. Since the flesh was fearful, one day the Lord appeared in an intellectual vision, for I felt him but did not see him, and he told me, "Olives and the grape must pass through the winepress of martyrdom to give their liquid; all my friends have gone down this road," and the vision disappeared, telling me, "That's how I want you." This awoke a new courage in me, for I had been downhearted, and taking heart I offered myself anew for whatever God wanted of me. I really and truly put my heart in his hands. I felt my determination was agreeable to him.

Another day after Communion I was thinking about the words that a father had told me, how it was not good or necessary that nuns go to France among so many heretics, since they would not be preaching to them. I was seeing the truth in this when the Lord appeared to me and told me, "Don't pay any attention to that, for just as honeycombs attract flies, so will you attract souls." This was when the debate was underway about the French who had come seeking nuns from Spain, and there were different opinions about whether it was a good thing or not.[56] Since all of those involved in it

---

56. Various members of the French church hierarchy had for some time been seeking to establish the Discalced Order in France. With this goal in mind Pierre Bérulle (see the volume editor's introduction), Jean de Quintanadueñas Bretigny (1556–1634), and others arrived in

were learned people and those who doubted were great servants of God, it made my soul wonder whether it was God who had spoken to me, although the confessors assured me that it was God and encouraged me. I was quite afflicted at seeing the possibility of a change of country and afflicted by my doubts as well, because of wanting to do God's pleasure. And since this was pulsing in my spirit, God showed through other souls what he wanted, so that I would not doubt so much. His Majesty made me talk with a nun in our house who was very saintly. She lamented that I was going to France; she wanted to hinder it and said, "How, Lord, can you want this sister to go so far away?" The Lord responded to her, saying that it had to be, that it was not right for her to want anything different. Replying that she feared what I would suffer, the Lord told her, "Those who take honey from the hives get stung, but they get the honey."

Everyone in the house and the whole village commended me to God, for they feared my going to foreign lands, full of heresies. In the convent all were distressed, for it's a house of God where all love each other, and although I didn't deserve it, they loved me in excess, and I loved them as saintly souls. They all did all they could so that the prelate would not give me permission, but the French were so obsessed that it could not be denied; my poor soul was so upset and fearful that I didn't know where to turn. Afraid that it might be the devil who wanted to deceive me, I did not cease lamenting day and night, asking the Lord not to let me be deceived.

On the other hand, the Lord did battle with me, showing me that I should be faithful to him and carry out what I had offered to him at other times. I carried about this exterior and interior battery, which was no small cross. It cannot be believed. The devil and the flesh assaulted my spirit, telling me I was old, didn't know the language, was useless without the language of those who were taking me there, and would die on the road. [I was also told] that I should not go because I would be ruined and persecuted and scorned by all, that my friends didn't like it, and that I would suffer grave hardships away from them. [Finally], I should see that I was well loved, where did I want to go, that there in Ocaña I had all repose and rest for my soul.

All this I suffered in my soul, a poor weak woman, under great pressure. In these afflictions, the Lord pressed me and other friends and told me one day, "Don't delay going; if you don't go, nothing will be done; all the others

---

Spain at the end of 1603 to negotiate the transfer to France of some of the nuns who had been associates of Saint Teresa. There was a great deal of ambivalence among the Carmelites about the French foundations. There was also a good deal of uncertainty about whether or not Ana de Bartolomé should be among the founders in France. Although the negotiations had been under way since 1585, the first group of Spanish nuns did not arrive in France until 1604.

will come back once they get there." And that's how it was, for a few days after we were in Paris, they had sent me to Pontoise, and they [the other founders] sent to me to ask whether I wanted us to go back to Spain; [they said] they weren't adjusting and wanted to go back. I sent a message to them to go, that I wanted to persevere in what we had started. They got angry with me and didn't dare go back.

Before leaving, our Lord spoke with another sister in the house and told her, "Tell her to go there now and not to fear, that I tell her what I tell my disciples. She will be afflicted and scorned, but her troubles will turn into joy." This that the Lord told my friends gave me more strength than I had had until then.

Another day, while I had this worry, I fell half asleep, and a youth appeared to me, a very fine gentleman wearing a soldier's uniform. He told me, "You can't fail to go, take heart." I believed it was the angel Saint Michael, to whom I have been devoted since I was a girl, and I prayed to him each day.

All of us who were supposed to go came together in our convent at Avila on Saint Bartholomew's Day, and we were there until the day of the beheading of Saint John the Baptist.[57] In those days, a month before leaving you could see stars in the sky day and night, before we knew the ones who would go. The stars were very resplendent, some larger than others. And that's how we were. I was the least of all.

Another time before leaving, while in the struggle I have just spoken of, the Lord told me, "Go, for just as birds stick to birdlime, souls will attach to you, and they will remain with me forever."

The whole way, my soul was very commonly frequented by the presence of its beloved with great comforts and favors and with a peace and tranquility from heaven. Only once was I very distressed, because I had seen the whole way that my companions were much displeased at bringing me, that they saw I was not good for anything, and they were right.[58] It seemed a reckless thing for me to go, since I am worth so little, and as they showed me such displeasure, this day, as I say, I found myself very afflicted. But the Lord appeared to me in a vision, crucified and loving of my soul. He consoled me, saying, "Daughter, take heart, I will help you and be with you."

---

57. From August 24 (Saint Bartholomew's Day) until August 29 (Day of the Death of Saint John the Baptist), 1604.

58. The nuns who accompanied Ana de San Bartolomé to France were Ana de Jesús, who had professed at Salamanca in 1571; Isabel de los Ángeles, who professed there in 1591; Beatriz de la Concepción, who also professed at Salamanca in 1593; Leonor de San Bernardo, who professed at Loeches in 1598; and Isabel de San Pablo, who professed at Burgos in 1590.

This same day,[59] crossing a bridge over a big river, in the middle of it the evil spirit tried to throw us in the river. The horses got upset, and the coach rose up on one side, and my companions, fearful, cried out to God. With the uproar the coach went off the bridge, falling, and you could see it was the devil causing it because in leaving the bridge he threw it into a small ditch full of many thorns. I went toward the door, and the coach fell over on that side and everyone fell on me. People screamed and were saying, "She's dead." I didn't feel the thorns or any other difficulty, as though God had me in his palm, and while the others were on top of me, I could hear them scream loudly, and I didn't know what about. One had a wounded foot, and the other an injured eye that the stick from the stirrup gave her, so it was necessary to send to the village for a surgeon to care for them. They were strong, and since I was weak and a nothing, the Lord would not abandon me for anything.

MOTHER ANA DE SAN BARTOLOMÉ

Arriving at Paris,[60] where the Lord continued the favors and delights of the road for me, I went, with the prelate's permission,[61] to cook the food with great pleasure, as I had always done in that office—which was that of a laysister—and although the Holy Mother in her life desired that I take the veil and proposed it to me a few times, I had resisted, saying that it would be an affliction to leave my vocation, and so she had let me alone, because she loved me and looked more to giving me pleasure than to taking any herself, which was a great concern for me. But my self-love made me believe that what I wanted was of greater perfection, and I had resisted it. The mother superiors then decided that I had to take the veil. There was another tempest in my soul, no less than the last, for it seemed to me that I had erred in not giving pleasure to the Holy Mother and that I had to do it now for foreigners. The prioress didn't want it. I was alone, and she had me in a cell a whole hour telling me things of great temerity: that I shouldn't believe

---

59. September 20, 1604.

60. October 15, 1604.

61. Ana de Jesús (Lobera) (1545–1621) was the first prioress at Paris. She professed at the convent of Saint Joseph in Avila in 1571. Saint Teresa selected her as prioress of the foundation at Beas, and she also founded the convent at Granada in 1582. Along with María de San José, Ana de Jesús was a leader of the "nuns' revolt" of 1590. After the foundation in Paris in 1604, she did another foundation in Dijon. In 1607, she went to Flanders where she was a founder at Brussels, Lovaina, and Mons. She died in Brussels in 1621.

them, that I would be the cause of my own damnation, and that because of me the order in France and Spain would become lax and be ruined.

I was conflicted by great fears, as can be imagined, because in coming to talk to me the prelates said the opposite and that it had to be, that the Superior General of the Spanish Order[62] had told them to do this as soon as I arrived in France. All of my companions were against the opinion of the prelates, except for Mother Leonor de San Bernardo, who was always of this opinion. On the roads and there in Paris she consoled me, saying that it was very necessary, and some days passed in give and take. Since the mother[63] was strong in her opinion and the prelates in theirs, I was caught between two waters that were besieging me. Father Coton, a Jesuit,[64] came; the prelates brought him to persuade me to do what they wanted. He, seeing me so perplexed, told me, "All those in my convent and I will say masses and prayers for nine days so that God will shed light on this matter, and what we decide you must obey in conscience."

In these nine days the Lord appeared to me two or three times, which consoled me and was very necessary. He was very beautiful and very happy and spoke to me with good grace. Once he told me with sweet and loving words, "Take heart, for it cannot be otherwise." At the end of this novena, the Jesuit father asked me how I was. I told him I was very troubled without telling what had happened with the Lord and the saint, who had also appeared to me and consoled me. He told me that in conscience I was obliged to obey, and he said, "I think that I can command you to do it in obedience on behalf of God, and I am doing so; you will sin if you do otherwise."

He told this to the superiors, who wanted it. And, in the end, I obeyed, my spirit quite disturbed, for I was not certain of anything. As the saint was not telling me anything, nor did she come to me, I felt it deeply, because she came only once to console me. I was very reliant upon what she used to tell me. In this condition, the Lord brought to mind how before I left Spain my Holy Mother had appeared to me and in her presence I saw that I had the black veil and I asked her, "Mother, can I take off this veil?" She told me, "Leave it alone" and showed a kind of sadness at what I had to suffer in this. Another mother came with her, a very holy woman, who had been my teacher in the novitiate. She carried in her hand a little plate with a liquor,

---

62. Francisco de la Madre de Dios. He professed at the monastery at Pastrana in 1579 and died as Prior at Madrid in 1616. He had been generally opposed to establishing the Discalced Carmelites in France.

63. Ana de Jesús.

64. Father Coton was a celebrated Jesuit theologian and confessor to Henry IV of France.

which seemed a heavenly thing, and told me, "Take some of this and fortify yourself, you need it." She gave me a spoonful; and then she showed me a happy and courageous spirit. This consoled me a little on the occasion of which I speak.

And then they tried to take me to Pontoise. This was another day, after it had already been arranged.[65] My worry and affliction of heart increased greatly, more than I can say here. I went to prayer, and the Lord told me, "Courage, for I have you in my heart. I will be in yours."

These talks and the presence of the Lord always comforted me, but my weakness was such that I would go back to my concern and great fear about my incapacity.

All of the aldermen from half a league outside the village came with the whole town, in a procession of such solemnity and devotion that you could hardly get through the streets because of the many people who came out; so we were detained from entering the house until the night. The devotion with which the people received that foundation was something to praise the Lord for; today they have it for themselves, and God, through those sisters, does and has done much good for the town. All this distressed me more, seeing that I was the one who had to attend to it. It was as though I were sentenced to death and so mortified that it seemed to me that the office was infamy for me, that I had never had an occasion of more humiliation for body and soul, and that I was no more than a worm. This is the truth; I am a worm, but I didn't really know it in this situation with the same conviction as now.

[DIVINE FAVORS IN PONTOISE]

Once while I was before the Holiest Sacrament, asking that he look to his honor and help me—for I found myself very alone—he told me, "Here I am. Like the light of my eyes I see you."

Another day I went to ask him to show me (since I had no other teacher) what I was to do, that I had to do a chapter and I was greatly concerned about it and that this feeling had left me without strength and as though spiritless to advise and teach what was necessary. As the Mass that the convent was hearing ended, the Lord told me, "Look at the rule, there you will find the strength you need." At this I took heart and went to do my chapter, and I told the sisters things that God put before me for their initiation. The truth was that although I wanted to serve and comfort them, I found myself very incapable; but I trusted in God and in the virtues and long desires they had had of

65. They left for Pontoise on January 14, 1605.

seeing the Order of Our Holy Mother. [I believed] that the Lord would help them and the Lord would satisfy them, although the means was weak.

In this and all the rest, as though I understood their language and they understood mine, we understood each other. After the chapter, I saw that all were crying and told them, "I think you're sad at not understanding my language," and they told me, "Everything you've said we've understood without missing a word, and this has given us such joy that we cry."

In these trials they wrote to me from Spain and told me how a nun had died like a saint. I, envious of her, was thinking about what merits she might have had, for she had worked hard, and the Lord answered me, "It is not best for people who have greater obligations to be active, but rather to die to themselves and all their passions and inclinations." In all of these talks, although they occurred quickly, there remained much light and new spirit for me to know God's goodness, and I felt obliged again to be faithful to him.

The kind of prayer I had then on some days was a kind of attendance and reverence to a light that was in my soul, for it seemed certain that all my faculties had lost their being and that I had no other except what I was receiving from this light. It isn't like seeing Christ, as I usually do, nor any other presence, but rather as if all of the Holiest Trinity were with me. The soul doesn't see anything but feels the reverence as if it saw it. The vision that I carry at other times in my soul is like a little silkworm, and how it is cared for and fed, and when it is properly grown, it begins to spin through its mouth a thin thread of silk and make its cocoon, and with the pleasure and sweetness that there is in that, it doesn't feel that it's dying until in giving the goodness that it has, it closes itself in its cocoon and dies. In this way did I see my soul, or was shown it, and with the same sweetness and silence, it is giving of itself what it has and has received from God. Like the worm, it encloses itself in a being of nothingness, and with the sweet love that it is always threading through my heart I no longer want to exist, for in dying is the life of the soul. I would like to have one thousand lives to spend, so that God would grant his grace to me; nothing is suitable for me except to give my life for the Beloved.

Another day I was complaining to our Lord that I was not adequate for what he was ordering me, and I told him of my little worth, that I was like a straw, and the Lord told me, "With straws I light the fire."

Another time too, thinking about my little worth and my own nothingness, the Lord spoke to me and told me, "That's how I want you, without being or knowing anything, in order to do through you what I want to do. The wise men of the world with their human prudence don't listen to me, for they think that they know everything."

While I was here, one of the prelates wrote asking that I commend to God one of the novices we had received in Paris; she was the first,[66] who it was expected would be of the administration. Since they loved her a great deal, they didn't stop writing to me that I ask God and our Holy Mother for her life, and they almost became angry that the saint didn't obtain this favor for them from our Lord. Seeing them like this, I persisted in asking our Lord for it, and His Majesty told me, "Can you want something other than what I want?" At this, I left it and the nun died. The Lord showed me his will.

I was now very peaceful in this convent, and those daughters were of great comfort to me in their observance of the rule and constitutions. I saw that the prelates were looking toward returning me to Paris as prelate. I resisted greatly going back to be prioress there, because it was a court town and pretentious. While I was recollected one day I had a kind of interior worry, because I was confused at not being very resigned to going to Paris; it seemed that God wanted it, and I had scruples at refusing it. And so I once again made a great effort and told the Lord, "Do with me, Lord, what serves you; I see quite well that I am not right for this, and I have great fears; furthermore, it is a great source of humiliation for me to achieve any honor. Why, Lord, do you want to give me this trouble?" And the Lord appeared to me in his humanity and glory. There was such a great clarity from the sky where he was appearing to me, as though he were near, and he told me, "That is how those who do God's work have to go about, as I went about on earth, afflicted with honors and dishonors." At this I felt joy and comfort and love, and I was amazed. Again I took heart to come back to Paris.

[PRIORESS OF CARMEL IN PARIS]

At this time, before a year was finished, being, as I have said, content there with those holy souls, once while in the refectory I was a little recollected, and in this short period the Lord appeared in this way: he was in his glory and in heaven, very far from me, not like other times, and he showed me that soon they would take me to Paris and I should prepare myself, that greater hardships than in the past awaited me as well as humiliations. Like the weak person that I am I was sorry, because the Lord had me there as though in heaven because of the many favors he did for me. It seemed that he was there for everything I had to do, talking to me and showing me what I should do like a father to his children. I was also sorry to leave those

66. This first French novice was Andree de Tous les Saints (Levoix), who made her profession before dying and was buried on Good Friday, April 8, 1605.

souls who seemed to be angels that the Lord carried in his palm, according to their comforts and spiritual happiness; and the people of the town, so Christian and good that it seemed I had been born among them. When they began to fear that they were going to take me away, the people in the town were prepared to resist it; it was necessary to take me out in the middle of the night, and they made the nuns keep quiet under obedience.

One of the prelates came for me and brought with him a nephew of mine[67] who was studying in Paris. So that people wouldn't recognize me, they took off my white cape and put on my nephew's short cape and hat, and that's how we went until we were outside the town, for in that town they don't lock their gates. The nuns didn't know it until it was time for Mass, when the one who remained in my place went to make them sing the Mass, and they cried so that it became known in the town. There was no small uproar, and most of all from the parents and relatives who had their daughters there, and they, the daughters, were quite disconsolate, the poor things.

Arriving at Paris[68] I was well received by all the novices; there was no professed nun except Mother Leonor de San Bernardo, to whom I owed much on this occasion and others. Since we had many novices, they gave them to me and ordered me to take charge of them, although I was prioress. Mother Ana de Jesús and her two companions had gone to a foundation in Burgundy with the intent of going from there to Spain, and they wrote to the father general[69] that he go there for them, but he played deaf and didn't go.

The first year I was there was very peaceful. It was a great comfort to me that all the novices were so observant in all that had to do with religion and so favored by God that, although most were high ranking ladies, they seemed like girls who had returned to a state of innocence, for such was their simplicity of spirit. They were very open and affable with me, as though I had raised them. Although on the one hand I took comfort at seeing that those souls were doing so well, my interior worries were not lacking in the office of prioress and its duties, for although, as I say, I was among angels, I was not capable of marking the place in the readings and other things, for I didn't know how to read the breviary, and they made me pray as though I knew.

This distressed me greatly; it seemed the greatest disgrace and humiliation I had ever had, and everything was afflicting me, so that I didn't know

---

67. Toribio Manzanas. He had accompanied his aunt, Ana, on the Carmelite expedition from Spain to France, where he became a student of theology in Paris. He and Ana corresponded regularly and died in the same year, 1626.

68. They left Pontoise on October 5, 1605, and arrived at Paris on the same day.

69. Francisco de la Madre de Dios.

whether I had erred in what I had done and whether those who had ordered me to do it had erred. Once I wanted to put the breviary away, and the Lord spoke to me and told me, "Don't put it away, mortify yourself and say whatever you know. That is what I want." This he told me in prayer. I was encouraged by this and did it, and at night, after all had retired, I spent hours looking in the book at what I had to say the next day. I went back over what I had prayed in the choir; for as the Lord had told me to do this, I had scruples about not looking at it thoroughly, although I was sweating with anguish. After this, Our Lord did me such favors that I felt him next to me in the choir. I went about with such light and comfort that I understood Latin as though I knew it during the time that I felt his company, which didn't happen when he left me. Sometimes he was so close that I asked him to withdraw a little, for my heart burned so in his presence that I couldn't bear it, and he did. At other times, he granted me favors but didn't come so close; but my soul seemed to be among angels, and it seemed that those who prayed with me were angels. One night in dreams I found myself saying the breviary, and I saw that a good-looking youth was looking at me as though I was not getting it quite right. I was flustered by his attention. He told me, "Don't be upset, for what we desire to do is what matters most in our deeds," as though he had said that I should take care of the rest, that although I didn't know it well I should not stop saying it and that I should humble myself.

One day one of the prelates commanded me to commend to God the question of who would be best for our visitor,[70] and I went to the Holiest Sacrament. While I was doing this, a great recollection and comfort came over me with a clear view of how God loved souls and how he wanted us who had come there to be sweet. The Lord told me, "You will be the salt of the earth." I was amazed because I expected an answer to what I had asked for, and he gave me one so far from what I expected that I was surprised.

At the end of this first year, the devil, father of discord, put suspicions in the superiors about me. Until then they had loved me in the extreme. This displeasure with me began because of their fear that I had all the nuns in the palm of my hand, so that if the Religious of the Order came to France [from Spain], all would stay with me under obedience to them. It was true, for they were not planning anything different from this, because some said that everything they saw me do was holy. With these fears, the superiors used a very fine scheme, ordered by the father of lies, and little by little they

---

70. The visitor was an ecclesiastical official appointed by the vicar general or ordinary of a diocese who visited religious communities with the purpose of maintaining orthodoxy and discipline.

won over the nuns; and when they had them in their good graces, they told them, "Don't discuss your souls with the mother, for her spirit is not for you. She is a foreigner and furthermore, Spanish. Don't trust her, for she wanted the friars, and they will give you a very hard life. They're harsh. Their rule is not for you."

I knew nothing of this at the beginning. I saw the nuns withdrawing from me; rather than the openness they had shown me, it was quite the opposite. Amazed, I told the prelate[71] one day that I didn't know what it was, that the nuns didn't speak to me or direct themselves to me after they professed as they had before, nor did they speak of anything to me; that I found them changed in the extreme. He told me, "It isn't necessary that they speak to you nor you to them, for your spirit is bad. We don't want it to attach to them, for you have demons and hatred against us," and other such things, that if I had one demon, she who consulted with me would have two.

I was already troubled, and this really troubled me, in such a way that you could well see that this thing was of the evil spirit.

This same day after Communion I had retired, and in a vision I was shown a great cross that seemed impossible to carry. I comforted myself as best I could and embraced it; and I was confused at not knowing what it was. The afternoon passed in what I have just said.

From this beginning, the quarrels grew from day to day. The demon in my soul did what he could, for since I have always been such a sinner and remiss in doing penance, perhaps for not having done it and being compensated for some of my errors, God was irritated and was seemingly very far from me (as he had shown me in Pontoise, he was in his heaven and saw me from afar). With his absence and the continuous situations of discord, I was quite imperfect and practiced quite badly the virtue to which I was obliged. Sometimes the superiors sent nuns of lower category to me (sometimes certain nuns and other times, others) in order to inform me of my faults and whatever the superiors wanted. I regretted it because of what they were losing of their simplicity and the spirit with which they had started.

The Lord came, little by little, from day to day and gave me some comfort with words of love, and then he left and I went back to my solitude. Once they sent me a nun who had loved me greatly. She came very freely and determined and began to scold me, as though she were prioress. She said I didn't have mortification, how could I resent what the prelates were doing with me, and other very insolent words. I was greatly grieved, as I have said, at seeing the extent of her ruin. I had been bled and had a fever, and my weak

71. Pierre Bérulle

character resented it greatly; the devil brought me so many reasons why I should respond to her in such a way that she would not dare say anything else another day. But what I told her was to go away and leave me alone. I went to the choir to commend it to God. And the Lord responded to me, "What are you sad about? Shouldn't you be comforted by what they say of you and that they take you for simple and of little worth? They said it of me and other worse things. The laws of the world are different from mine. Suffering, mortification, and patience please me most."

[DIFFICULTIES WITH DON PEDRO DE BÉRULLE]

Another time after Communion, having been some days without feeling the Lord's company, His Majesty returned to my soul and I was recollected with his presence. Then he showed me a sheet full of little crosses, as though they were stuck on that cloth, and as I looked at it the thing that occurred to me was what the Lord showed to Saint Peter, which was a cloth full of little animals, but this one had crosses. They invited me to embrace them; and with the Lord's presence that I had, I consented to embrace them and feel them in my soul. As I consented they came into my soul in all its parts and feelings and became one with me. Then the Lord was absent again, and I went about all crucified in my soul; the situations on the outside grew worse, so that it seemed that day and night the superiors were coming out with lies and malice.

I had nowhere to turn my head or rest my soul because, although I asked for a confessor, they never gave me one. I went to confess with one of the prelates, the one who was making most war against me,[72] and it seemed to me I was in mortal sin confessing with him, because the resistance and vehemence with which I went to him could not have been greater. I told him, "Give me another confessor. I confess with you with distress, and many things that you tell me I don't believe, because I see the opposite." He said he didn't want to and that God showed him my sins. I didn't believe it nor was I satisfied, and I was in a true purgatory by day and night, and with such distrust in my salvation that many times I thought that there was nothing but to believe this and that God had abandoned me.

The lies with which he spoke to me and dealt with me were such that if I had not had this distress, they would have given it to me, as the French do. The Princess of Longueville[73] came into the house; she was a founder and knew what was happening. The nuns told her, for I had some who were

72. Bérulle.
73. Catherine d'Orleans. She was influential in bringing the Spanish Carmelites to Spain.

faithful to me, and she also knew who was saying these things to ridicule me; when Mother Ana de Jesús returned there on the road to Flanders (she had been in Dijon as I have said), she found me in that affliction. I didn't say anything, although I exhibited contentment to her. But the princess told her about it: that she should take me with her, that she feared they would kill me. She [Ana de Jesús] told me this: that if I wanted to go with her she would be pleased. I told her no, that I had not yet done anything nor employed the desire for suffering for which I had come there.

Once, in this situation of distrust that I have spoken of, I happened to go into a shrine to our saint with my broom in hand (we were all sweeping). Upon entering I went down on my knees. It seemed to me that my knees were obliging me to stop there, and I saw that a light like a column was coming out of my heart; it was coming down from the Holy Spirit and went up and out of the dark depths of my soul, arriving, as I have said, at the Holy Spirit. In this brief recollection, I think I had only put one knee on the ground; this column had such a clear light that it seemed that from my heart to heaven all the heavens were clear. It left my soul and all my bones and members with such a sweet fervor that it seemed they had anointed me with rich oils, and my body was so light that all the grace in my soul was communicated to it. All of this without saying a word; in a brief silence I was completely renewed and made a different person.

Another time the Lord showed me in these afflictions how the husband tells the wife to give him a kiss on the mouth.[74] He was on the cross and crowned with thorns, and this kiss was from his wife the church; and what he had shown me at the beginning in Avila (when he showed me the virtues in perfection while he was on the cross), that now I should try harder to win them. I felt this more clearly even than if it had been spoken. These visits happened quickly.

And those gentlemen didn't abandon or slacken their wiles. They put some people who had been looking after the monastery at the door to the outside to see if I wrote or spoke with anyone, and on the inside, they put a portress whom they trusted most, so that she would become my friend and draw out my thoughts, for coming into my cell as someone familiar, she could see if I had written anything and take it from me. I saw through it all and pretended that I didn't notice and showed good will to win her trust, pretending that I trusted her, when I really felt very differently. I was so fed up with their tricks that, although it was not my disposition, I said that one act of slyness would be cured with another; and so I used malice

74. Song 1:1.

in dissembling in many things, and this was no small cross to me, for I was abandoning my natural way of being.

I spent whole nights without sleeping, asking the Lord to help me and show me his will; and in the morning I awoke the nuns to go to prayer; God did me the favor that even with these anxieties, I attended to all the community's matters, although many times my heart was breaking and I almost became faint from the effort I was making.

There was a figure of Christ in the chapter, of stone, large, and very bound. I was very devoted to it and every day (in the two years that this tempest lasted) upon rising in the morning I took it a bunch of flowers, and when there weren't any, green branches of laurel or other similar things, and when I found pansies, which they call a kind of grass, I would take them to the statue and put them on the wounds on its feet and I asked him to give me good thoughts through his wounds. The hours that I could during the day I withdrew there alone and prayed, like someone who preaches to himself where no one hears him. One day at the hour of rest and silence I went there, and because of the affliction that enveloped my soul, upon entering I went up to the wall and became faint, and it seemed to me that my life was ending. In this distress, Christ spoke to me, showing me his agony, for he came with hands bound as when they untied him from the column after he'd been crowned with thorns and was naked, seated on a rock. He came to me and said with much sweetness, "Daughter, look at me, how I am for your sake, tied and my hands bound, and how I am waiting for them to do what they want with me." And then he said, "That's how much I love you as a friend." Then he disappeared. With this favor I came back to myself with the courage to go through whatever would come.

Another time I had been bled. This prelate[75] came to the turnstile and called me; and he began to make complaints about what had happened. I told him to leave it for another day, that I'd been bled, and he told me, "It doesn't matter, be still." He was a good hour arguing in matters of the constitution and the rule about some things he wanted to change. I contradicted him, and he said that he knew these matters as well as I. I told him that was not so, that he would know well from his reading, but not from experience as I did, about matters of the order, and I would not consent to it. He told me that Spain was one thing and France was another. I said that the rule and constitutions always had to be one and the same here and there and that I would not consent to it. This lasted so long that when I left I was so sick that I had to be bled again; and the blood they took from me startled the doctor

75. Bérulle.

so that he called one of the nuns aside and told her, "Look after this Mother, for she is dying, and it is a matter of conscience. You can see her afflictions in her blood, and she is a foreigner; you are obliged to look after her health."

These struggles occurred every day; they wanted only to change and do things their way; and since I didn't want to consent to it, everything was a quarrel, which distressed me. I had no one to help me on the outside or the inside. Although some of those who had come there with me advised me to leave—for they had already abandoned the fight—I thanked them for their kindness and said, "It is not time for me to abandon the cross. If they kill me, I came determined to that; and although I'm not yet dead as I would like to be, for my wretched body won't die, I won't abandon at present what the Lord has put in my hands. I came to suffer, and until now I haven't suffered anything."

Although it was as if my soul was in a dark night, at each occasion that presented itself, however vexed I might be, I was never of a mind to avoid the trouble. Rather, I don't know how it was, I seemed like a sick person in convalescence, and although she sees that the dish they put in front of her will be bad for her, she can't keep herself from it because of her hunger. Although they tell her, "This will kill you," she wants it and loves it. That's how my weak soul was at feeling sorrow, sick with a hunger for hardships, so that I couldn't rid myself of them, but rather I took strength from my soul's weaknesses in them. What distressed me most was confession, that I had to confess with this man, for we were opposed because of things that I saw as against the order and that a laywoman and layman, married people,[76] governed the convent more than I. I had a great deal to murmur about in this, and my soul was fearful. I wanted to forgive them and I could not, because things were so clear that I couldn't blind myself to them. This gave me so many scruples that I feared for my salvation and that I was in sin; I didn't seem to have the satisfaction that I wanted from them, and on the other hand, they seemed to be good. The Lord left me alone in this struggle and permitted it for my good. Once, in my cell, with these afflictions, I wrote these verses, I don't know how; they came into my mind and I entertained myself with them.

76. These two lay people were Madame Acarie and Michel de Marillac. Barbe Avrillot (1566–1618) played an important role in bringing the Discalced Carmelites from Spain to France. A cousin of Cardinal Bérulle, she recruited a number of young French noblewomen for the order, and after the death of her husband, Pierre Acarie, she herself professed at the convent at Amiens, taking the name of Marie de l'Incarnation. Her three daughters also became Carmelite nuns. She died in the convent at Pontoise in 1618 and was beatified in 1791. Michel de Marillac (1560–1632) belonged to a family of powerful French aristocrats. A friend and benefactor of the Discalced Carmelites in France, he was also the uncle of Saint Louise de Marillac, a cofounder of the Daughters of Charity of Saint Vincent de Paul.

If you see my shepherd,
Speak to him, Llorente
Tell him of my pain
See if he feels it.

Ask carefully
And well stated, shepherd
Why he has closed
My heart this way.
And being the Lord
Why he absents himself
From me this way
Tell him of my pain
See if he feels it.

Return the light to me
My dear, good friend,
And let the cross come
As you may be served
For this is the way
That love requests.
Tell him of my pain
See if he feels it.

The night is dark
And brings great fear
And the plunderers
Who won't be careless;
And then you conceal yourself,
My good safeguard.
Tell him of my pain
See if he feels it.

Don't be so harsh
The test is done
And it's enough;
Because as you see
It is uncertain
On ground that's weak
And without any vigor

Tell him of my pain.
See if he feels it.

Why have you put me
In so fierce a breach
And hidden from me
Leaving me in it
On a narrow road
Ignorant of where I go?
Tell him of my pain
See if he feels it.

If you understand me,
Why don't you respond
To my sorrowful sigh
Which you certainly hear?
This saddens me more
And makes me fearful
Tell him of my pain,
See if he feels it.

Tell him how I am
And all my trials
With great sorrow
At seeing his absence
And in foreign lands
Where the fear is greater.
Tell him of my pain
See if he feels it.

Tell him to hurry
Because I am dying
And I find no one
Who can console me
If I don't see him
In my heart
Tell him of my pain
See if he feels it

Ask him the hour
I should await him

Let him choose it
That he order me
And that I find him
As my shepherd.
Tell him of my pain
See if he feels it

Having arrived in Flanders, Mother Ana de Jesús, since she had left me in such affliction, sent to me to ask if I wanted to come to Flanders with her. I didn't answer until I had commended it to God for fifteen or twenty days, and at the end, while beginning prayer one morning, I felt that the Lord came to me as though he were alive and told me, "Say that you will do what obedience orders." Without saying another thing, he disappeared, and I told this to one of my superiors. He said he didn't want it, that if I wanted to go to Spain he would send me, but to Flanders, no. At this I said no to Mother Ana de Jesús, and although I had more troubles, I was not of a mind to make a change if God didn't reveal it to me.

I attended to the acts of community of the choir and refectory and the chapter with punctuality as prioress, but in the rest I was no more than one of the lowest nuns in the house. They had taken the hand of governance as if they were priors, and for the novices they did the same. They made that laywoman and layman come to consult with them and ask them for an account of how they were doing. I was aggrieved, not for myself in particular, but for the order, because I saw that they were introducing things well outside of the religious observance for which they had brought us there; and when I told them so, they told me to leave them alone, that they knew very well what the constitution was.

I did all that I could to be patient, which was really necessary, and the time that remained after the choir I spent in part doing the humble jobs of the convent, like the poorest of all, which I was, but I did them with great pleasure.

[PRIORESS AT TOURS]

After I was there for three years, a gentleman requested nuns to found a convent in his land,[77] with the condition that I go to found it. So they sent me with three others, daughters of the house, whom they trusted.

---

77. Antoine du Bois de Fontaines (1541–1627). He was a secular founder of the convent at Tours and the father of Madeleine de Saint-Joseph, one of the most important French prioresses.

In this city there are a lot of heretics and schismatics. When they saw us coming, they said, "If only they had drowned before leaving the river and had never left at all." The heretics took a great hatred against me and said I was a wicked woman, an idol of the papists. As my luck would have it, a devotee of the house, a great servant of God, converted a public woman with her good reasoning and brought her one day to our church and kept her until nightfall in the messengers' room. I didn't know about it, and at night, so that they [the heretics] wouldn't take her from their control, they took her to another house with other women. The heretics, who were looking for her and saw her go into the church and the messengers' house, said that we were other women of the same kind and that we had children in the house. This was done with such malice that the very Catholics of the house were doubtful, and this wickedness had gained such ground that it was necessary for me to call someone from the magistrate's office who was a friend. I told him that I wanted his advice to make some rooms in the house because it was not made to be a monastery and was uncomfortable; I asked that he do us the favor of going into even the barns and lower part, whatever seemed best to him.

I did this because they were saying I had a door upstairs where men came in, and without telling my intent to this man, he went in and saw it and said afterwards, "I know the innocence of these nuns and that what they are saying about them is false, that they had doors. I've been through the whole house and the cloister."

These were things that didn't trouble me because sooner or later the truth would be seen, and although they said more, I laughed at it all. This rumor spread for twenty leagues, which is all heretics' towns, and they couldn't bear to see us. One of the prelates came from Paris, which was sixty leagues away; and he came posthaste to find out how that wicked tale was spreading.

In this tempest I remembered that on the way to this foundation the Holy Mother came out to the road as though she were alive, and I saw that with her we passed through thorns and they didn't scratch us. The saint came up to me and said, "Go with courage, for soon I'll accommodate you a little better." And it was true, because after I distanced myself from these people who were governing differently from many things that the rule mandated, I had more peace and liberty to do what they didn't allow me to do in Paris; so these dishonors and false testimonies, which were all because of me, were like thorns far away that could not hurt me.

He became a widower in 1600, ordained as a priest by 1605, and was chaplain of the convent at Tours while Ana was prioress.

After this, since the heretics continued to hate us, one day in the house of a great, rich heretic, a servant of his made a hole in the corral where we had some chickens. I made him close it, saying that one of his servants wanted to take my chickens and that I thought the lord of the house, who was very honorable, didn't know about it. It confused him that we didn't think he was a heretic, and they told me that he returned to being a true Christian at seeing that we didn't complain to the people from the magistrate's office who had come to investigate and that we considered him honorable. They said, "These Teresian women that we didn't want will convert all of us to their faith."

In truth, I desired it. I treated them with much respect and honor. I had there good nuns who desired it and prayed for them. With all the dishonors, that monastery gave off such an aroma of virtue that wealthy and high-ranking ladies came from far away to request the habit, and once there were twenty asking for it at the same time, which was to praise the Lord.

God did me many favors there, although I was without a confessor, alone, and without anyone to whom I could communicate my spirit, because the one I had didn't know a word of Spanish and I didn't know a word of French. He confessed me in faith, and the prelates came from year to year, but it didn't bother me. I was very comforted by God there. He did favors for me that he had taken away from me at other times; and he did some favors that left me strong in his spirit for many days with exercises of penitence and virtue that could be done with great facility. The troubles seemed to have doubled my strength, and without feeling it I found myself recollected in the Lord's presence. I said that God was giving me the spirit of Saint Paul, and I felt that it was he himself who was giving me that spirit, and from this experience I said, "Who will separate me from Christ? Not hardship nor the lack of necessary things."[78] I was drunk with love, so that if God, who was giving me this love, hadn't given me the strength, I could not have withstood it alone. As Saint Paul had said, I also said on this occasion that I wished to be an anathema in order to die for my brothers and sisters and Christ, my Lord.[79]

And since on these occasions the soul offers itself with love and is resigned to his will without any conditions, the Lord told me at this same

78. Rom 8:35: "Who will separate us from the love of Christ? Will hardship, or distress, or persecution, or famine, or nakedness, or peril, or sword?" (New Revised Standard Version [NRSV]).

79. Rom 9:3: "For I could wish that I myself were accursed and cut off from Christ for the sake of my own people, my kindred according to the flesh" (NRSV). Paul is referring to the Jews when he says "my own people."

place, "This is the glory of the just, to do my will." He told me this with loving words, that the glory of the just consisted in doing his will. It created such a sweet love in me that I was as though outside myself, suspended.

While I was in this house, the Abbess of Fontevrault,[80] who lived two leagues more or less from there, was sick, and her nieces, the princesses of Longueville were with her; since the older of the sisters knew me, she wrote me often of her aunt's illness. I wanted to serve them in what I could; they had been favorable to me without my deserving it and had comforted me in my needs. I commended the sick woman to God, desiring that God do with her whatever might be for her salvation, because I feared for her. She had many monasteries under her in that abbacy; with the wars and heresies many of them had been ruined and lost; and as I say, I feared for her. One day she and her nieces sent to ask that I pray for her urgently, that she was dying, and God showed it to me. The doctor who cared for her went there and came to tell me how she was. On the day when he arrived, God had already shown me that she was at the end and that she needed me to pray for her. Recollecting in prayer, I saw many bands of demons were entering the room, and the poor soul was quite afflicted. I was also upset by this travail, and trusting in God with this distress, I turned to him in the hope that he would do me a favor. Then I saw Jesus Christ come in as he was in the world. He came dressed as a pontifical, very beautiful, with a wondrous majesty, accompanied by a great number of angels and saints. Upon entering the room of the sick woman, all those evil spirits fled; they couldn't leave fast enough, and the blessed soul left its travail, and the Lord took her with him. She, they said, was very good, and she had been a great religious woman in all that she had been able to do and kind to her nuns in hardships.

Other times occasionally other people, alive but absent, have appeared to me. Father Gracián,[81] in hardships and afflictions, appeared to me two or three times alive and showed me his troubles. Later in Turkey, when they

---

80. Eleanor of Borbon (1532–1611), aunt of Henry IV; she was named abbess of Fontevrault in 1575.

81. Jerónimo de la Madre de Dios (Gracián) (1545–1614). A confessor and confidante to Saint Teresa, he was at the center of much of the discord that afflicted the order following her death. He was at odds with Nicolás Doria on many of the central issues of Discalced Carmelite life and was finally expelled from the order by Doria in 1592. Prior to his expulsion he had occupied many positions of authority in the order, including that of the order's first provincial. Gracian was captured by the Turks but was a captive in Tunisia, not Turkey. He wrote a version of Ana's spiritual experiences entitled *Diálogos sobre su espiritu. Espíritu y revelaciones y manera de prozeder de la madre Anna de San Bartholome* [Dialogues about her Spirit. Spirit and Revelations and Manner of Proceeding of the Mother Anne of Saint Barholomew], as well as autobiographical accounts of his own experiences.

tried to martyr him, he showed me the fire and how they wanted to burn him. But I didn't see everything or whether it was another martyrdom, but I saw the fire that was prepared and that some Moorish women were praying that they release him. And I saw that the martyrdom didn't proceed and that the father was very distressed.

Another time a nun from our house in Valladolid left after she professed, because her parents got a brief from the pope and took her to another order, which was of Saint Francis.[82] It seemed to her that she aspired to stricter things. And so she was thinking that she would be more comforted and that they wouldn't esteem her as much, because she lamented greatly that they esteemed her, because she was a daughter of a commander of Castile. The blessed soul deserved to be loved for her nature and virtue, leaving aside who she was, and since she was humble, for the time that our saint was in that convent she accompanied her, for the saint esteemed her, and when she couldn't speak to her [Saint Teresa] she was with me night and day. It was a very great friendship that we had. When she left that house, we weren't there. She appeared to me alive in Avila, as she was, very distressed, and she told me, "O my sister! How sorry I am to be where they have put me!" It was a great concern, because I was very fond of her. I had asked that they bring her to Avila to take her away from her family. When this happened, I was a good thirty leagues from her.

Another time, while I was in France, Father Tomás de Jesús[83] was in Rome. I didn't know that he was having difficulties, but the Lord showed him to me as very afflicted. It was because the pope had called upon him to govern a seminary that he was making to educate souls that they were going to convert to the faith in the Indies. His Holiness wanted the seminary to be Carmelite, but the order didn't want him to go, and they contradicted His Holiness. I saw him as very distressed, but the Lord told me that upset would soon pass, and it did.

In Tours, although I was comforted because the prelates were far away, it didn't last long, because I had a subprioress who was completely one of

---

82. Casilda de Padilla, whose entrance into the order is narrated in chapters 10 and 11 of Saint Teresa's *Book of Foundations*. She left the Discalced convent at Valladolid to enter the Franciscan Convent of Saint Luis in Burgos in September of 1581.

83. Tomás de Jesús (Sánchez Dávila) (1564–1627). Strongly influenced by the writings of Saint Teresa, he entered the order in Salamanca, became a professor of theology in Seville, and was attracted to missionary work. After working in the Italian congregation in Rome for several years, he went to Belgium where he helped organize the Discalced province. He also helped to organize the famous Mission School of Louvain and combated "heresy" from his position as professor at the university there.

them. She informed them that I had a doorkeeper whom I trusted, and they
took her away and put in another to their liking. They had two keys put on
the turnstile, and neither of the two would open the turnstile alone, so that
they could see if I was writing to Spain;[84] the nuns would take the letters
and send them to the prelates, the ones that came from Spain as well as the
ones that I sent there.

Although this could have bothered me, because I saw through it, I acted as
though I didn't notice it, and I wrote things that I didn't care at all if they saw,
because what I wanted was to see our reformed priests in France. I was already
certain of that. The Lord had shown me that it would happen, because while I
was in Paris, before coming to Tours, he revealed it to me. I saw many religious
men in white capes throughout France, with which the Lord consoled me, revealing to me that he desired it. On account of this, I wasn't troubled that their
wiles would impede it. The nuns were very fond of me, and the Holy Mother
appeared to me at times and comforted me. Once, in particular, she came to
me as though she were alive and took my hand and led me along a long road
out of France; that's how it was that I soon came to Flanders.

Another time, she showed me that she was quite angry with the French,
for they didn't love the order. This vision was like a dream: while in prayer
in the choir the nuns came to me and told me, "Our saint is here, and she
has covered herself with the veil and didn't want to see us." I went, and upon
arriving, she revealed herself to me and embraced me. She did this favor to
show me that she wasn't happy that they were accommodating themselves
outside the order with those people, because it weakened everything.

That time that I have said that she took me on a long road, she had
taken me by the hand, and throughout that whole day, although I washed
and went about from one thing to another, the fragrance of her relics did
not leave me.

[ANOTHER STAY IN PARIS]

The three years ended[85]; I asked them to bring me to Paris, because although I didn't say why, the priests had arrived, and I wanted to speak to
them in order to go over to the order.[86] But still I feared returning to Paris,

---

84. It is not clear from her description exactly what the situation was at the turnstile. It is possible that the two keys would have necessitated two doorkeepers or greater control over Ana's
visitors and correspondence.

85. 1608–11.

86. To place herself under the exclusive jurisdiction of the Discalced Carmelite Fathers.

and the Lord told me, "Come, don't be afraid. Everything will turn out well." Like a weakling and sinner, I was afraid.

With this, they let me choose which house in France I wanted to go to. I said Paris, because aside from the intent I had of speaking with the priests, I had a desire to make a general confession with that superior who had made such a commotion because of my displeasures. I wanted to do it and so the Lord arranged it for me. I came and did it to the great satisfaction of my soul and of his [the superior's] also, for he recognized many truths, and I think he had been deceived. At this time they asked me insistently to stay with them and give them obedience. I refused. I said freely, "I want to return to the order where I professed and where they have nurtured me and suffered my sicknesses of body and soul."

They were greatly offended at this and didn't think I would get my way in it, so they favored me and showed me much grace. Since I spoke with our Discalced fathers sometimes, I told them my desire and that if the prelates ordered me in obedience to leave the obedience in which I was, it would comfort me greatly.

They had great kindness in my case, because they sent me a patent and priests to accompany me. The day this patent came I didn't know anything about it; I went before the hour of prayer to visit the shrines and walked through these stations with a presence of God that had me recollected and actually offering myself to God for whatever he might order me. Upon entering a shrine of the cross, as soon as I got on my knees Christ appeared to me with open arms, very resplendent; he came toward me and embraced me like a father embraces a small child and told me, "Don't fear anyone. Here I am, I will help you; go back to Carmel." He left me with a vision of a flowering Carmel to which I was returning.

This consoled me and gave me infinite spirit and a clear truth with which I could not fear anything that presented itself to me.

Late at night, the prelate with whom I had made my general confession[87] called me. He was one who knew a little Spanish, and he said to me, "They've given me here a patent for you; they are ordering you to Flanders. Have you said you will obey?" I said yes. He became so angry that he ordered me to go to my cell and not leave it or speak with anyone without his permission. I went, very content, and was there ten days with complete contentment, waiting for them to order me to go after all, although they didn't want to.

87. Bérulle.

And in these ten days this father called me two times and asked me if I had changed my mind and if the Lord was telling me something different. Since I told him no to one thing and the other, he was very upset and sent me two or three times a nun who they believed had contact with God to tell me something, as though on her own. She came in and told me that she wanted to tell me in secret something from God that was important for me, and it was that God didn't want me to leave that house; that I should be careful; that he would become angry and other similar things. She told me that the perfection of that house would decline. All of this was a scheme of the prelates, because they had told those on the outside that I wanted to stay in obedience to them. They didn't like me or want me for anything except vanity, to tell the world that Saint Teresa's companion found their governance good and wanted to stay with them.

They've done a lot of good in France, and God has a crown reserved for them; but they've lost much of the prize for having wanted to take up the governance of the nuns, because in this, it is quite clear, they haven't been right. It will soon be seen that they are not Carmelites, nor will this rule and the constitution as the Holy Mother left them to her daughters remain intact. With the desire I had for this I suffered seven years, the most humiliating years I have ever had. I did my duty to show that I loved them and the sisters well, but when I saw that they were becoming stronger every day, I came out and said it clearly. Many times I told them I couldn't be where the rule was not kept but was becoming weaker.

Many who desired obedience to the order and hoped that through me they would be in it were quite upset.

I go back to how I was in my cell. As I was in my cell, Saint Francis's Day arrived at the end of these ten days, and on the eve of the saint's day the prelate sent to tell me that after Saint Teresa's Day, he would order me to go, for they were hoping that on that day the saint would order me to stay. It was the opposite, because on the night of Saint Francis's Day, which was when God took her from this world, she appeared to me accompanied by other daughters who, together with her, were enjoying God's company. I, upon seeing her, was thinking that she came for me to take me out of so many dangers. But as I told her with great joy, "Mother, take me with you," and she didn't say anything, the sisters turned to her and asked her to take me, because I was suffering greatly. She responded to them severely, "I will not take her, for it is necessary that she live now and do what I would have done."[88]

88. 1611–12.

[IN FLANDERS]

The next day after the saint's day I left, for although I hadn't wanted to come to Flanders, I came very consoled by God and I remembered that before I left Spain I had had a vision that didn't seem trivial, for I saw that I would not complete seven years in France and that during these years I would go down to the Low Country, and that's how it's been; only about five or six days were missing to complete seven years.[89]

Before I came to Tours the Lord showed me a light and in it a house; coming to Flanders, in our first house of the foundation at Antwerp I recognized this house; the first young woman who was received I recognized as the one I had seen in that vision, and now she is called Teresa de Jesús.

When I got to Mons with the priests who were accompanying me, I was well received and was there exactly a year. Then the foundation at Antwerp was arranged, where I did not think they would order me to go, because I thought they would send others more capable than I. One day after I knew that that was the will of obedience, while I was commending it to God after Communion, I asked him to give me grace to do his holy will and if this foundation was not it, to take the idea out of the superiors' minds. The Lord consoled me, for I was quite worried because there was no lack of people to put it in the prelate's heart not to bring me, [to tell him] that someone else was more appropriate, and this troubled me, because I didn't want to come, but they ordered me to against my own convenience; and now I saw that they wanted something else. With this, as I have said, I took Communion, and after receiving the Lord I recollected; His Majesty consoled me as he has done on other occasions and told me, "Take heart and go, for this foundation will be a lit torch that will give light to that whole country."

With this I took courage to embrace the cross, and I don't doubt that it will be as the Lord told me, because in these beginnings the Lord brings souls very capable of spirit, beautiful and noble people, to the great wonder of all the worldly. I am sure that the saint governs this house and takes particular care of it, and our Lord too, as is seen in many things through experience; because we came here in such poverty that we had only fifty borrowed lorins. The Jesuit fathers gave us the equipment to say the first Mass, for we had nothing and the magistrate's people didn't want us. They wanted to send us back, and God has straightened it all out in such a way that this monastery is esteemed by the whole village. In the three years we've been here it is better furnished for the church than others of ten years.

89. The departure from France for Flanders was on October 5, 1611.

We've bought the best place in the village. I have not had any care nor hardship because God brought me in truth with such faith and sureness that His Majesty was caring for this convent and that the saint is the prioress, that usually I imagine that I am serving her, as I did when she was alive, and that she does all the rest. Many times without it being my imagination, I have actually felt that she is with me and that she is doing everything. In this God has given me such peace and comfort that no one could believe it, and the prayer has been continuous and favorable. Sometimes the spirit is as strong as at the beginning. Being in the Divine Office many times I could not endure the Lord's presence, and I would tell him, "Go away, Lord, for I am not strong or capable of attending to the Divine Office if you are so near me."

One day the saint appeared to me, very happy, and told me, "Now daughter, you have to do me a favor." I asked her, "What is it?" and she answered, "A father will tell you." That same day in the afternoon, a letter came from a prelate in Rome,[90] which gave me an order that the other monasteries resisted accepting and the nuns here also found difficult, but since I was firm that obedience must be done and they are good souls, they yielded right away to what I told them. The prelates were quite content with these daughters and there was no difficulty at all. From this I have felt favorable comforts, as though God and the saint were obliged to me for this resignation and this favor, but also, in my body God gives me such a facility for things as though I didn't have a body or a nature that is contrary to the practice of virtues.

In this I am quite perplexed because even having this help, I don't practice the virtues; rather I go about with such carelessness and negligence that it's a disgrace. I've had this help ever since I began to serve God when I was a girl, in whatever serious difficulties presented themselves. Only in Paris did the Lord leave me in such darkness and shadows that it really seemed like a dark night because the visits he made to me were so brief that the comfort lasted only a little, and my body was usually completely sick. In the rest I cannot say that the Lord has failed me with his strength in anything.

Once something happened to me that I am going to tell so that the goodness of the Lord may be seen, which was that in the house at Avila His Majesty permitted a nun to get leprosy.[91] God wanted to test that soul, which was holy, and also the others in the house. The doctors said that in

90. Urkiza suggests that Ana is referring to a letter from the Provincial General Juan de Jesús María, who wanted to curtail the freedom of prioresses to select confessors.
91. Ana de San Pedro (Wasteels). Born in Flanders, she professed at Avila in 1571 after the death of her husband and died at Avila in 1588.

good conscience it was best to take her out of the house to care for her because otherwise everyone would catch it. God gave me and another sister the desire to care for her and confine her to the house. We went to the prioress who was very distressed and confused at not knowing what she would do, for she lamented in her soul that this nun would have to be cared for on the outside. On our knees we asked that she give us the sick one, that we would cure her. She, the prioress,[92] was consoled to see our spirit, and so she gave her to us. The doctors ordered very harsh sweats and cures for her, though the house was in such poverty that there were very few sheets for what was necessary. Since the sweats were many, what was dirtied during the day I washed at night for the next day. They were full of material, and they and her body smelled as foul as a dead body, so that if it were not for God that it was being done, it could not be tolerated. During the day I served her in everything. At night I stopped sleeping in order to wash the clothes. I had this work for forty days. I went to the turnstile because there were few nuns, and this I did with such lightness and ease as though God were giving me recreation in everything. The smell was such that the others couldn't go near the infirmary because the stench was overwhelming.

She, as I have said, was good, and God loved her. He must have liked that we served her, because not only did I not feel the exhaustion or the lack of sleep or food, but rather it seemed that God was with us. My companion said the same thing. After the forty days, the sick one was healthy, as though she'd never had this disease. She suffered greatly, and her condition at that time was that of a leper, even though she was an angel.

One day, feeling sorry for her, I asked the Lord to alleviate her troubles, for she was suffering greatly. The Lord showed her to me very beautiful and in the high state of perfection that he had reserved for her, and His Majesty told me, "It's not completely earned yet; it's not time to take away her hardships."

These favors are due to God, because although I could think that other people deserved them, I have not deserved them nor known how to ask for or give thanks for them. May he be completely blessed.

[MYSTICAL FAVORS]

Since I came here[93] the Lord has especially bathed me in this love and charity so that I have almost always found myself in God's presence, sometimes more

---

92. María de San Jerónimo.
93. Antwerp, October 17, 1612.

assiduous in charity and the desire for the good of others, other times more assiduous for the salvation of souls and zeal for the church, for in this latter case, I can truthfully say that I suffered with my heart and could not resist it.

Once on Holy Thursday the Lord showed me the great mystery of that day and the great love that His Majesty has for souls, and my soul enjoyed these divine mysteries. He gave me to understand that if we thought each day about his divine Passion and the love with which he suffered it for us, however little it might be [i.e., however little they thought about it], it would be enough for our salvation and to receive great favors. God's love was so great that I felt that my soul was leaving my body and that my time had come, and if that impulse had not passed, I could not have endured it. My soul was so peaceful and afire in his love from this favor that I wanted to put all my sisters and all creatures in my heart, and I became much stronger than I was.

Another time, while a nun was professing I recollected with a great impulse of the love of God, and I saw how, as she was making the vows, the Child Jesus took her vows with him and offered them to the Eternal Father.

Another time while two nuns were professing in this house I saw that the Holy Mother was between them with a very great majesty from God.

Another time, in Paris, it was the same. The Holy Mother and Christ Our Lord were between the two nuns professing.

Once while I was in the choir commending a sick man to God, the Lord showed me that he had him in his heart.

I forgot to say in its place that while the Holy Mother was alive and doing a chapter for her nuns in Avila, the Lord showed me how Christ Our Lord was at her side with such splendor that all the nuns in my view seemed deified, and they left the chapter with great joy and happiness.

Another time, the day of our Lady of the Presentation,[94] having made the vows in the chapter in imitation of our Holy Mother—for she left us the custom that it be on that day that the Virgin presented herself in the temple—we came to the choir to present the vows to the Holiest Sacrament. God did me the favor that as I was recollected there for a moment, he showed me how that action had been agreeable to him and that the sisters were in his grace for that act that they had done for him from the heart.

Sometimes the Lord shows himself to me as more familiar than other times and gives me more complete confidence. He considers what I ask him to be agreeable.

94. November 21, 1622.

One eve of the day of Saint Catherine while I was in this house, they brought me a letter in which they showed in words my little worth and poor administration. I stayed calm, without having a bad thought, and I went to the choir and said to the Lord that I loved only him and his honor. He appeared to me as when he was in the world, with a face of peace and great majesty and he was at my side for a while. With this great favor my soul recollected, and the favor lasted for some days.

Around the Conception of Our Lady and its octave I felt a great presence of the Virgin and this mystery; and one day in particular in the octave I saw her intellectually with great splendor. But this vision didn't last long. Another time while I was asking for someone's health, Our Lord showed me that it was not convenient for her to have good health at that time.

Another time while I was quite perplexed at not having done the penance I wanted because of my age and weakness, Our Lord showed me that not everything is great exterior demonstrations and actions. A good heart was what pleased him and what His Majesty wanted. This must be understood when we can't do things and we want to.

Once, in the Octave of the Kings, while recollected and meditating upon that mystery for which God has given me particular devotion, I saw Our Lady with the Child Jesus in her arms, and she was like that in my heart many times.

Sometimes the Lord has shown me how I should govern, and this has been a great grace for me because I am ignorant and simple.

Other times the Lord does me other great favors without my deserving them or knowing how to best use them; [he does me great favors] even more now, on the Day of All Saints and Souls, on whose holiday I have always received favors, but this past year and all of the octave, he does them for me, showing more love, for you can't believe the love which he has for this poor ungrateful soul. Many times I feel the Lord as united with my soul as though they were two brothers.

One day he woke me as I slept, and upon waking I found all my soul so aflame with his love that I couldn't bear it, and the Lord came closer and closer to me. He opened his heart to me and put me inside. And my soul rested there from that dizziness of love. The love was great, and I think the trance was no less great, but it was sweet and without complications, for it consumed itself. This love is not always this way. It comes and goes. This feeling of Jesus Christ at my side is such that although I don't see him, it seems to me that I have him more surely than if I did see him. In the time that I feel this precious company, I don't think I am practicing the virtues, for there is simplicity in my soul, although there are occasions that cause sorrow.

Other times it's like water falling on stones, which runs off them without moistening them on the inside; and so little do I practice the things of faith, that it seems that I see more than I believe.

In these needs of the church my soul has great emotion. God shows me such a great love when I ask him to forgive sinners and calm his anger that I don't know how to say what my soul feels. It is as though it were outside subjection to the flesh and in a region of sweetness and delights and that only with its Beloved and Lord does it find what it might desire. But it wants nothing for itself, but rather the honor and glory of its Beloved, and for this reason it is always asking, "Lord, make yourself known to everyone so that they love you. Don't permit, my Lord, that all souls be ignorant of who you are." The soul says this with great love and confidence, "I know, Lord, that if you reveal yourself and make yourself known, that all will love you." He likes this so much that more and more he shows me that he loves me.

O infinite goodness! What confusion when this vision is withdrawn, to see that this goodness heeds not my wickedness nor does it look to anything but making itself known so that I love it; it is love itself, and it begins with a tiny light and sweetness, like a little fire is lit with straws and throwing wood on it makes a great fire that cannot be withstood!

Someone asked me if I thought it would be right to make truces again.[95] I commended it to the Lord and he told me, "Don't make peace with enemies, for they will become strong in their errors and we, in the midst of them, will be lost." It seemed to me that the Lord was showing that we should die to defend his church and faith, that he was not pleased with the laxity of Christians, and that they show it most in wanting peace and not war.

During the war with Germany, Our Lord gave me a great zeal for the church, day and night, which did not seem to subside. Another time the royal princess[96] asked me to commend to God if she should make a truce or peace. And the Lord responded to me, "Peace will please me, and truces just the opposite."

In this time that I have said of Germany,[97] that the Lord showed himself so loving, he concealed himself from me after a few days, and my soul was as though in a desert, alone and dark, with such dryness as though it had not known God; fearful, thinking that the favors from before had been a trick, I

---

95. It is not clear who this person was or exactly when this occurred. The truce between Spain and Holland to which this refers began in 1609 and ended in 1621.

96. Phillip II's daughter, Isabel Clara Eugenia, who, together with her husband, the Archduke Albert, ruled the Low Countries. She asked Ana for advice concerning the truce in a letter written at the end of January 1621.

97. This appears to be a reference to the Thirty Years' War (1618–48).

resigned myself in everything to God's will. I felt a tightness of my heart as though they had it in a press. It was the Christmas holidays, which I spent very differently from other times. On Three Kings' Day, arriving at Communion with a great fear of my little inclination, the Lord showed himself to me lovingly, and before taking Communion a very loving impulse and recollection of love came over me. Taking the host the Lord told me, "I will be your companion until I take you with me." My soul was as though inflamed in his love and full of reverence and grateful to His Majesty that he did me such a favor without my deserving it. This vision and feeling passed quickly, but afterwards I had God's presence for some days, peace and comforts ordinarily, and a desire to begin the road to virtue, which I have never done.

Another time in another Christmas holiday while saying my prayers, I was adoring the wounds on Christ's feet and the memory came, "Now, Lord, you come as a child, and you are on the cross. What must I do to see you always like this, O Child?" At this moment the Virgin with the child in her arms appeared to me, showing him to me, naked and tiny, as she had carried him in her holy womb. He had the wounds marked on his tiny feet, like wounds with some drops of blood that seemed to have fallen, as though indicating the nails he would have and that I should always go to his wounded feet, whether he was a child or an adult. This vision was of the brevity of others. Ordinarily, the presence of mother and child has stayed with me.

Another time after this, a great inner affliction came back to me, no less troubling than the last, and it lasted some days. Since my soul was in this same apprehension, I went to prayer and began to consider the poverty and solitude that Christ had in this world and his sorrows and humiliation. The Lord gave me to know it better because I had never felt these mysteries as I did then. I would like to know how to tell it or make it understood, but I can't, because he showed me such great things in what I have said that even if I thought about it my whole life I couldn't understand or feel what the Lord let me feel in that moment. My soul was in such turmoil that my strength would have been too scarce for what I was feeling if God had not helped me.

At Mass, I got up to take Communion with great effort; when I arrived at Communion the Lord was there like a man in love and told me, "Do you see all that I have suffered? It is all for you." I almost left myself. Without saying a word, I had in mind the words that Saint Augustine spoke, "Lord, if I were God and you were Augustine, I would become Augustine, so that you would be Lord. So great is the love I have for you." I could speak with the same love and emotion, for I felt it in my soul with great excess.

After some days, in the morning, while at prayer, Our Holy Mother appeared to me as though alive, showing me love and grace. This occurred three times. Wanting to wake up from my recollection, I opened my eyes and she was there; she embraced me, and I embraced her. She was with me for a bit and disappeared. Being very recollected and looking at the good Jesus and his mother who were in my heart, as I have said, suddenly I saw in my spirit a majesty of the Holy Spirit, and the father was above Jesus Christ as when they came to the baptism, when Saint John baptized him. This vision passed quickly, but my soul remained so full of God that I think I can say what Saint Paul said, "I do not live, but Christ lives in me."

Some days since, I still feel this presence of Our Lord Jesus Christ, and also his blessed mother.

After this, one morning upon waking, glorious Saint Joseph showed me all the favors that God had done for me, making me more and more obliged to perfection.

Another time in prayer, the Lord showed me the glory of all the saints; in the midst of them my Holy Mother. At this vision my spirit rose up in great happiness, and I said to her, "Is it possible, Mother, that I, such a sinner, have lived with someone of such glory?"

Another time, half asleep and half awake, I saw that the saint was taking two of the earliest nuns in the order with her. They were on a riverbank in a very beautiful green meadow. I told the saint, "Mother, take me with you." And she replied, "Not now, because you have to be here and do what I would have done."

These sisters died; one, María de la Cruz in Valladolid,[98] was twenty leagues from where I was. The other, who was in our house, was María de San José, two of all the first nuns, but I forgot to describe it in its place.

Another time, while our fathers were in a chapter in Valladolid,[99] I was in Avila, and having just taken Communion I was commending them to God; I had scarcely recollected when the Lord showed me, above the monastery where they were meeting, a resplendent cloud like a sun, and in the middle of it our father, Saint Elijah, who was above the chapter, his cape extended like a father who was sheltering them. After the chapter the provincial came to our convent in Avila. The mother prioress asked him how the chapter had been, and he said, "It is certain, Mother, that it's been from

98. María de la Cruz (de la Paz) was originally a servant of Dona Guiomar de Ulloa, a patroness of the Convent of Saint Joseph at Avila, in whose palace she met Saint Teresa, who selected María as one of the first four nuns at this initial foundation. She professed in 1562. Eventually Teresa took her to Valladolid as a cofounder, where she died in 1588. According to Urkiza, Ana has mistaken the name of the second nun. He believes that she is referring to Ana de San Pedro, who died in Ávila on May 8, 1588.

99. April 19–25, 1587.

God. Once we entered, we were all as though full of God and inflamed in love, for there was no contradictory disposition."

Returning to the things here, asking the Lord what would please him most, and being asleep, I found myself entering to pray to the Christ of the Column, which is in Avila, and upon entering, I got on my knees at his feet. The Christ looked at me with a gaze so loving that it penetrated my heart.

This penetrating was such that it cannot be told. All those days before I had been asking him to show me in what I could serve him most; and as I lay prostrate at his feet, not saying anything to him, he told me these words, "Patience, humility, and love," and disappeared. These words have remained with me with the same feeling that I felt before, for although it might not be as intense, it is almost the same. I awoke with the same love in my heart, so that it was necessary to distract myself from what I was feeling.

While I was ill and could not go to the choir during the Christmas holidays, I was lamenting it. But since the Lord is good, the Child Jesus appeared to me in the doorway there where I was, which consoled me greatly.

One day of the Holy Mother the Lord showed me a little cloud over this house that signified new graces that he would do for this convent.

Another time, I was going about somewhat more recollected than usual, and I felt in my soul a tabernacle and the Holiest Trinity in it, with the three powers. It can be well believed, but not told, that the Lord showed these great things to my soul.

At the beginning of this foundation[100] I commended this house to our saint, that she be the prioress and watch over it; and sometimes, asleep, she showed me the mistakes that were being made and that I didn't see. Once she took me by the hand, led me to the doorway, and told me to correct something there that was not going well.

Sometimes I notice that although the love of God that his Majesty gives me is not of the same strength or impulse as at other times, it is more delicate so that it causes more suffering than at other times.

This Octave of the Purest Conception of Our Lady[101] it has been more continuous, particularly at the hour of morning prayer. This was so strong that it seemed to me that it would not have been much to die from God's love. I wanted many people to feel what I was feeling and something occurred to me to represent it, or it was shown to me, which is this: when there are springs of water in the fields, these are usually in sandy ground and the water does not come out altogether through one conduit but rather bubbles

---

100. Ana founded the Antwerp convent on November 6, 1612.

101. Possibly December 8, 1623.

among the sands and shakes the sands, which don't stop moving; the water comes out over them clear and pure like crystal, and although it goes along covering them, they are always moving with a great happiness. In this same way I felt at this time my soul and all its movements drenched in this love throughout, and it was being shaken and undone in all parts, so that if God didn't moderate it, my life would end.

This grace took away a great sorrow that I had at this time, for at the same time that the Lord does favors, he dispenses suffering; and since he has always done me favors without my deserving them, now he usually gives me very great interior afflictions. It must be two or three years now,[102] and the afflictions are so great that if I hadn't known and enjoyed the Lord's goodness, I could be distrustful of them. But he has left me this favor, that always, however anguished I might be, I find myself resigned to his will and its disposition. From the suffering that I had earlier from that excess of love that has been spoken of, a kind of cloud came into my soul that was darker than the darkest night you can see outside. This one is interior and comes with a power that, although it is dark and all bitter and makes the hair on your head tremble sometimes, the soul embraces it and shows a very great pleasure and resignation. With this it delivers itself into the soul, and it seems that this is what it is to be dying, and life is ending and the soul doesn't want to take it away, although it could, but rather wants to die, if it pleases God, more than to resist.

I don't know how it is that all the passions and powers occupy me in such a way that I am in myself as though I really were not in myself. All is in silence, and the soul is in freedom, without knowing from whence it comes, because the suffering is so interior that it seems I am in a strange region. Nothing that delights is seen or heard; rather, all is dark, and the soul is in such restriction that it is as though it were in a press.

There is only comfort in that the soul is not superficial as in other matters and forms of prayer; it is firm in not diverging from anything that can cause it scruples. The dying and ending of life would be a rest for it, but it does not ask for it, nor desire it, nor is there movement toward desiring anything other than to be resigned. God gives the soul to feel that abandonment that he had in this world in everything, particularly at the time of his Holy Passion.

This feeling and the light with which he shows it to me are so delicate that they cannot be told nor meditated upon if His Majesty doesn't make them felt.

102. Probably the years 1621–24.

When this feeling subsides, another comes over me no less perceptible and great, namely, savoring the excessive pain that he suffered in all his wounds until he gave up his life in that abandonment. But it shows the soul that what killed him was love. Arriving at this feeling, the soul cannot suffer it and leaves itself saying, "Lord, steal my heart," and "I want to be undone and not to exist, but rather in my undoing for you to become greater and greater in all creatures and that they know you and I remain all undone and consumed in you."

I cannot tell the way in which the soul comes undone in the presence of God and as though he had need of it, saying, "May you, Lord, be, and may I be all undone." Truly where love is, it disconcerts and causes oblivion and has the effect of madness, if it can be said this way.

Another time I was three days in such a darkness and constriction of soul that I didn't know where I was, and on Saint Matthew's Day in this year of 1624 I went to the choir in the afternoon and sat there, after having adored the Holiest Sacrament as best I could. Just as a ray of light enters a dark room through a crack, so a little sliver of light entered my soul, and I understood that they were telling me, "The Beloved loves you well and is not content at seeing you suffer." With this little light my spirit rose up and I came out saying this verse that the bride, somewhat disguised, says in the Song of Songs:

> O crystalline fountain!
> If only you could form
> Suddenly on your silver surface
> The beloved eyes
> I carry inscribed within me![103]

This satisfied and gave fullness to my heart, which had been hungry and faint; nothing that I saw or that presented itself satisfied me, nor could meditating comfort me, as it usually does; now none of that was doing me any good.

Blessed be this Lord, who cannot suffer that we suffer without consoling us, and so he well deserves that we love him with the pureness he wants. That's what he showed me a little while ago. As I was about to take Communion on Saint John's Day I had a scruple—that I had told someone that friendships among servants of God were not good. I saw that it troubled her. I asked the Lord for forgiveness, that he pardon me if I had offended him in

---

103. A verse from Saint John of the Cross's *Cantico espiritual.*

this. He told me no, rather that those who truly look to their welfare should fear any attachment, although it might be as light as a small piece of dust, if they want to find God's grace. This the Lord responded to me.

Another time, a good man who trusted me told me things of his soul. I commended him to God. The Lord told me that I should tell him that at the hour of death little things, even the smallest imperfections, are shown to a soul.

In this last illness, after receiving the Holiest Sacrament, I had a fainting spell. I thought my hour had come. While I was like that, I saw at a little distance in my very cell three very venerable people, and all three were of a kind and very beautiful, dressed in pontifical robes. I knew that it was the Holiest Trinity; my soul was dying to get close to them and leave this body. But they didn't call me. More and more I strove to get close, and they disappeared. I came back to myself and took more heart. But one thing in this vision made me suspect that it wasn't God, because I was two days without resigning myself to staying here on earth. But with this scruple I resigned myself to whatever God wants, to live or to die, and that's how I have remained, so that when the desire to die comes over me, I remove it and resign myself to his will.

APPENDIX A
"AN ACCOUNT OF THE
FOUNDATION AT BURGOS"

O ur Holy Mother, Teresa of Jesús, arrived at this house of Saint Joseph of Avila, in the year of 1581 at the beginning of the month of September. She came from the foundation of the monastery at Soria, and because at this house of Saint Joseph they had always wanted to have her as prelate, they undertook this upon her arrival; and she who was then the prelate[1] of this house persuaded the provincial father[2] to absolve her from the office in order to elect our Holy Mother, and that's what was done.

This was at a time when the house was in extreme material need, and it was to praise the Lord that from that very day it has never lacked the necessary things; rather, it has increased them, so that even with many debts the Lord has arranged it in such a way that not only are these paid but also the house can get by without all the struggle and bother that there had been. If I had to speak about spiritual matters, there would be much to say, but this should be for the prelates to say, as those who know best, for I don't have to do more than give this account, which our provincial father has ordered.[3]

With everyone very happy to have our Holy Mother here as prelate of this house, Our Lord began to move a person from the city of Burgos[4] to

1. María del Cristo (del Aguila) professed at Avila in 1568 and died in Málaga in 1590.

2. Jerónimo Gracián de la Madre de Dios. Friend and confidante of Saint Teresa and also a strong supporter of more autonomy for convents. He was embroiled in conflicts with the conservative superior general of the Discalced Carmelites, Nicolás Doria , after Teresa's death and was finally expelled from the Discalced Order by him.

3. According to Urkiza, this provincial could be either Nicolás Doria (see the volume editor's introduction) or Gregorio Nacianceno (1548–99). Father Nacianceno entered the order in 1576 and occupied various high positions, including the vicar provincial of Castilla la Vieja and provincial of lower Andalucía. He died in Madrid in 1599.

4. This person was Catalina de Tolosa, a native of Vizcaya. She professed at Palencia in 1588 under the name Catalina del Espíritu Santo. Several of her children (four daughters and one

make a monastery there, and she wrote to Our Mother to come found it. She answered that she [the person in Burgos] should seek the license of the Lord Archbishop[5] and advise her upon obtaining it. This was not with the intent of going herself but rather of sending nuns. After this decision, she came to understand that it was God's will that she go in person to found it, and this is really the truth, because if she hadn't gone it would have been impossible to do it because of all the hardships and adversities that were experienced, as will be seen later on.

At this time, Father Friar Juan de la Cruz,[6] the first Discalced friar in our order, came to Avila. He brought saddles and provisions to our Holy Mother for the foundation in Granada because they thought that as it was the first foundation in that kingdom, it was best that she do it. As the Holy Mother saw that she couldn't go because of the foundation in Burgos, she chose two nuns who were suitable for that trip; one had been the prioress of this house when they elected our Holy Mother, and the other was a nun of much spirit and perfection. But because the account of that foundation will contain all there is to be said about them, I will say no more here except that in this house they left behind much regret and loneliness [because we were] missing such good company.

They left on the eve of Saint Andrew, and our Holy Mother left for Burgos the day after New Year's of 1582. The two nuns she had brought from Alba for this purpose and her companion[7] went with her. The provincial father Jerónimo de Madre de Dios and two friars he brought with him went with her. Throughout most of the day on which they left it rained and snowed, which caused her palsy to commence, for this ailment plagued her at times. And so we arrived at Medina with great effort because of rain the whole way. She stayed in this house for three days; from there we went on to Valladolid where the illness bothered her so much that the doctors told her that if she didn't leave right away a greater illness would befall her and it

---

son) entered the reformed Carmelites. Saint Teresa speaks of her at length in chapter 32 of the *Book of Foundations.*

5. Cristobel Vela, a son of Blasco Nuñez Vela, the first Viceroy of Peru, was elected the Archbishop of Burgos in 1580. He died in Burgos in 1599.

6. San Juan de la Cruz (1542–91). Born Juan de Yepes, he entered the Carmelites as Father Juan de Santo Matia in 1564. He met Saint Teresa in 1567, while she was founding the convent at Medina del Campo, and quickly became one of her disciples and favorite sons. One of the three first members of the reformed male Carmelites, he took the name Juan de la Cruz and suffered persecution from the Calced Carmelites who imprisoned him for his part in the reform. Most famous as one of Spain's greatest mystic poets, his works include *Cántico espiritual, Noche oscura del alma,* and *Subida al monte Carmelo.*

7. Ana refers to herself as Saint Teresa's companion.

wouldn't be possible to leave, so we went right away from there to Palencia where one of our houses had been founded a year earlier. At that time the townspeople had shown such devotion to our Holy Mother that when they knew she was coming so many people gathered that she and the nuns had to get out of the carriage; we could do so only with great difficulty because people crowded around to speak to her and ask for her blessing, and those who couldn't do this were satisfied to hear her speak.

Upon entering the monastery, they received her with a "Te Deum" as they did at all the monasteries. The happiness and joy of the nuns could well be seen in the way they had adorned the courtyard, where altars and other things were not lacking, so that they seemed to have made a little heaven. The days we were in this monastery our Holy Mother was quite ill, and the weather was very rainy. All of this was not enough to dissuade the saint from wanting to continue on the road to Burgos. They told her that she couldn't possibly set out on the road in such weather because she could perish, and so they sent a man to find out the condition of the roads. He returned with very bad news about how they were.

While the Holy Mother was in this anguish of not knowing what to do, it was understood later that Our Lord told her to leave, that he would help us. It became very clear later, given the dangers in which we found ourselves, that if His Majesty hadn't watched over us, death would have been very certain in the midst of the journey. Going along a riverbank, the mud was so deep that it was necessary to get down because the carts were getting stuck. Having escaped this danger, while going up a hill, we now saw another, greater one, and it was that the Holy Mother saw her nuns' cart upset in such a way that they were about to fall in the river, and the hill was so steep that even many people were not sufficient to free them from this danger or keep the cart from falling. At this moment, one of the boys we had with us saw it and grabbed the wheel and held the cart so that it wouldn't fall. He seemed more like a guardian angel than a man, because it was not possible for him to hold it back alone if God had not wanted to save them.

It was a great hardship for our Holy Mother to see this because she thought that her nuns were going to drown; and after she saw it, she wanted to be in the lead, so that she would be the first in other dangers that might present themselves. To rest from this travail, we arrived that night at an inn where there was nothing with which to make a bed for Our Mother. Even with this slight shelter, it seemed good to stay there some days because of the news that they were giving us about the roads, that the rivers were so high that the water rose above the bridges by more than two feet. The innkeeper was such a good man and was so sorry for us that he offered to go ahead to guide us through the water, because it was so murky, the bridges were covered, and it was impossible to see the road we had to follow. The bridges were so narrow and made of wood, that the wheels just fit on them, and if they swerved just a bit, we would fall into the river. To face this danger, we confessed and asked our Holy Mother to give us her blessing like people who were going to die, and we said the creed. The Holy Mother, seeing us so disheartened, encouraged us, and since she had more faith that our Lord would deliver us safely from this danger, she told us with great happiness, "Look, my daughters! What more could you want than to be martyrs here for love of Our Lord?" She said more: that she would go first, and if she drowned, she asked us not to continue but to return to the inn. In the end it served God that we were freed from this danger.

With all these travails, our Holy Mother was so ill and her tongue so tied by palsy that it was pitiful to see her. We arrived at a town before midday, and then she wanted the father provincial to say Mass. She took Communion and her tongue was loosened and she was better. From here we went to Burgos that night, and we arrived in such great rain that the streets were like rivers. The woman who was waiting to put us up in her home was such a kind person that she had a very good fire for us and she housed us very well.

Since our Mother was so wet, she stayed longer in front of the fire that night than usual. It did her such harm that that very night she had a fainting spell and such vomiting from an already irritated throat that a sore developed that oozed blood. The next day she could not get up to negotiate the business of the foundation, but was lying on a little cot that they put next to a window that opened onto a hallway where those who wanted to speak to her did so. They went to tell the archbishop that she had arrived. He asked, Why did she bring nuns, since he had said that only she should come to negotiate? When they asked him permission to place the Holiest Sacrament in the house and say Mass, because the monastery was to be there in that very house, His Lordship answered that we should not worry because this matter [the foundation itself] had to be looked at slowly. They took some people to speak to him, but nothing worked. Our father provincial went to him, and the answer he brought back was that we could go back, that there was no need for reform in his town, that the monasteries were quite reformed. After some days another person went to talk to him, and he answered that he thought we had left, that we could very well go back.

At this time the Holy Mother was very ill, so that she could eat only liquid food because of her bad throat, and since she was in this state, not even in a condition to get out of bed, it was a great effort for her to go hear Mass on holy days, and for this reason they went to ask the archbishop's permission to say Mass in the house. Moreover, the nuns were so grieved to see themselves among the laypeople in the church that they left the ground wet with their tears. The solution His Lordship gave for this concern was to say that it didn't matter, that they would be setting a good example. It should be understood that this did not arise from His Lordship's lack of charity, since all know of his great sanctity. Rather, the Lord ordered it thus so that the Holy Mother and the sisters would suffer. This could well be seen in the conformity and perfection with which the Mother took it, because so many people went to speak to him and came back disgusted and irritated to see the little they had achieved. The Holy Mother made such excuses for him and spoke such words to them that they forgot the annoyance with which they had come. Some weeks were spent in this, so that with all her sickness she went on holy days to hear Mass and take Communion, with the streets very difficult in the bad weather. All this was not the greatest hardship she had, but rather seeing the father provincial with the disgust and worry that this was causing him and also for the woman who had brought us to found the monastery;[8] for it happened that she [Catalina de Tolosa] went to confess and he didn't want to absolve her, because we were in her house and she had been the cause of our coming.

When she was feeling a little better, the Holy Mother went to see the lord archbishop to see if she could do what the others had not been able to, and while she was there, the sisters were taking a discipline; they arranged this in such a way that it lasted the whole afternoon while the Holy Mother was with the lord archbishop. While she was with him, she told him, "Look, Your Lordship, my nuns are disciplining themselves." To this he responded that "they could just keep disciplining themselves because he was not of a mind to give permission," and so the Holy Mother returned without it. When we saw her coming we went out to ask her what she was bringing, because her face showed great contentment. When we learned that she didn't bring the license, we were very distraught, showing our grievance with the lord archbishop. She began to comfort us, saying that he was a saint and gave very good reasons that satisfied her and that she had enjoyed her time with him, that we shouldn't worry and must trust in God, that it would be done.

Seeing that there was no solution for the license for the monastery or [for our desire] to say Mass in the house despite how much the Holy Mother and all of us disliked going outside to hear it, the order was given to

8. Catalina de Tolosa.

go somewhere where we could hear Mass without leaving the house, and so we went to a hospital; there they gave the provincial father a room upstairs where there was a little balcony where we could hear Mass. This room was available because it was in such condition that no one wanted to live in it; its reputation was that nowhere in all of Burgos did more hobgoblins congregate than there. There must have been something in what they were saying because one thing or another did happen while we were there. And apart from this, it was a very uncomfortable room for the Holy Mother's illness. She underwent great hardship, and since we were feeling sorry about it, she responded that it was too good a place for her, that she didn't deserve it, and that she was sorry for us, but for herself she had no worry, that she didn't deserve to be received in that hospital. When they made her a wretched little bed she said, "Oh, my Lord, what a lovely bed this is, and you on the cross!" Each time she ate, blood came out of the sore in her throat, and as we were sorry for her; she told us, "Don't be sorry for me, for my Lord suffered more for me when he drank gall and vinegar."

One day she said that since she was so uncomfortable she might eat some sweet oranges, and that very day a woman sent them to her. When we brought her a few very good ones, upon seeing them she put them in her sleeve and said she wanted to go down to see a poor man who had complained a great deal; so she went and distributed the oranges among the poor. When she came back we asked her why she had given them away. She said, "I want them more for them than for me; I'm very happy that they gave them so much pleasure." You could well see the contentment on her face. Another time they brought her some limes, and when she saw them she said, "Blessed be God, for he has given me something to take to my dear poor ones." One day they were curing some abscesses for someone, and he was screaming terribly, so that he was torturing the others. Taking pity on him, the Holy Mother went downstairs, and upon seeing her, the poor man became quiet. She said to him, "My son, why do you scream so? Won't you bear it with patience for the love of God?" He responded, "I feel like they are tearing my life out." After the saint had been there for a bit, he said the pain had ended and later, although they were working on him, we never heard him complain again.

The poor told the nurse to bring them that holy woman many times, that it consoled them a great deal just to see her, and it seemed that their ills were relieved. The same nurse told us that when they found out we were leaving, she had found them crying and very afflicted at knowing that the Holy Mother was leaving. We were very distressed on the eve of Saint Joseph because the time when they would turn us out of the hospital was approaching. They had given us only until Easter, and if we didn't have a house by then, they could turn us out; and the house had still not been found. As we were in that state that I have said on the eve of Saint Joseph, Our Lord provided the house for us in a way that seemed more a miracle than anything else. Because I understand that our Holy Mother has spoken of this foundation, I will say no more of this here.

Once this house was arranged, we moved to it within two or three days, and from then until Easter was spent in furnishing it. After we were in it, the lord archbishop went two or three times to see our Holy Mother and to see the convenience of the house for a monastery, giving her the hope that he would give us the license by Easter. While he was with us one day, he asked for a pitcher of water, and the Holy Mother had them take it to him with some little gift she had been sent. When he saw it, he said, "You've achieved quite a bit with me, Mother, because I've never taken anything from anyone in all Burgos like this that I take because it's from your hand." The mother responded, "I was also hoping to obtain the license from Your Lordship's hand." And when he didn't give it to her, she was as happy and praising the Lord as though he had given it, and she praised His Holiness greatly and how good such prelates were for the church of God; never did we hear her speak a word against him.

We were there until Easter awaiting the license. During Holy Week, we went to a church to hear the offices, and while we were there on Holy Thursday, some men wanted to pass by where the Holy Mother was. Since she didn't get up as quickly as they wanted, they kicked her to one side to go by. When I went to help her get up, I found her all smiles and contentment at this, which made me praise God. We were waiting for them to bring the license to say Mass in the house on Easter Sunday. Here God wanted to test the Holy Mother's patience even more, or rather that of the sisters, for she had patience to spare. It did not come on any of the three days in time to keep us from going outside to Mass during all of Easter. The last day the sisters were so exasperated as well as the woman who had brought us there [Catalina de Tolosa], that she took her leave of the Holy Mother and her nuns, not to see them again until she knew the foundation was done. At this time, the Holy Mother was quite troubled at seeing the distress of this woman and the sisters, and at this very moment a gentleman to whom we owed much came in with the archbishop's license to make the monastery;[9] and he was so happy that upon entering, before he told us anything, he went with great haste to ring the bell that was there. At this we knew

9. Hernando de Matanzas, an alderman of Burgos.

that he brought the license. The rejoicing by all was great; and the Holiest Sacrament was placed there the next day, and the first Mass was said, where we now could be enclosed, which was greatly desired by all. Some fathers of the Order of Saint Dominic said the Mass and placed the Holiest Sacrament there, for those of this order have always helped and favored our Holy Mother in her needs.

After a few days, the habit was given to the daughter of the woman who had arranged our monastery to be founded there. The lord archbishop preached at this ceremony with so many tears and such humility that it caused great bewilderment for all of us and devotion in the rest of the public. He showed, among other things he said, that he regretted having delayed our business. He praised greatly the woman who brought us to that city, and he evinced great love for our Holy Mother.

From then on the house became so well-known that some important people began to visit our Holy Mother, among them a woman who for some years had been wanting God to give her children. And she commended it to our Mother to ask God for it with such faith that her wish was fulfilled. She was very grateful for this favor that God did for her.

At this time, when our Mother and all of us were very happy in our house and at seeing ourselves enclosed and that everything had turned out very well, Our Lord wanted to temper this happiness with a trial that came upon our house and the whole city. On Ascension Day[10] the river rose so much that a great amount of water entered the city; the case was so extreme that the monasteries were evacuated so as not to be flooded. We also were in danger, and because of it they advised the Mother to leave the house. She never wanted to accept this, but rather she had the Holiest Sacrament placed in a high room where she made us all withdraw and say litanies. In the end, the travail came to such a pass that the dead were disinterred and houses sank, and ours was in the most danger because of being on flat ground and closest to the river. Finally, so as not to draw this out, although there is much to say about it, I conclude by saying that the voices of many people, especially the Archbishop, were saying that because our Holy Mother was there, she had tied God's hands so that the town didn't perish.

After this difficulty, which was much greater than what I have shown here, while the Mother was with Our Lord, she said to him, "Lord, are you happy now?" And the answer he gave her was to tell her, "Go on, there is another greater travail awaiting you soon." At the time she didn't understand the meaning of this. Later it was evident in the hardships she went through

10. May 24, 1582.

from then until she arrived at Alba, in her poor health as in other serious difficulties that presented themselves, because while she was in Burgos worried about not knowing if she was leaving immediately or if she was staying there longer, Our Lord told her to leave, since there was no more to do there, that now it was finished. So she left straight away for Palencia,[11] and from there, for Medina, with the intent of going directly to Avila.[12] She found there the provincial vicar Antonio de Jesús who was waiting for her to send her to Alba. With all the favor God had granted her in this virtue of obedience, she was so aggrieved at this, thinking that he was making her go there at the duchess's request,[13] that I never saw her regret anything that the prelates ordered her to do as much as this.

We left here in a carriage that traveled so poorly that when we arrived at a little place near Peñaranda, the Holy Mother was in such pain and weakness that she had a fainting spell, which made us all feel great pity for her. We had nothing to give her for this except a few figs, which had to last her the whole night, because not even an egg could be found in the whole place. I was suffering at seeing her in such need and with nothing to help her. She consoled me, telling me not to worry, that the figs were too good for her, that many poor people had less. She said this to comfort me; but as I knew her great patience and suffering and the joy for her in suffering, I believed her travail was greater than she showed. To remedy her need we went the next day to another place, and what we found to eat were some boiled cabbages with a lot of onions, which she ate, although it was very bad for her health. This day we arrived at Alba,[14] and our Mother was so ill she could not keep company with her nuns. She said she felt so broken in health that she didn't seem to have one healthy bone. From this day, which was the eve of Saint Matthew, she went on with her work until Saint Michael's Day, when she went to take Communion.

Upon returning from Communion, she came straight back and lay down on the bed, for she had a hemorrhage, from which it is understood that she died. Two days before her death she asked that they give her the Holiest Sacrament, because she knew that she was dying. When she saw that they were bringing it to her, she sat up in bed with such strength of

11 They left Burgos on July 26, 1582, and arrived in Palencia on July 28.

12. They left Palencia on August 25, 1582, and arrived in Medina del Campo on September 15 or 16.

13. María Enríquez de Toledo, wife of Duke Fernando, asked that Teresa be present when her daughter-in-law, María Enríquez de Toledo y Corona, gave birth.

14. September 21, 1582.

spirit that it was necessary to hold her back, because she seemed to want to throw herself out of bed. She said with great happiness, "My Lord, it's time to go, may it be for the good and may your will be done." She gave God many thanks that she was a daughter of the church and that she was dying in it, saying that through Christ's merits she hoped to be saved. She asked all of us to ask God to forgive her sins and not look at them but rather to look at his own mercy. She asked all for forgiveness with much humility, saying not to look at what she had done and the bad example she had given.

When the sisters saw that she was dying, they implored her to tell them something for their benefit. What she told them was for the love of God to keep her rule and constitutions carefully. She did not want to tell them anything else. After this, all that she spoke was to repeat many times that line of David's that says, "A spirit given as sacrifice to God; do not reject, O God, a contrite and humble heart."[15] Especially the part beginning "contrite heart," was what she said until speech left her. Before it left her, she asked for Extreme Unction and received it with great devotion.

On Saint Francis's Day at nine o'clock in the evening,[16] Our Lord took her with him, leaving all with such sadness and travail that if I had to tell it here, there would be much to say. Some things I learned that happened while the Holy Mother was dying I will not put down here, because they were notable; if it seems right to the prelates, they will tell them.[17]

The following day they buried her with all the solemnity possible in that place. They put her body in a coffin and loaded so much stone, chalk, and bricks on it that the coffin broke and all of this fell into it. The person who endowed this house, Teresa de Laiz, did this; no one could keep her from doing it, for she thought that by loading it down, she would be more certain that they would not take her out of there.

After nine months, the provincial, who was then Jerónimo Gracián de la Madre de Dios, went to that house, and her [Teresa's] sisters pressured him to open the tomb, saying that they were worried about how that holy body was. At their request, he began to try to open it, but since it was loaded down with stones and all the rest, they told us that he and a companion spent four days removing what was on top of it. They found the holy body so full of earth and damaged because the coffin had broken that it was a pity to see. They say it was as fresh as if she had just died, very swollen

15. Ps 51:19.

16. October 4, 1582.

17. There are many other accounts of Teresa's death. Carlos Eire compares and analyzes these accounts in detail in *From Madrid to Purgatory*, chap. 2.

from the humidity and full of mold;[18] the clothing was and all rotted as well. With all of this, the body was so without corruption, and so whole, that no part of it was decayed, and not only did it not have a bad odor, but rather it had as good a fragrance as it still has today.

They put other clothes on her and placed her in a large casket in the same place where she was before, and after two and a half years when they went to take her out to bring her to this house of Saint Joseph in Avila, again they found her clothes almost rotted, and her holy body as without corruption as before, although very shriveled, and with such a good odor that it is to praise God, may he be blessed forever.

That God has done this favor for our Mother in that her body is like this has not surprised those of us who saw her and dealt with her, because if I had to explain here the travails and humiliations she suffered and the patience with which she bore them, principally on this last road from Burgos, when she left here from Avila until she returned to Alba where God took her, it was all a prolonged martyrdom, which cannot be set forth now. For some good reasons I will tell a word that I heard from her, which, for one of her great spirit and soul was much to say, which is that, of the many travails that she had endured in the course of her life she "had never seen herself as afflicted and harassed as at this time." I don't marvel at this, because I can certainly say in all truth that many times it seemed to me that God had given permission to the demons to torment her, and not only to them, but to all sorts of people who dealt with her, in order, to say it better, to fashion her crown. For when I remember now what I saw then, I cannot contemplate it without great tenderness and compassion, and so I saw well fulfilled the words that our Lord told her in Burgos, that another greater travail was awaiting her soon. May he be blessed forever, that he is so liberal in giving worthy matters to his chosen ones. May His Majesty give me the grace to be one of them.

---

18. It was common for cadavers of the saintly to emit a fragrance of freshness or flowers and to show no evidence of decomposition. Despite the seemingly contradictory description, that seems to be what Ana is trying to communicate with this passage.

APPENDIX B
"PRAYER IN ABANDONMENT"
(1607)

My God, help me in this tribulation.[1] Let me not lack your grace, your light, and your spirit so that I am faithful to you on all occasions, for as long as I am faithful to you and have this grace from Your Majesty I will fear no adversity, however great it might be. Your grace makes my soul the mistress of all things; nothing has strength or life against you.

As I did at many other times I implore you to give me the gift of being faithful to you, and may all my senses and members obey you in the way that you command. Don't fail me, Lord, for you know that I seek only you and your grace in all my travails and joys.

Look, Lord, I have left my homeland, my well-known and dear sisters of my soul, and the spiritual fathers through whose counsel my soul found you and was comforted in its doubts and moved to your service; for in order to do you greater service and accompany you in this exile, I left that land with good will. I know well that you are not a God of deceit, that you will stay with me and will fulfill the words you gave me through some of your servants. You know very well the love I have and have had in serving you, placing myself in all disgrace and travails for your love. Don't reject me for my sins and defects, don't leave me in tribulation; be in my favor, for to the extent of my abilities, I will be in yours.

My God of my soul, dearest Beloved! Help me and give me some minister who will help me in your name and who I can be very sure is from you. Look, Lord, at my solitude and the confusion of my soul. It is yours; don't abandon me, dear Beloved, well-being of my soul. Grant me that I be faithful to you in believing the matters of our faith and in not believing all spirits.

1. The tribulation refers to her situation of being without a confessor who satisfied her and of being relieved of her duties as prioress. See the volume editor's introduction.

If I am obliged to believe what it is that is tormenting me these days, show it to me, through you yourself or one of your ministers in whom I can be satisfied, for I am little or not at all satisfied with the case that you, my God, know is worrying me these days.

Although I know well that you know everything, I want to tell you my trouble and rest in telling you what you already know, Lord. The father who is confessing me[2] tells me that Your Majesty has told him to beware of me. He does this and shows me resentment, disgust, and disbelief of my ideas and doesn't tell me why. I had held this father to be one whom I trusted, and now I can't because I don't believe, Lord, that it is you who speaks, for you are not a God of confusion, and this is a great confusion: telling me to have a care and not telling me of what. For when you wish to warn someone who is wrong, and wish to correct them, you send someone to warn them; you tell him [the person being sent to warn—Ed.] what you want him to tell them [the people being warned—Ed.] so that they will amend themselves, with love and sweetness and in charity and in secret. But creating discord between the confessor and the penitent and stirring up hatred, I cannot believe this is you. My will doesn't deserve this, although the sins and disrespect I have committed might deserve it.

Well you know that I have a will desirous to please you, so how could I believe of yours that it would permit me to be deceived and that it would reveal my sins to another and not to me? For the things they charge me with do not pertain to prayer and spiritual matters, but rather are things that, if they exist, are defects, which I must confess. Well, if I leave nothing unconfessed, am I to believe, Lord, that you tell them that I don't confess all my sins? That is not your way. If this person had told me that he thinks worse of me than what I tell him, I would believe him, because my self-love is such that it blinds me, and in many things I don't know myself; this I believe as I am saying it, and that I am more wicked and deceitful than any creature on earth. But you, Lord, are the refuge of sinners. In you all have found an open heart to imprison wicked acts without revealing them except through the mouths of the sinners themselves, who with your light reveal them to show your mercy more clearly. That is what the Samaritan woman did, for you revealed to her alone what sins she had.[3] Also, to the good thief you gave permission to exercise his profession in your kingdom and treasures, thereby covering his sins.[4] You also did this with the

2. Pierre Bérulle.

3. Jn 4:18.

4. Lk 23:42–43.

adulteress.[5] And always, Lord, you have been and will be merciful with sinners. I, more than anyone, have good experience of the many graces and mercies that I owe you; and I believe, my Lord, that if you had done this thing, it would be by means of peace and tranquility. But neither does he who tells me this have peace, nor does he inspire it in me. I also believe of your mercy that if you gave me a hardship, you would have also given me a person to remove my doubts. But this is just the opposite and all is anguish. Among such people you scarcely know if those with whom you speak are completely Catholic, for although there are many good ones, for this ministry they are few.

I give you thanks, my God, my true comfort and all my well-being, my refuge, that you never fail those who call upon you, and in the scant capacity of men, you, Lord are abundant and fill all the emptiness of the soul and the senses. You don't allow your handmaiden to suffer much, for in all that is sorrow and trials, you have granted that she find delight, strength, and all wisdom. Certainly, men of the world will never be as favored in their delights as is the soul that you, Lord, incline to the cross and humiliations. As long as the soul does not make its seat in pain and scorn, it is not strong in the truth of its own iniquity, and it is all vanity.

In that vision that I have spoken of, when Christ appeared to me crucified and showed me the virtues in perfection, I was very bewildered because I saw that I didn't have them and that there was always an impediment to attaining them on my part. My nature always looked to its whims, and because of them the soul stopped being faithful to God. As one day and another went by and I didn't look to my obligations, Your Majesty, like a true father, gave me a whole matter to attend to and has taken me out of myself, forcing my soul to ask you for travails and that you place me in situations where my nature will be mortified, even though I might not want it. That's how I am now, but I am not certain that I will emerge well from this business that is in my hands. But I see well, as the Lord says, that the kingdom of God requires strength and that to have virtue is to reign, that you have to suffer greatly. Many have stayed in the road for not having this strength, and I can be one of them if God doesn't give me his hand for all that presents itself, as is His Majesty's wont. For although it seems that he leaves me sometimes, he doesn't go far away, he knows well that he can't entrust the treasure of suffering to me alone. I see in His Majesty a great concern that I don't lose this treasure. All the times that he wishes to grant me a new travail, he comes to me first and forewarns me, although he doesn't tell me what it will be. It

5. Jn 8:11.

is a light in which I am given to understand whether the cross will be great or small.

One day after taking Communion, a recollection came over me, and I saw that they were showing me a great cross and encouraging me to die upon it if necessary. Not many days passed before I saw myself in a great affliction and in matters of much conscience, without having anyone with whom to discuss them; because I could not be certain that in some things anger would not rule those who had taken part in the matter, while in other things I saw that they were sympathetic. This was not enough to keep my soul from being greatly distressed. This worrisome situation had occurred only a short time ago, when, as I was again in the choir and had just taken Communion, I saw another kind of cross, which was of the same type as when they showed Saint Peter a sheet full of little animals. This sheet had many little crosses, which seemed to suit each sense and emotion. The sight of them returned me to a great celestial joy so perfect that through them I saw the perfect virtues. I felt a great reverence and the passage into my soul of strength from the light with which I saw them. I see that all are acting in many ways; I find myself stronger, although it is not my own strength, because sometimes my soul is as though in a dark night, defenseless and surrounded by enemies who are trying to kill it, but it doesn't yield or lose its courage. I don't know how it happens that without thinking or knowing what it is, it disappears, and the majesty of God enters my soul and completely overwhelms it. Everything is like this as long as it lasts, but one and the other disappear quickly; and without a confessor it's uncertain and very troubling.

Sometimes because of the sick, other times because of other occupations, I have postponed this, which is for our own good. Now let us return again with a new spirit and awareness that we are nothing and that any little thing hinders us and keeps us from our goals and that without God our acts are in vain and empty. Although the imperfections are bad, the good that can be had from seeing this is that we see who God is and who we are and that we fear seeking anything at all for ourselves, although it might seem good. And so, I think we can most serve His Majesty by giving him our hearts and free will without asking him for this or that, but rather [by asking] that he avail himself of us as he wishes and as is good for his honor and glory. Let us not desire to know anything about what he wants of us, but rather, with sincerity, like a small infant who doesn't know of good and evil and looks to his father to see if he tells him anything and with that is happy, let us look that way at Our Father who orders us to love him with our whole heart, and not at our own likes and personal matters and benefits, but rather whatever is properly the glory and honor of God. And let us all ask him very truly that we have no other happiness than what might be his greater glory and pleasure, that we not be ignorant of what this is, that we abhor ourselves and not look at ourselves as more than something that doesn't exist. No artifice is necessary for this truth, for in truth we are abhorrent while we are not in God's grace. Charity is grace, and God is in the soul that has it. Let us love one another with God's charity; let their good or bad things be as our own, like those of our own soul, and let us look at them and conceal them as each would desire for herself.

I say all this so that we don't seek for ourselves in anything; that we abhor ourselves and consider ourselves poor; and let us look at the peace of the poor, for since they have no goods to watch over, nor do they care if the sky is clear or cloudy, nothing bothers them, they have nothing to lose. And so the truly poor man doesn't fear or love or need anyone; he looks for nothing from earthly creatures but rather says with the prophet, "There is no one richer or freer or more powerful than he who knows how to abandon himself and all things and put himself in the place of his nothingness." Let us seek this road with sincerity and life in our deeds, so that the Holy Spirit will come into our souls and strengthen them as he did for the apostles, in hardships or sorrows, unpleasantness and humiliations, as he did for them. And let us await him with patience as they did, for although they had been with Christ, he didn't tell them on what days this consolation of the Holy Spirit would come.

And so that not everything be of the spirit, I ask you in charity whether any of you has a need of the soul or of the body, that you tell me with openness, for my desire to help you and comfort you in all that I can is very great. I think that you will do it and that you have understood my will and desire for your good.

And let us all be happy in Christ and for Christ, for His Majesty doesn't need our services; let us not give them to him grudgingly nor desire to see our rewards in so short a space of time as this life, since an eternity awaits us.

Let us be faithful to God, for His Majesty will be with us and will be seated in our hearts, which is the seat of the soul and the throne of its repose, just as His Majesty says that his delights are with humanity. It's certain that there is no better place in us for God than the heart, and it's true that where our treasures are there is the heart and in the heart is heaven. If we knew how to do this, we could say with Saint Paul, "Our conversation is in heaven," because the good that is in heaven is in the heart. Happy the poor who know how to dispossess themselves and abandon their desires and properties, for they will fill the emptiness with that infinite grace and divine wisdom and will receive one hundred graces for one!

As long as we don't have a great disillusionment in ourselves nor feel pleasure and strength in the trials and humiliations that come to us, let us not be self-assured in our deeds and goals, although they might seem good. In this and in everything, holy fear is necessary while we are in the flesh, to guard us and free us from many falls, because falling is certain since our vision is very short and crude and more accustomed to looking at our own matters than at the divine. If there is any of this divine vision, with the use of our own and self-love we give it a different feeling and are pleased with ourselves, attributing some grace to ourselves. Holy fear is a lighted candle with which the soul sees God and how vain and mistaken is man when he is self-confident. For truly our whole condition consists of vanity as long as we don't die to ourselves and are not scorned by our own will. So, my dearest ones, let us have holy fear as our strength. And I call it strength that we have it without limit in not esteeming ourselves, but rather place our hopes and love in God, as a father who is not surprised by our faults and wants us to go to him with the love of daughters and respect for a father. He does not wish to treat us as slaves, and so he says, "Come to me all you who are tired, and I will refresh you."[1]

I greatly desire that all keep in mind the calling that God made to each one of us and that is renewed with those flames that you felt were in your souls. What desires to suffer, to be scorned, to undergo all manner of hardship, solitude, and poverty! What a letting go of parents, family and friends, and all that used to be a delight and comfort to us! And what a flame and light each one carried over her head to see this truth and perfection and the importance of following it! Well, if we spent a little time each day renewing these desires, as is our obligation, you would not be distracting yourselves nor wasting time on irrelevant things, for if you knew how precious time is, you would not use it badly. It is not a trivial matter, nor more or less what we have come here to do, to go through it with such carelessness and negligence; being cold is something that God detests, for he himself says that he vomits out those who are lukewarm in their faith. Well, let's look, my sisters, at what we are doing and what we are lacking of what we had when we came here and how we are losing it, for God doesn't order us to do it because of how much he needs us or our services, nor does he desire it from ill will, but rather from good will and pleasure.

Now that we have left the world and God has gathered us here in the Carmelite spirit, I want to see you desirous of lofty goals in everything, and I am not saying lofty so that you think you have to seek contemplation through its measures and techniques, for this would be mistaken, but rather, once your goal is set, [that you seek] to follow it with truth. Let us not seek anything but the greater glory and honor of God and that this be always the beginning and end of our prayers and our continuous and efficacious desires. Without doubt, our works and goals will be lofty and glorious and eternal, because our souls will be oblivious of themselves and their own welfare and because they will look only to God and God will be found in them whenever they seek him. Just as in a lake, looking at it at midday in the strength of the sun, you will see the sun in its depths wherever you look, because it faces only the sun and the sun puts its rays in it; so will we, if we are stripped of our

---

1. Mt 11:28: "Come to me, all you that are weary and are carrying heavy burdens, and I will give you rest" (NRSV).

self-love, see only what is God's glory, for although we are of earth and water, our deeds will be eternal and our ends glorious. But if we forget this obligation and let ourselves be guided by self-love, all our deeds will be in vain and we will become vanity itself and everything will be like this.

Let us take the Mother of God, our lady and patron, for our advocate. Let us call upon her in all our needs and desires for virtue and let us look to her as a perfect model of it, for from the moment she opened her eyes it was to look upon God, and she never took her eyes from this vision. God was seen in her as in a mirror and infused his being in her in such a way that he made her like him; and one saint says that if there were no God he would have adored her as God. May he be blessed who makes the things he beholds so like himself! Well, who better to obtain this vision for us than she who always had it perfectly? And who would have more compassion for our failings than she who has most knowledge of what we are? Through this light of knowing she always had God, and seeing that mankind didn't know him, she regretted greatly our loss and ignorance and blindness, for where there is no light all is darkness and shadow.

Well, my dearest ones, we've come here to seek light and remedy for our wickedness, and for this we have approached the Virgin and taken her habit. If we know how to ask for it with humility, she will obtain the virtues of God's grace for us, as she is the one who is most in his grace and more like his grace than any other creature.

It is a good God who infuses in this way his being, his virtue, his flavor and color and actions in the soul that looks only to him and his greater glory. This vision was so habitual in the Virgin Mary that there is nothing told in the Holy Scriptures of the excess and ecstasy that she might have shown, because since it was her custom to look upon that eternity, it was all as though her own, as were the messages that the angels brought to her from there. She only became troubled at hearing that she was to be the Mother of God, because of the reverence and knowledge she had of him. For although she more than anyone wished to see him made man, it had not entered her heart to be Mother of God, and because of this great humility she was troubled. But her joy was greater and more excessive because of the great charity she had toward humanity and her desire for its redemption. So we see that on the day of the Visitation, when she saw that Christ was revealing himself to Saint John and his parents, she expressed admirable joy, saying these words of the Magnificat: "My soul increases and praises the Lord." I have no doubt that all souls who consider the joys of the Virgin each day—if only for a quarter of an hour—will achieve victory in the virtues they seek in this manner and in all manner of need that they take to this lady.

I have good experience of some needs that seemed very doubtful of fulfillment, and in a short space of time I saw them done without knowing how, except that the Mother of God was doing them easily. In the first monastery that our saint founded, which is Avila, all of the nuns have great devotion to this lady [the Virgin] and the mystery of the Visitation. Of the things that devotees of the house have commended to her, there have been some very clear miracles. Once a man whose young daughter had gone blind came to commend it to God, and the nuns went to Our Lady, feeling great compassion for this request, and she was cured and had all her vision restored. A bishop and his canons were in great discord and great travail and went to the nuns to commend them to God; and upon praying to the Mother of God, the discord stopped and they were friends. Many other troubles have been solved upon asking for help, and many sick persons cured upon asking her through these joys [prayers]. You can well consider how infinite they would be; for the Virgin's charity is infinite and desirous of our redemption. We are very obliged to this lady, and the Carmelites even more than most, for she is our patron and naturally we are more her children than other religious since Our Lady came from the prophets, those of Mount Carmel.[2]

POVERTY

In poverty one must watch carefully that it be from a heart that is honest and pure and not deceitful, for many times and in many things we think we are doing well, and we don't look into the interior and depths of the soul. Our self-love blinds us, and we are deceived, and we deceive the world. To make a vow to be poor and think that we are is deceit and no less than a mortal sin—not to keep the vow after it is promised. It is not a joke or a matter of little importance to promise it easily and with little attention to the weight that it has, but rather as though [it were something that we have] on credit that will not fail us. It is deceit and a facade of virtue, and not virtue itself, to want to be poor in name and not in will.

If we are not content, content with what is necessary to dress and eat each day, then we are looking for what is necessary for the next day and arranging it so that it will be sure and certain and not fail us. If in this we keep the things that seem good to us and make them our property and love them so much that if they are taken away we are disconsolate, and if it seems we don't know this virtue [i.e., poverty—Ed.] nor do we keep it unless it serves

2. This refers to the Carmelite tradition that the order was founded by the Old Testament prophets Elijah and Elisha.

our purpose, oh, how far we are from true poverty! Because [in that case] we worship undesirable things and love them like idols and are oblivious of the obligation we have to keep the vow. We are unfaithful to God and faithful only to our whims and self-love and we are always slaves to ourselves.

And apart from the danger we are in of sinning against the vow, we lack the happiness and interior freedom that true poverty brings to the soul that possesses it. We don't have the faith of our forefathers, for they never thought God would fail them in their needs; they neglected themselves as though they had no bodies, and God took care of them. Just see if God failed our father Elijah when he saw him, for he sent him an angel with bread, and also Elisha [whom he helped] with the good woman, and Saint Paul in the desert, and many other saints who left everything to God and trusted truly in him. Well, God would do the same now if we trusted in him and forgot ourselves, for he is the same now as then and has the same power to attend to us and grant us his riches, for he desires only our welfare and benefit.

Take heart, sisters! Let us not waver nor desire virtue for the reward that they will give us for it but only for the pleasure of God and for his greater glory, which is to be his imitators as his true daughters. Well, what child doesn't take pride in being like his father and forgetting himself in order to serve his father in something? To the poor in spirit His Majesty has made a promise, for he will never go back on his word, which says, "Happy are the poor in spirit, for theirs is the kingdom of heaven."[3] But where will this truly poor person be found? Very far away and very high is his value.

For it doesn't consist of seeming poor or dressing like a pauper, or of giving all your estate to the poor, or of having a very tender and fervent devotion to them, or of having the appearance and concerns of a poor and great contemplative person, but it consists of just one thing, which is to come out of yourself completely and so completely that nothing personal or of self-love is left to you. Such a one could say with the prophet, "I am one alone and poor." There is no one richer, nor freer, nor more powerful than he who knows how to abandon himself and all things and places himself in the lowest place, which is that of his nothingness.

OBEDIENCE

Well, about the vow of obedience, it is difficult to obey other people as one should; and it is one thing to obey with respect for obedience and another to do it with disrespect. For obedience, after having been promised, must

3. Mt 5:3.

not be seen as obeying other people, but rather God. The vow is made to him, and anyone who is in his place is his minister. To the extent that you respect and obey him [the person in God's place], you obey and respect God, and to the extent that you disrespect him, you disrespect God. You won't have the slightest excuse, whether he who is in the place of God is good or bad, for you didn't make that condition when you promised obedience. The one who is in his place may well err, as he or she is a weak man or woman and subject to failings like everyone, but the one who obeys will not err if his obedience is true and honest, as our obligation, which is not small, requires. Don't think that it is fulfilled by saying, "I will obey until death," willingly or unwillingly, since it is promised. This is not true obedience, nor is physical death alone what should be understood, for if we have not died to ourselves for obedience, we will not deserve the rewards of obedience.

Obedience must be blind in small things and great things, without excuses in anything. After all, it is to die to ourselves and to our own judgment and will and, finally, to all our passions that resist obedience and any difficulty, until dying for Christ. Blessed are those who keep their vows this way, for these will be the dead of whom the Lord says, "Blessed are the dead who die in Christ," for he will live in them in eternity.

Let the one who gives orders look well to his obligation and he will need a good conscience. And let him look also at the little freedom that he has the day that he assumes that office and becomes more a slave and a subject than the subjects themselves, because he is obliged to be perfect, to do works with the taste and flavor of perfection, and to adjust to the condition of all and accommodate himself to each one according to his need and capacity, taking care that the souls not be troubled or separated from God by him. Let him not presume with too much zeal to test and mortify them unwisely, but with the love of a father await their cooperation at a pace that they like. And let him have the humility to hear his faults, and that they know by the love with which he treats them that they are obligated to him and so have new love for their prelate. What prelate, considering that he is doing the work of God and that God is watching him, does not humble himself and feel bewildered and hold himself to be the smallest of all and does not truly know the love and charity that obliges him to look to the progress of his subjects. And what prelate would not consider what the Lord would tell them, if he spoke to them on this or that occasion, and what are his places of refuge? As His Majesty says with his own mouth in the Gospel, "My delights are with the children of mankind."

Well, who could be better than those who have left everything for his love just to follow his words? What conscience would, instead of helping them in their holy purposes, with an unwise manner and lack of love and esteem that their holy purposes deserve, upset them and put them in such confusion that many times they are sorry to be religious in this order and sorry that they don't find God as they had longed to? Woe to him who proceeds in this manner, for it would be better for him not to have a name in this life! For on earth and in the shrines of the Lord he has gotten lost and has not known how to profit but rather has lost his gains and those of the workers in his charge; the day will come on which the Lord will call the chosen and will remove him from his seat of power.

THE RESPONSIBILITY OF THE RELIGIOUS VOCATION

Many times we speak of keeping the rule, and we bring it into conversation, but I don't know if we know well what the rule is, because it must seem to us that in being cloistered and following the choir and refectory and keeping order in the community, it is done. That is good and obligatory, and everything that is external order is good and very necessary. But we should not content ourselves with just this, for in many religious orders an external order is kept in such a way that they appear to be angels and many times there is no more than what is seen on the outside, and that is vanity and a road to perdition, as has been seen in many cases through experience.

In the chronicles of Saint Dominic, which came out a few years ago, composed by Friar Hernando del Castillo of the same Order of Saint Dominic, he tells of a case to fear greatly, for many deceased and grave religious of the order who on the surface had been of great composure and with the reputation of educated men appeared in a vision one day with God's permission; and they told who they were and that they were all in hell because of the pride and vanity that they had had in wanting to be great religious and men of letters, without respect for other rules, which are the ones we commit ourselves to on the day we become religious. For there is a rule and level inside us that is always looking to our obligations that are many times concealed, concealed not because God wishes to conceal them, but rather because we don't see them, nor do we enter our interior being, where we would see with the light of grace a law and perfect rule that will give us all the strength and virtue to rule our passions and deeds according to God's will. For God, like a true father, desires that we live with him in truth and justice.

Indeed, if it were for no other reason than to please God without attending to any other interest (for to whomever considers it well there is no greater interest than this), we should be very just in all our deeds, thoughts, words, and feelings, and with a pure and sincere vision, always looking to what God wants, how we will please him, how we will keep his law. If we liked, as the Lord says, how gentle he is and the wisdom he has, we would run to him, as the Holy Scripture says, just as the worldly run to silver and gold. Nothing is said about God's praise of Saint Simeon, except that he was just and fearful of God. Indeed a great praise, to be just and fearful of God, for each one of these two virtues makes deeds holy; because holy fear comes from knowing that which is loved and fear of losing it, for where there is no esteem or knowledge of what is loved, there is no fear of losing it. Happy the soul that has this knowledge and esteem of God, for it will keep justice, and its deeds will be just and flourish forever over the palms!

It can well be seen that to say the rule is a very harmonious thing and that in this monastery of interior virgins, where there are both prudent and imprudent virgins, let all be governed by a holy wisdom and mortification through which our passions, the crazy virgins, will be ruled, for if we listen to them they will always lead us to wickedness; so a great vigilance is necessary to keep them subdued through interior mortification. This virtue is so precious and praiseworthy that, wherever it is, the soul will always be in honest and holy perfection. For that which is true mortification is a total dying to all our natural desires and inclinations; while they live in us, we cannot consider ourselves true religious nor lovers of God, but rather we love ourselves and our whims, as is said of the children of Israel, who, having been freed from the captivity of the pharaoh and placed in the desert, cried for the onions of Egypt. That is how we religious are who are not mortified or have rule over our passions, nor do we know from what God has freed us in taking us out to the desert of religion so that we know him through the example and good habits that we see in our sisters. If we truly like mortification and spiritual rules, we would find that all things seem as we had wished them, and we would see how the Red Sea opened and drowned our enemies and that we had become mistresses of ourselves. But few retire from the world to see this victory.[4]

---

4. This final sentence continues briefly with the words, "and so, instead of . . ." but is incomplete. Ana may have intended to complete it at some future point but never actually did.

APPENDIX D
CHRONOLOGY OF THE LIFE OF
ANA DE SAN BARTOLOMÉ

1549	Ana is born in El Almendral, the daughter of Hernán García and María Manzanas.
1558–59	Ana's parents die.
1562	St. Teresa of Avila founds the first Discalced Carmelite convent, San José of Avila.
1570	Ana enters the Convento de San Jose in Avila as a Discalced Carmelite.
1572	Jerónimo Gracián takes the Discalced Carmelite habit at Pastrana.
1575–77	Period of illness during which Ana is unable to accompany Teresa in the foundations.
1577	The mitigated or Calced Carmelites intensify their opposition to the Teresian reform. San Juan de la Cruz (St. John of the Cross) is arrested and imprisoned at Medina del Campo. Ana becomes Teresa's assistant and companion.
1580–82	Ana assists Teresa in foundations at Villanueva de la Jara, Palencia, Soria, and Burgos. Teresa dies on October 4, 1582.
1585	Ana completes her initial version of *The Final Years of St. Teresa.*
1588	Nicolás Dora becomes Vicar General of the Discalced Carmelites and begins to place limits on Discalced convents' autonomy. The Spanish Armada is defeated. The Nun of Lisbon (María de la Visitación) is revealed to be a religious fraud.
1590	The "revolt of the Nuns." Some Discalced nuns, led by Ana de Jesús, and María de San José, secretly obtain a Papal brief, which confirms the 1581 Constitution of the Order and requires papal approval for any modification.

1591	Ana accompanies María de San Jerónimo to Madrid.
1592	Jerónimo Gracián is expelled from the order.
1593	The Discalced Carmelites separate completely from the Old Observance of the Order.
1594	Doria dies. Ana returns to the Convent at San José de Avila with María de San Jerónimo.
1595	Ana accompanies Maria de San Jeronimo to Ocaña. She testifies in the beatification proceedings of Teresa of Avila.
1604	Ana leaves for France with five other nuns to establish the Discalced Order in France. The Discalced Convent is founded in Paris with Ana de Jesús as its first prioress.
1605	Ana takes the black veil and becomes a choir nun. Accompanied by Ana de Jesús, Ana founds the Discalced convent at Pontoise and is named its prioress. She returns to Paris and is named prioress of the convent there.
1606	The difficulties between Ana and Pierre Bérulle begin. The Princess Regent Isabel Clara Eugenia writes to Ana from Flanders inviting her to found the Teresian Carmelites there.
1608	Ana resigns as prioress in Paris. She leaves Paris to found a convent in Tours and becomes its prioress.
1611	Ana leaves France for convent at Mons, Flanders
1612	Ana founds the Discalced convent at Antwerp.
1614	Gracián dies. Teresa of Avila is beatified.
1619	Ana helps the English Discalced Carmelites found a convent in Antwerp.
1622	Maurice of Nassau, Prince of Orange, attacks Antwerp at night, but a storm foils his attempt. Ana is credited with saving the city through her prayers.
1623	The English Carmelites separate from the jurisdiction of the Order and place themselves under the Archbishop of Antwerp.
1624	Ana is once again credited with saving Antwerp from an attack by the enemy. The city is about to be occupied when another storm destroys the enemy's plans.
1626	Francisca de Jesús (Cano) Ana's cousin and childhood friend dies on February 19 at Medina del Campo. Ana dies on June 7 at the convent in Antwerp.
1632	Crisóstomo Enríquez publishes the first biography de Ana de San Bartolomé.
1917	Ana is beatified by Pope Benedict XV.

SERIES EDITORS'
BIBLIOGRAPHY

PRIMARY SOURCES

Alberti, Leon Battista (1404–72). *The Family in Renaissance Florence*. Trans. Renée Neu Watkins. Columbia: University of South Carolina Press, 1969.

Arenal, Electa and Stacey Schlau, eds. *Untold Sisters: Hispanic Nuns in Their Own Works*. Trans. Amanda Powell. Albuquerque: University of New Mexico Press, 1989.

Astell, Mary (1666–1731). *The First English Feminist: Reflections on Marriage and Other Writings*. Ed. and Introd. Bridget Hill. New York: St. Martin's Press, 1986.

Astell, Mary and John Norris. *Letters Concerning the Love of God*. Ed. E. Derek Taylor and Melvyn New. The Early Modern Englishwoman 1500–1750: Contemporary Editions. Aldershot: Ashgate Publishing Co., 2005.

Atherton, Margaret, ed. *Women Philosophers of the Early Modern Period*. Indianapolis: Hackett Publishing Co., 1994.

Aughterson, Kate, ed. *Renaissance Woman: Constructions of Femininity in England; A Source Book*. London: Routledge, 1995.

Barbaro, Francesco (1390–1454). *On Wifely Duties*. Trans. Benjamin Kohl in Kohl and R. G. Witt, eds., *The Earthly Republic*. Philadelphia: University of Pennsylvania Press, 1978, 179–228. Translation of the Preface and Book 2.

Behn, Aphra. *The Works of Aphra Behn*. 7 vols. Ed. Janet Todd. Columbus: Ohio State University Press, 1992–96.

Blamires, Alcuin, ed. *Woman Defamed and Woman Defended: An Anthology of Medieval Texts*. Oxford: Clarendon Press, 1992.

Boccaccio, Giovanni (1313–75). *Famous Women*. Ed. and trans. Virginia Brown. The I Tatti Renaissance Library. Cambridge: Harvard University Press, 2001.

———. *Corbaccio or the Labyrinth of Love*. Trans. Anthony K. Cassell. Second revised edition. Binghamton: Medieval and Renaissance Texts and Studies, 1993.

Booy, David, ed. *Autobiographical Writings by Early Quaker Women*. Aldershot: Ashgate Publishing Co., 2004.

Brown, Sylvia. *Women's Writing in Stuart England: The Mother's Legacies of Dorothy Leigh, Elizabeth Joscelin and Elizabeth Richardson*. Thrupp: Sutton, 1999.

Bruni, Leonardo (1370–1444). "On the Study of Literature (1405) to Lady Battista Malatesta of Moltefeltro." In *The Humanism of Leonardo Bruni: Selected Texts*. Trans.

and Introd. Gordon Griffiths, James Hankins, and David Thompson. Binghamton: Medieval and Renaissance Studies and Texts, 1987, 240–51.

Castiglione, Baldassare (1478–1529). *The Book of the Courtier*. Trans. George Bull. New York: Penguin, 1967; *The Book of the Courtier*. Ed. Daniel Javitch. New York: W. W. Norton & Co., 2002.

Christine de Pizan (1365–1431). *The Book of the City of Ladies*. Trans. Earl Jeffrey Richards. Foreward Marina Warner. New York: Persea Books, 1982.

———. *The Treasure of the City of Ladies*. Trans. Sarah Lawson. New York: Viking Penguin, 1985. Also trans. and introd. Charity Cannon Willard. Ed. and introd. Madeleine P. Cosman. New York: Persea Books, 1989.

Clarke, Danielle, ed. *Isabella Whitney, Mary Sidney and Aemilia Lanyer: Renaissance Women Poets*. New York: Penguin Books, 2000.

Couchman, Jane and Ann Crabb, eds. *Women's Letters Across Europe, 1400–1700*. Aldershot: Ashgate Publishing Co., 2005.

Crawford, Patricia and Laura Gowing, eds. *Women's Worlds in Seventeenth-Century England: A Source Book*. London: Routledge, 2000.

"Custome Is an Idiot": Jcobean Pamphlet Literature on Women. Ed. Susan Gushee O'Malley. Afterword Ann Rosalind Jones. Chicago: University of Illinois Press, 2004.

Daybell, James, ed. *Early Modern Women's Letter Writing, 1450–1700*. Houndmills: Palgrave, 2001.

De Erauso, Catalina. *Lieutenant Nun: Memoir of a Basque Transvestite in the New World*. Trans. Michele Ttepto and Gabriel Stepto; foreword by Marjorie Garber. Boston: Beacon Press, 1995.

Domestic Politics and Family Absence: The Correspondence (1588–1621) of Robert Sidney, First Early of Leicester, and Barbara Gamage Sidney, Countess of Leicester. Ed. Margaret P. Hannay, Nowl J. Kinnamon, and Michael G. Brennan. The Early Modern Englishwoman 1500–1750: Contemporary Editions. Aldershot: Ashgate Publishing Co., 2005.

Elizabeth I: Collected Works. Ed. Leah S. Marcus, Janel Mueller, and Mary Beth Rose. Chicago: University of Chicago Press, 2000.

Elyot, Thomas (1490–1546). *Defence of Good Women: The Feminist Controversy of the Renaissance*. Facsimile Reproductions. Ed. Diane Bornstein. New York: Delmar, 1980.

Erasmus, Desiderius (1467–1536). *Erasmus on Women*. Ed. Erika Rummel. Toronto: University of Toronto Press, 1996.

Female and Male Voices in Early Modern England: An Anthology of Renaissance Writing. Ed. Betty S. Travitsky and Anne Lake Prescott. New York: Columbia University Press, 2000.

Ferguson, Moira, ed. *First Feminists: British Women Writers 1578–1799*. Bloomington: Indiana University Press, 1985.

Galilei, Maria Celeste. *Sister Maria Celeste's Letters to her father, Galileo*. Ed. and trans. Rinaldina Russell. Lincoln: Writers Club Press·of Universe.com, 2000; *To Father: The Letters of Sister Maria Celeste to Galileo, 1623–1633*. Trans. Dava Sobel. London: Fourth Estate, 2001.

Gethner, Perry, ed. *The Lunatic Lover and Other Plays by French Women of the 17th and 18th Centuries*. Portsmouth: Heinemann, 1994.

Glückel of Hameln (1646–1724). *The Memoirs of Glückel of Hameln*. Trans. Marvin Lowenthal. New Introd. Robert Rosen. New York: Schocken Books, 1977.

Harline, Craig, ed. *The Burdens of Sister Margaret: Inside a Seventeenth-Century Convent*. Abr. ed. New Haven: Yale University Press, 2000.

Henderson, Katherine Usher and Barbara F. McManus, eds. *Half Humankind: Contexts and Texts of the Controversy about Women in England, 1540–1640*. Urbana: Indiana University Press, 1985.

Hoby, Margaret. *The Private Life of an Elizabethan Lady: The Diary of Lady Margaret Hoby 1599–1605*. Phoenix Mill: Sutton Publishing, 1998.

Humanist Educational Treatises. Ed. and trans. Craig W. Kallendorf. The I Tatti Renaissance Library. Cambridge: Harvard University Press, 2002.

Hunter, Lynette, ed. *The Letters of Dorothy Moore, 1612–64*. Aldershot: Ashgate Publishing Co., 2004.

Joscelin, Elizabeth. *The Mothers Legacy to her Unborn Childe*. Ed. Jean leDrew Metcalfe. Toronto: University of Toronto Press, 2000.

Kaminsky, Amy Katz, ed. *Water Lilies, Flores del agua: An Anthology of Spanish Women Writers from the Fifteenth Through the Nineteenth Century*. Minneapolis: University of Minnesota Press, 1996.

Kempe, Margery (1373–1439). *The Book of Margery Kempe*. Trans. and ed. Lynn Staley. A Norton Critical Edition. New York: W.W. Norton, 2001.

King, Margaret L., and Albert Rabil, Jr., eds. *Her Immaculate Hand: Selected Works by and about the Women Humanists of Quattrocento Italy*. Binghamton: Medieval and Renaissance Texts and Studies, 1983; second revised paperback edition, 1991.

Klein, Joan Larsen, ed. *Daughters, Wives, and Widows: Writings by Men about Women and Marriage in England, 1500–1640*. Urbana: University of Illinois Press, 1992.

Knox, John (1505–72). *The Political Writings of John Knox: The First Blast of the Trumpet against the Monstrous Regiment of Women and Other Selected Works*. Ed. Marvin A. Breslow. Washington: Folger Shakespeare Library, 1985.

Kors, Alan C., and Edward Peters, eds. *Witchcraft in Europe, 400–1700: A Documentary History*. Philadelphia: University of Pennsylvania Press, 2000.

Krämer, Heinrich, and Jacob Sprenger. *Malleus Maleficarum* (ca. 1487). Trans. Montague Summers. London: Pushkin Press, 1928; reprinted New York: Dover, 1971.

Larsen, Anne R. and Colette H. Winn, eds. *Writings by Pre-Revolutionary French Women: From Marie de France to Elizabeth Vigée-Le Brun*. New York: Garland Publishing Co., 2000.

de Lorris, William, and Jean de Meun. *The Romance of the Rose*. Trans. Charles Dahlbert. Princeton: Princeton University Press, 1971; reprinted University Press of New England, 1983.

Marcus, Leah S., Janel Mueller, and Mary Beth Rose, eds. *Elizabeth I: Collected Works*. Chicago: University of Chicago Press, 2000.

Marguerite d'Angoulême, Queen of Navarre (1492–1549). *The Heptameron*. Trans. P. A. Chilton. New York: Viking Penguin, 1984.

Mary of Agreda. *The Divine Life of the Most Holy Virgin*. Abridgment of *The Mystical City of God*. Abr. by Fr. Bonaventure Amedeo de Caesarea, M.C. Trans. from French by Abbé Joseph A. Boullan. Rockford: Tan Books, 1997.

Moore, Dorothy. *The Letters of Dorothy Moore, 1612–64: The Friendships, Marriage and Intellectual Life of a Seventeenth-Century Woman*. Ed. Lynette Hunter. The Early Modern Englishwoman 1500–1750: Contemporary Editions. Aldershot: Ashgate Publishing Co., 2004.

Mullan, David George. *Women's Life Writing in Early Modern Scotland: Writing the Evangelical Self, c. 1670–c. 1730.* Aldershot: Ashgate Publishing Co., 2003.

Myers, Kathleen A. and Amanda Powell, eds. *A Wild Country Out in the Garden: The Spiritual Journals of a Colonial Mexican Nun.* Bloomington: Indiana University Press, 1999.

Ostovich, Helen and Elizabeth Sauer, eds. *Reading Early Modern Women: An Anthology of Texts in Manuscript and Print, 1550–1700.* New York: Routledge, 2004.

Reading Early Modern Women: An Anthology of Texts in Manuscript and Print, 1550–1700. Ed. Helen Ostovich and Elizabeth Sauer. New York: Routledge, 2004.

Russell, Rinaldina, ed. *Sister Maria Celeste's Letters to Her Father, Galileo.* San Jose: Writers Club Press, 2000.

Teresa of Avila, Saint (1515–82). *The Life of Saint Teresa of Avila by Herself.* Trans. J. M. Cohen. New York: Viking Penguin, 1957.

———. *The Collected Letters of St. Teresa of Avila. Volume One: 1546–1577,* trans. Kieran Kavanaugh. Washington, DC: Institute of Carmelite Studies, 2001.

Travitsky, Betty, ed. *The Paradise of Women: Writings by Englishwomen of the Renaissance.* Westport, CT: Greenwood Press, 1981.

Weyer, Johann (1515–88). *Witches, Devils, and Doctors in the Renaissance: Johann Weyer, De praestigiis daemonum.* Ed. George Mora with Benjamin G. Kohl, Erik Midelfort, and Helen Bacon. Trans. John Shea. Binghamton, NY: Medieval and Renaissance Texts and Studies, 1991.

Wilson, Katharina M., ed. *Medieval Women Writers.* Athens: University of Georgia Press, 1984.

———, ed. *Women Writers of the Renaissance and Reformation.* Athens: University of Georgia Press, 1987.

———, and Frank J. Warnke, eds. *Women Writers of the Seventeenth Century.* Athens: University of Georgia Press, 1989.

Wollstonecraft, Mary. *A Vindication of the Rights of Men and a Vindication of the Rights of Women.* Ed. Sylvana Tomaselli. Cambridge: Cambridge University Press, 1995. Also *The Vindications of the Rights of Men, The Rights of Women.* Ed. D. L. Macdonald and Kathleen Scherf. Peterborough: Broadview Press, 1997.

Woman Defamed and Woman Defended: An Anthology of Medieval Texts. Ed. Alcuin Blamires. Oxford: Clarendon Press, 1992.

Women Critics 1660–1820: An Anthology. Edited by the Folger Collective on Early Women Critics. Bloomington: Indiana University Press, 1995.

Women Writers in English 1350–1850: 15 published through 1999 (projected 30-volume series suspended). Oxford University Press.

Women's Letters Across Europe, 1400–1700. Ed. Jane Couchman and Ann Crabb. Aldershot: Ashgate Publishing Co., 2005.

Women's Life Writing in Early Modern Scotland: Writing the Evangelical Self, c. 1670–c. 1730. ed. David G. Mullan. The Early Modern Englishwoman 1500–1750: Contemporary Editions. Aldershot: Ashgate Publishing Co.,m 2003.

Wroth, Lady Mary. *The Countess of Montgomery's Urania.* 2 parts. Ed. Josephine A. Roberts. Tempe: MRTS, 1995, 1999.

———. *Lady Mary Wroth's "Love's Victory": The Penshurst Manuscript.* Ed. Michael G. Brennan. London: The Roxburghe Club, 1988.

———. *The Poems of Lady Mary Wroth.* Ed. Josephine A. Roberts. Baton Rouge: Louisiana State University Press, 1983.

de Zayas Maria. *The Disenchantments of Love*. Trans. H. Patsy Boyer. Albany: State University of New York Press, 1997.

———. *The Enchantments of Love: Amorous and Exemplary Novels*. Trans. H. Patsy Boyer. Berkeley: University of California Press, 1990.

SECONDARY SOURCES

Abate, Corinne S., ed. *Privacy, Domesticity, and Women in Early Modern England*. Aldershot: Ashgate Publishing Co., 2003.

Ahlgren, Gillian. *Teresa of Avila and the Politics of Sanctity*. Ithaca: Cornell University Press, 1996.

Akkerman, Tjitske, and Siep Sturman, eds. *Feminist Thought in European History, 1400–2000*. London: Routledge, 1997.

Allen, Sister Prudence, R.S.M. *The Concept of Woman: The Aristotelian Revolution, 750 B.C.–A.D. 1250*. Grand Rapids: William B. Eerdmans Publishing Company, 1997.

———. *The Concept of Woman*. Volume 2, *The Early Humanist Reformation, 1250–1500*. Grand Rapids, MI: William B. Eerdmans Publishing Company, 2002.

Altmann, Barbara K., and Deborah L. McGrady, eds. *Christine de Pizan: A Casebook*. New York: Routledge, 2003.

Ambiguous Realities: Women in the Middle Ages and Renaissance. Ed. Carole Levin and Jeanie Watson. Detroit: Wayne State University Press, 1987.

Amussen, Susan D. And Adele Seeff, eds. *Attending to Early Modern Women*. Newark: University of Delaware Press, 1998.

Andreadis, Harriette. *Sappho in Early Modern England: Female Same-Sex Literary Erotics 1550–1714*. Chicago: University of Chicago Press, 2001.

Arcangela Tarabotti: A Literary Nun in Baroque Venice. Ed. Elissa B. Weaver. Ravenna: Longo Editore, 2006.

Architecture and the Politics of Gender in Early Modern Europe. Ed. Helen Hills. Aldershot: Ashgate Publishing Co., 2003.

Armon, Shifra. *Picking Wedlock: Women and the Courtship Novel in Spain*. New York: Rowman & Littlefield Publishers, Inc., 2002.

Attending to Early Modern Women. Ed. Susan D. Amussen and Adele Seeff. Newark: University of Delaware Press, 1998.

Backer, Anne Liot Backer. *Precious Women*. New York: Basic Books, 1974.

Ballaster, Ros. *Seductive Forms*. New York : Oxford University Press, 1992.

Barash, Carol. *English Women's Poetry, 1649–1714: Politics, Community, and Linguistic Authority*. New York: Oxford University Press, 1996.

Barker, Alele Marie and Jehanne M. Gheith, eds. *A History of Women's Writing in Russia*. Cambridge: Cambridge University Press, 2002.

Battigelli, Anna. *Margaret Cavendish and the Exiles of the Mind*. Lexington: University of Kentucky Press, 1998.

Beasley, Faith. *Revising Memory: Women's Fiction and Memoirs in Seventeenth-Century France*. New Brunswick: Rutgers University Press, 1990.

———. *Salons, History, and the Creation of Seventeenth-Century France*. Aldershot: Ashgate Publishing Co., 2006.

Becker, Lucinda M. *Death and the Early Modern Englishwoman*. Aldershot: Ashgate Publishing Co., 2003.

Beilin, Elaine V. *Redeeming Eve: Women Writers of the English Renaissance*. Princeton: Princeton University Press, 1987.

Bennett, Lyn. *Women Writing of Divinest Things: Rhetoric and the Poetry of Pembroke, Wroth, and Lanyer*. Pittsburgh: Duquesne University Press, 2004.

Benson, Pamela Joseph. *The Invention of Renaissance Woman: The Challenge of Female Independence in the Literature and Thought of Italy and England*. University Park: Pennsylvania State University Press, 1992.

——— and Victoria Kirkham, eds. *Strong Voices, Weak History? Medieval and Renaissance Women in their Literary Canons: England, France, Italy*. Ann Arbor: University of Michigan Press, 2003.

Berry, Helen. *Gender, Society and Print Culture in Late-Stuart England*. Aldershot: Ashgate Publishing Co., 2003.

Beyond Isabella: Secular Women Patrons of Art in Renaissance Italy. Ed. Sheryl E. Reiss and David G. Wilkins. Kirksville, MO: Turman State University Press, 2001.

Beyond Their Sex: Learned Women of the European Past. Ed. Patricia A. Labalme. New York: New York University Press, 1980.

Bicks, Caroline. *Midwiving Subjects in Shakespeare's England*. Aldershot: Ashgate Publishing Co., 2003.

Bilinkoff, Jodi. The Avila of Saint Teresa: Religious Reform in a Sixteenth-Century City. Ithaca: Cornell University Press, 1989.

———. Related Lives: Confessors and Their Female Penitents, 1450–1750. Ithaca: Cornell University Press, 2005.

Bissell, R. Ward. *Artemisia Gentileschi and the Authority of Art*. University Park: Pennsylvania State University Press, 2000.

Blain, Virginia, Isobel Grundy, and Patricia Clements, eds. *The Feminist Companion to Literature in English: Women Writers from the Middle Ages to the Present*. New Haven: Yale University Press, 1990.

Blamires, Alcuin. *The Case for Women in Medieval Culture*. Oxford: Clarendon Press, 1997.

Bloch, R. Howard. *Medieval Misogyny and the Invention of Western Romantic Love*. Chicago: University of Chicago Press, 1991.

Bogucka, Maria. *Women in Early Modern Polish Society, Against the European Background*. Aldershot: Ashgate Publishing Co., 2004.

Bornstein, Daniel and Roberto Rusconi, eds. *Women and Religion in Medieval and Renaissance Italy*. Trans. Margery J. Schneider. Chicago: University of Chicago Press, 1996.

Brant, Clare, and Diane Purkiss, eds. *Women, Texts and Histories, 1575–1760*. London: Routledge, 1992.

Briggs, Robin. *Witches and Neighbours: The Social and Cultural Context of European Witchcraft*. New York: HarperCollins, 1995; Viking Penguin, 1996.

Brink, Jean R., ed. *Female Scholars: A Traditioin of Learned Women before 1800*. Montréal: Eden Press Women's Publications, 1980.

———, Allison Coudert, and Maryanne Cline Horowitz. *The Politics of Gender in Early Modern Europe*. Sixteenth Century Essays and Studies, 12. Kirksville: Sixteenth Century Journal Publishers, 1989.

Broude, Norma and Mary D. Garrard, eds. *The Expanding Discourse: Feminism and Art History*. New York: HarperCollins, 1992.

Brown, Judith C. *Immodest Acts: The Life of a Lesbian Nun in Renaissance Italy*. New York: Oxford University Press, 1986.

——— and Robert C. Davis, eds. *Gender and Society in Renaisance Italy.* London: Addison Wesley Longman, 1998.

Brown-Grant, Rosalind. *Christine de Pizan and the Moral Defence of Women: Reading Beyond Gender.* Cambridge: Cambridge University Press, 1999.

Burke, Victoria E. Burke, ed. *Early Modern Women's Manuscript Writing.* Aldershot: Ashgate Publishing Co., 2004.

Burns, Jane E., ed. *Medieval Fabrications: Dress, Textiles, Cloth Work, and Other Cultural Imaginings.* New York: Palgrave Macmillan, 2004.

Bynum, Carolyn Walker. *Fragmentation and Redemption: Essays on Gender and the Human Body in Medieval Religion.* New York: Zone Books, 1992.

———. *Holy Feast and Holy Fast: The Religious Significance of Food to Medieval Women.* Berkeley: University of California Press, 1987.

Campbell, Julie DeLynn. "Renaissance Women Writers: The Beloved Speaks her Part." Ph.D diss., Texas A&M University, 1997.

Catling, Jo, ed. *A History of Women's Writing in Germany, Austria and Switzerland.* Cambridge: Cambridge University Press, 2000.

Cavallo, Sandra, and Lyndan Warner. *Widowhood in Medieval and Early Modern Europe.* New York: Longman, 1999.

Cavanagh, Sheila T. *Cherished Torment: The Emotional Geography of Lady Mary Wroth's Urania.* Pittsburgh: Duquesne University Press, 2001.

Cerasano, S. P. and Marion Wynne-Davies, eds. *Readings in Renaissance Women's Drama: Criticism, History, and Performance 1594–1998.* London: Routledge, 1998.

Cervigni, Dino S., ed. *Women Mystic Writers. Annali d'Italianistica* 13 (1995) (entire issue).

——— and Rebecca West, eds. *Women's Voices in Italian Literature. Annali d'Italianistica* 7 (1989) (entire issue).

Charlton, Kenneth. *Women, Religion and Education in Early Modern England.* London: Routledge, 1999.

Chojnacka, Monica. *Working Women in Early Modern Venice.* Baltimore: Johns Hopkins University Press, 2001.

Chojnacki, Stanley. *Women and Men in Renaissance Venice: Twelve Essays on Patrician Society.* Baltimore: Johns Hopkins University Press, 2000.

Cholakian, Patricia Francis. *Rape and Writing in the Heptameron of Marguerite de Navarre.* Carbondale: Southern Illinois University Press, 1991.

———. *Women and the Politics of Self-Representation in Seventeenth-Century France.* Newark: University of Delaware Press, 2000.

Christine de Pizan: A Casebook. Ed. Barbara K. Altmann and Deborah L. McGrady. New York: Routledge, 2003.

Clogan, Paul Maruice, ed. *Medievali et Humanistica: Literacy and the Lay Reader.* Lanham: Rowman & Littlefield, 2000.

Clubb, Louise George (1989). *Italian Drama in Shakespeare's Time.* New Haven: Yale University Press

Clucas, Stephen, ed. *A Princely Brave Woman: Essays on Margaret Cavendish, Duchess of Newcastle.* Aldershot: Ashgate Publishing Co., 2003.

Conley, John J., S.J. *The Suspicion of Virtue: Women Philosophers in Neoclassical France.* Ithaca: Cornell University Press, 2002.

Crabb, Ann. *The Strozzi of Florence: Widowhood and Family Solidarity in the Renaissance.* Ann Arbor: University of Michigan Press, 2000.

The Crannied Wall: Women, Religion, and the Arts in Early Modern Europe. Ed. Craig A. Monson. Ann Arbor: University of Michigan Press, 1992.

Creative Women in Medieval and Early Modern Italy. Ed. E. Ann Matter and John Coakley. Philadelphia: University of Pennsylvania Press, 1994.

Crowston, Clare Haru. *Fabricating Women: The Seamstresses of Old Regime France, 1675–1791.* Durham: Duke University Press, 2001.

Cruz, Anne J. and Mary Elizabeth Perry, eds. Culture and Control in Counter-Reformation Spain. Minneapolis: University of Minnesota Press, 1992.

Datta, Satya. Women and Men in Early Modern Venice. Aldershot: Ashgate Publishing Co., 2003.

Davis, Natalie Zemon. *Society and Culture in Early Modern France.* Stanford: Stanford University Press, 1975.

———. *Women on the Margins: Three Seventeenth-Century Lives.* Cambridge: Harvard University Press, 1995.

DeJean, Joan. *Ancients Against Moderns: Culture Wars and the Making of a Fin de Siècle.* Chicago: University of Chicago Press, 1997.

———. *Fictions of Sappho, 1546–1937.* Chicago: University of Chicago Press, 1989.

———. *The Reinvention of Obscenity: Sex, Lies, and Tabloids in Early Modern France.* Chicago: University of Chicago Press, 2002.

———. *Tender Geographies: Women and the Origins of the Novel in France.* New York: Columbia University Press, 1991.

———. *The Reinvention of Obscenity: Sex, Lies, and Tabloids in Early Modern France.* Chicago: University of Chicago Press, 2002.

D'Elia, Anthony F. *The Renaissance of Marriage in Fifteenth-Century Italy.* Cambridge: Harvard University Press, 2004.

Demers, Patricia. *Women's Writing in English: Early Modern England.* Toronto: University of Toronto Press, 2005.

Dictionary of Russian Women Writers. Ed. Marina Ledkovsky, Charlotte Rosenthal, and Mary Zirin. Westport: Greenwood Press, 1994.

Diefendorf, Barbara. *From Penitence to Charity: Pious Women and the Catholic Reformation in Paris.* New York: Oxford University Press, 2004.

Dixon, Laurinda S. *Perilous Chastity: Women and Illness in Pre-Enlightenment Art and Medicine.* Ithaca: Cornell Universitiy Press, 1995.

Dolan, Frances, E. *Whores of Babylon: Catholicism, Gender and Seventeenth-Century Print Culture.* Ithaca: Cornell University Press, 1999.

Donovan, Josephine. *Women and the Rise of the Novel, 1405–1726.* New York: St. Martin's Press, 1999.

Early [English] Women Writers: 1600–1720. Ed. Anita Pacheco. New York: Longman, 1998.

Eigler, Friederike and Susanne Kord, eds. *The Feminist Encyclopedia of German Literature.* Westport: Greenwood Press, 1997.

Engendering the Early Modern Stage: Women Playwrights in the Spanish Empire. Ed. Valeria (Oakey) Hegstrom and Amy R. Williamsen. New Orleans: University Press of the South, 1999.

Erdmann, Axel. *My Gracious Silence: Women in the Mirror of Sixteenth-Century Printing in Western Europe.* Luzern: Gilhofer and Rauschberg, 1999.

Erickson, Amy Louise. *Women and Property in Early Modern England.* London: Routledge, 1993.

Extraordinary Women of the Medieval and Renaissance World: A Biographical Dictionary. Ed. Carole Levin, et al. Westport: Greenwood Press, 2000.

Ezell, Margaret J. M. *The Patriarch's Wife: Literary Evidence and the History of the Family*. Chapel Hill: University of North Carolina Press, 1987.

——. *Social Authorship and the Advent of Print*. Baltimore: Johns Hopkins University Press, 1999.

——. *Writing Women's Literary History*. Baltimore: Johns Hopkins University Press, 1993.

Farrell, Michèle Longino. *Performing Motherhood: The Sévigné Correspondence*. Hanover: University Press of New England, 1991.

Feminism and Renaissance Studies. Ed. Lorna Hutson. New York: Oxford University Press, 1999.

The Feminist Companion to Literature in English: Women Writers from the Middle Ages to the Present. Ed. Virginia Blain, Isobel Grundy, and Patricia Clements. New Haven: Yale University Press, 1990.

Feminist Encyclopedia of Italian Literature. Edited by Rinaldina Russell. Westport: Greenwood Press, 1997.

Feminist Thought in European History, 1400–2000. Ed. Tjitske Akkerman and Siep Sturman. London: Routledge, 1997.

Ferguson, Margaret W. *Dido's Daughters: Literacy, Gender, and Empire in Early Modern England and France*. Chicago: University of Chicago Press, 2003.

——, Maureen Quilligan, and Nancy J. Vickers, eds. *Rewriting the Renaissance: The Discourses of Sexual Difference in Early Modern Europe*. Chicago: University of Chicago Press, 1987.

Ferraro, Joanne M. *Marriage Wars in Late Renaissance Venice*. Oxford: Oxford University Press, 2001.

Fletcher, Anthony. *Gender, Sex and Subordination in England, 1500–1800*. New Haven: Yale University Press, 1995.

Franklin, Margaret. *Boccaccio's Heroines*. Aldershot: Ashgate Publishing Co., 2006.

French Women Writers: A Bio-Bibliographical Source Book. Ed. Eva Martin Sartori and Dorothy Wynne Zimmerman. Westport: Greenwood Press, 1991.

Frye, Susan and Karen Robertson, eds. Maids and Mistresses, Cousins and Queens: Women's Alliances in Early Modern England. Oxford: Oxford University Press, 1999.

Gallagher, Catherine. *Nobody's Story: The Vanishing Acts of Women Writers in the Marketplace, 1670–1820*. Berkeley: University of California Press, 1994.

Garrard, Mary D. *Artemisia Gentileschi: The Image of the Female Hero in Italian Baroque Art*. Princeton: Princeton University Press, 1989.

Gelbart, Nina Rattner. *The King's Midwife: A History and Mystery of Madame du Coudray*. Berkeley: University of California Press, 1998.

Giles, Mary E., ed. *Women in the Inquisition: Spain and the New World*. Baltimore: Johns Hopkins University Press, 1999.

Gill, Catie. *Women in the Seventeenth-Century Quaker Community*. Aldershot: Ashgate Publishing Co., 2005.

Glenn, Cheryl. *Rhetoric Retold: Regendering the Tradition from Antiquity Through the Renaissance*. Carbondale: Southern Illinois University Press, 1997.

Goffen, Rona. *Titian's Women*. New Haven: Yale University Press, 1997.

Going Public: Women and Publishing in Early Modern France. Ed. Elizabeth C. Goldsmith and Dena Goodman. Ithaca: Cornell University Press, 1995.

Goldberg, Jonathan. *Desiring Women Writing: English Renaissance Examples*. Stanford: Stanford University Press, 1997.

Goldsmith, Elizabeth C. *Exclusive Conversations: The Art of Interaction in Seventeenth-Century France*. Philadelphia: University of Pennsylvania Press, 1988.

———, ed. *Writing the Female Voice*. Boston: Northeastern University Press, 1989.

——— , and Dena Goodman, eds. *Going Public: Women and Publishing in Early Modern France*. Ithaca: Cornell University Press, 1995.

Grafton, Anthony, and Lisa Jardine. *From Humanism to the Humanities: Education and the Liberal Arts in Fifteenth-and Sixteenth-Century Europe*. London: Duckworth, 1986.

The Graph of Sex and the German Text: Gendered Culture in Early Modern Germany 1500–1700. Ed. Lynne Tatlock and Christiane Bohnert. Amsterdam: Rodolphi, 1994.

Grassby, Richard. *Kinship and Capitalism: Marriage, Family, and Business in the English-Speaking World, 1580–1740*. Cambridge: Cambridge University Press, 2001.

Greer, Margaret Rich. *Maria de Zayas Tells Baroque Tales of Love and the Cruelty of Men*. University Park: Pennsylvania State University Press, 2000.

Grossman, Avraham. *Pious and Rebellious: Jewish Women in Medieval Europe*. Trans. Jonathan Chipman. Brandeis/University Press of New England, 2004.

Gutierrez, Nancy A. *"Shall She Famish Then?" Female Food Refusal in Early Modern England*. Aldershot: Ashgate Publishing Co., 2003.

Habermann, Ina. *Staging Slander and Gender in Early Modern England*. Aldershot: Ashgate Publishing Co., 2003.

Hacke, Daniela. *Women Sex and Marriage in Early Modern Venice*. Aldershot: Ashgate Publishing Co., 2004.

Hackel, Heidi Brayman. *Reading Material in Early Modern England: Print, Gender, Literacy*. Cambridge: Cambridge University Press, 2005.

Hackett, Helen. *Women and Romance Fiction in the English Renaissance*. Cambridge: Cambridge University Press, 2000.

Hall, Kim F. *Things of Darkness: Economies of Race and Gender in Early Modern England*. Ithaca: Cornell University Press, 1995.

Hamburger, Jeffrey. *The Visual and the Visionary: Art and Female Spirituality in Late Medieval Germany*. New York: Zone Books, 1998.

Hampton, Timothy. *Literature and the Nation in the Sixteenth Century: Inventing Renaissance France*. Ithaca: Cornell University Press, 2001.

Hannay, Margaret, ed. *Silent But for the Word*. Kent: Kent State University Press, 1985.

Hardwick, Julie. *The Practice of Patriarchy: Gender and the Politics of Household Authority in Early Modern France*. University Park: Pennsylvania State University Press, 1998.

Harris, Barbara J. *English Aristocratic Women, 1450–1550: Marriage and Family, Property and Careers*. New York: Oxford University Press, 2002.

Harth, Erica. Ideology and Culture in Seventeenth-Century France. Ithaca: Cornell University Press, 1983.

———. Cartesian Women. Versions and Subversions of Rational Discourse in the Old Regime. Ithaca: Cornell University Press, 1992.

Harvey, Elizabeth D. Ventriloquized Voices: Feminist Theory and English Renaissance Texts. London: Routledge, 1992.

Haselkorn, Anne M., and Betty Travitsky, eds. *The Renaissance Englishwoman in Print: Counterbalancing the Canon*. Amherst: University of Massachusetts Press, 1990.

Hawkesworth, Celia, ed. *A History of Central European Women's Writing*. New York: Palgrave Press, 2001.

Hegstrom (Oakey), Valerie, and Amy R. Williamsen, eds. *Engendering the Early Modern Stage: Women Playwrights in the Spanish Empire*. New Orleans: University Press of the South, 1999.

Hendricks, Margo and Patricia Parker, eds. *Women, "Race," and Writing in the Early Modern Period*. London and New York: Routledge, 1994.

Herlihy, David. "Did Women Have a Renaissance? A Reconsideration." *Medievalia et Humanistica*, NS 13 (1985): 1–22.

Hill, Bridget. *The Republican Virago: The Life and Times of Catharine Macaulay, Historian*. New York: Oxford University Press, 1992.

Hills, Helen, ed. *Architecture and the Politics of Gender in Early Modern Europe*. Aldershot: Ashgate Publishing Co., 2003.

Hirst, Jilie. *Jane Leade: Biography of a Seventeenth-Century Mystic*. Aldersgate: Ashgate Publishing Co., 2006.

A History of Central European Women's Writing. Ed. Celia Hawkesworth. New York: Palgrave Press, 2001.

A History of Women in the West.

    Volume 1: *From Ancient Goddesses to Christian Saints*. Ed. Pauline Schmitt Pantel. Cambridge: Harvard University Press, 1992.

    Volume 2: *Silences of the Middle Ages*. Ed. Christiane Klapisch-Zuber. Cambridge: Harvard University Press, 1992.

    Volume 3: *Renaissance and Enlightenment Paradoxes*. Ed. Natalie Zemon Davis and Arlette Farge. Cambridge: Harvard University Press, 1993.

A History of Women Philosophers. Ed. Mary Ellen Waithe. 3 vols. Dordrecht: Martinus Nijhoff, 1987.

A History of Women's Writing in France. Ed. Sonya Stephens. Cambridge: Cambridge University Press, 2000.

A History of Women's Writing in Germany, Austria and Switzerland. Ed. Jo Catling. Cambridge: Cambridge University Press, 2000.

A History of Women's Writing in Italy. Ed. Letizia Panizza and Sharon Wood. Cambridge: University Press, 2000.

A History of Women's Writing in Russia. Edited by Alele Marie Barker and Jehanne M. Gheith. Cambridge: Cambridge University Press, 2002.

Hobby, Elaine. *Virtue of Necessity: English Women's Writing 1646–1688*. London: Virago Press, 1988.

Horowitz, Maryanne Cline. "Aristotle and Women." *Journal of the History of Biology* 9 (1976): 183–213.

Howell, Martha C. *The Marriage Exchange: Property, Social Place, and Gender in Cities of the Low Countries, 1300–1550*. Chicago: University of Chicago Press, 1998.

———. *Women, Production and Patriarchy in Late Medieval Cities*. Chicago: University of Chicago Press, 1986.

Hufton, Olwen H. *The Prospect Before Her: A History of Women in Western Europe, 1: 1500–1800*. New York: HarperCollins, 1996.

Hull, Suzanne W. *Chaste, Silent, and Obedient: English Books for Women, 1475–1640*. San Marino: The Huntington Library, 1982.

Hunt, Lynn, ed. *The Invention of Pornography: Obscenity and the Origins of Modernity, 1500–1800*. New York: Zone Books, 1996.

Hutner, Heidi, ed. *Rereading Aphra Behn: History, Theory, and Criticism*. Charlottesville: University Press of Virginia, 1993.

Hutson, Lorna, ed. *Feminism and Renaissance Studies*. New York: Oxford University Press, 1999.

The Invention of Pornography: Obscenity and the Origins of Modernity, 1500–1800. Ed. Lynn Hunt. New York: Zone Books, 1996.

Italian Women Writers: A Bio-Bibliographical Sourcebook. Edited by Rinaldina Russell. Westport: Greenwood Press, 1994.

Jaffe, Irma B. with Gernando Colombardo. *Shining Eyes, Cruel Fortune: The Lives and Loves of Italian Renaissance Women Poets*. New York: Fordham University Press, 2002.

James, Susan E. *Kateryn Parr: The Making of a Queen*. Aldershot: Ashgate Publishing Co., 1999.

Jankowski, Theodora A. *Women in Power in the Early Modern Drama*. Urbana: University of Illinois Press, 1992.

Jansen, Katherine Ludwig. *The Making of the Magdalen: Preaching and Popular Devotion in the Later Middle Ages*. Princeton: Princeton University Press, 2000.

Jed, Stephanie H. *Chaste Thinking: The Rape of Lucretia and the Birth of Humanism*. Bloomington: Indiana University Press, 1989.

Jones, Ann Rosalind and Peter Stallybrass. *Renaissance Clothing and the Materials of Memory*. Cambridge: Cambridge University Press, 2000.

Jordan, Constance. *Renaissance Feminism: Literary Texts and Political Models*. Ithaca: Cornell University Press, 1990.

Kagan, Richard L. *Lucrecia's Dreams: Politics and Prophecy in Sixteenth-Century Spain*. Berkeley: University of California Press, 1990.

Kehler, Dorothea and Laurel Amtower, eds. *The Single Woman in Medieval and Early Modern England: Her Life and Representation*. Tempe: MRTS, 2002.

Kelly, Joan. "Did Women Have a Renaissance?" In her *Women, History, and Theory*. Chicago: University of Chicago Press, 1984. Also in Renate Bridenthal, Claudia Koonz, and Susan M. Stuard, eds., *Becoming Visible: Women in European History*. Third edition. Boston: Houghton Mifflin, 1998.

———. "Early Feminist Theory and the *Querelle des Femmes*." In *Women, History, and Theory*.

Kelso, Ruth. *Doctrine for the Lady of the Renaissance*. Foreword by Katharine M. Rogers. Urbana: University of Illinois Press, 1956, 1978.

Kendrick, Robert L. *Celestical Sirens: Nuns and their Music in Early Modern Milan*. New York: Oxford University Press, 1996.

Kermode, Jenny and Garthine Walker, eds. *Women, Crime and the Courts in Early Modern England*. Chapel Hill: University of North Carolina Press, 1994.

King, Catherine E. *Renaissance Women Patrons: Wives and Widows in Italy, c. 1300–1550*. New York: Manchester University Press (distributed in the U.S. by St. Martin's Press), 1998.

King, Margaret L. *Women of the Renaissance*. Foreword by Catharine R. Stimpson. Chicago: University of Chicago Press, 1991.

King, Thomas A. *The Gendering of Men, 1600–1700: The English Phallus*. Vol. 1. Madison: University of Wisconsin Press, 2004.

Krontiris, Tina. *Oppositional Voices: Women as Writers and Translators of Literature in the English Renaissance*. London: Routledge, 1992.

Kuehn, Thomas. *Law, Family, and Women: Toward a Legal Anthropology of Renaissance Italy.* Chicago: University of Chicago Press, 1991.

Kunze, Bonnelyn Young. *Margaret Fell and the Rise of Quakerism.* Stanford: Stanford University Press, 1994.

Labalme, Patricia A., ed. *Beyond Their Sex: Learned Women of the European Past.* New York: New York University Press, 1980.

Lalande, Roxanne Decker, ed. *A Labor of Love: Critical Reflections on the Writings of Marie-Catherine Desjardina (Mme de Villedieu).* Madison: Fairleigh Dickinson University Press, 2000.

Lamb, Mary Ellen. *Gender and Authorship in the Sidney Circle.* Madison: University of Wisconsin Press, 1990.

Laqueur, Thomas. *Making Sex: Body and Gender from the Greeks to Freud.* Cambridge: Harvard University Press, 1990.

Larsen, Anne R. and Colette H. Winn, eds. *Renaissance Women Writers: French Texts/ American Contexts.* Detroit: Wayne State University Press, 1994.

Laven, Mary. *Virgins of Venice: Enclosed Lives and Broken Vows in the Renaissance Convent.* London: Viking, 2002.

Ledkovsky, Marina, Charlotte Rosenthal, and Mary Zirin, eds. *Dictionary of Russian Women Writers.* Westport: Greenwood Press, 1994.

Lehfeldt, Elizabeth A. *Religious Women in Golden Age Spain: The Permeable Cloister.* Aldershot: Ashgate Publishing Co., 2005.

Lerner, Gerda. *The Creation of Patriarchy* and *Creation of Feminist Consciousness, 1000–1870.* 2-vol. history of women. New York: Oxford University Press, 1986, 1994.

Levack. Brian P. *The Witch Hunt in Early Modern Europe.* London: Longman, 1987.

Levin, Carole and Jeanie Watson, eds. *Ambiguous Realities: Women in the Middle Ages and Renaissance.* Detroit: Wayne State University Press, 1987.

Levin, Carole, Jo Eldridge Carney, and Debra Barrett-Graves. *Elizabeth I: Always Her Own Free Woman.* Aldershot: Ashgate Publishing Co., 2003.

Levin, Carole, et al. *Extraordinary Women of the Medieval and Renaissance World: A Biographical Dictionary.* Westport: Greenwood Press, 2000.

Levy, Allison, ed. *Widowhood and Visual Culture in Early Modern Europe.* Aldershot: Ashgate Publishing Co., 2003.

Lewalsky, Barbara Kiefer. *Writing Women in Jacobean England.* Cambridge: Harvard University Press, 1993.

Lewis, Gertrud Jaron. *By Women for Women about Women: The Sister-Books of Fourteenth-Century Germany.* Toronto: University of Toronto Press, 1996.

Lewis, Jayne Elizabeth. *Mary Queen of Scots: Romance and Nation.* London: Routledge, 1998.

Lindenauer, Leslie J. *Piety and Power: Gender and Religious Culture in the American Colonies, 1630–1700.* London: Routledge, 2002.

Lindsey, Karen. *Divorced Beheaded Survived: A Feminist Reinterpretation of the Wives of Henry VIII.* Reading: Addison-Wesley Publishing Co., 1995.

Lochrie, Karma. *Margery Kempe and Translations of the Flesh.* Philadelphia: University of Pennsylvania Press, 1992.

Longino Farrell, Michèle. *Performing Motherhood: The Sévigné Correspondence.* Hanover: University Press of New England, 1991.

Lougee, Carolyn C. *Le Paradis des Femmes: Women, Salons, and Social Stratification in Seventeenth-Century France.* Princeton: Princeton University Press, 1976.

Love, Harold. *The Culture and Commerce of Texts: Scribal Publication in Seventeenth-Century England*. Amherst: University of Massachusetts Press, 1993.

Lowe, K. J. P. *Nuns' Chronicles and Convent Culture in Renaissance and Counter-Reformation Italy*. Cambridge: Cambridge University Press, 2003.

Lux-Sterritt, Laurence. *Redefining Female Religious Life: French Ursulines and English Ladies in Seventeenth-Century Catholicism*. Aldershot: Ashgate Publishing Co., 2005.

MacCarthy, Bridget G. *The Female Pen: Women Writers and Novelists 1621–1818*. Preface by Janet Todd. New York: New York University Press, 1994. (Originally published by Cork University Press, 1946–47).

Mack, Phyllis. *Visionary Women: Ecstatic Prophecy in Seventeenth-Century England*. Berkeley: University of California Pres, 1992.

Maclean, Ian. *Woman Triumphant: Feminism in French Literature, 1610–1652*. Oxford: Clarendon Press, 1977.

———. *The Renaissance Notion of Woman: A Study of the Fortunes of Scholasticism and Medical Science in European Intellectual Life*. Cambridge: Cambridge University Press, 1980.

MacNeil, Anne. *Music and Women of the Commedia dell'Arte in the Late Sixteenth Century*. New York: Oxford University Press, 2003.

Maggi, Armando. *Uttering the Word: The Mystical Performances of Maria Maddalena de' Pazzi, a Renaissance Visionary*. Albany: State University of New York Press, 1998.

Maids and Mistresses, Cousins and Queens: Women's Alliances in Early Modern England. Ed. Susan Frye and Karen Robertson. Oxford: Oxford University Press, 1999.

Marshall, Sherrin, ed. *Women in Reformation and Counter-Reformation Europe: Public and Private Worlds*. Bloomington: Indiana University Press, 1989.

Masten, Jeffrey. *Textual Intercourse: Collaboration, Authorship, and Sexualities in Renaissance Drama*. Cambridge: Cambridge University Press, 1997.

Matter, E. Ann, and John Coakley, eds. *Creative Women in Medieval and Early Modern Italy*. Philadelphia: University of Pennsylvania Press, 1994. (sequel to the Monson collection, below)

McGrath, Lynette. *Subjectivity and Women's Poetry in Early Modern England*. Aldershot: Ashgate Publishing Co., 2002.

McIver, Katherine A. *Women, Art, and Architecture in Northern Italy, 1520–1580*. Aldershot: Ashgate Publishing Co., 2006.

McLeod, Glenda. *Virtue and Venom: Catalogs of Women from Antiquity to the Renaissance*. Ann Arbor: University of Michigan Press, 1991.

McTavish, Lianne. *Childbirth and the Display of Authority in Early Modern France*. Aldershot: Ashgate Publishing Co., 2005.

Medieval Women's Visionary Literature. Ed. Elizabeth A. Petroff. New York: Oxford University Press, 1986.

Medwick, Cathleen. *Teresa of Avila: The Progress of a Soul*. New York: Doubleday, 1999.

Meek, Christine, ed. *Women in Renaissance and Early Modern Europe*. Dublin: Four Courts Press, 2000.

Mendelson, Sara and Patricia Crawford. *Women in Early Modern England, 1550–1720*. Oxford: Clarendon Press, 1998.

Merchant, Carolyn. *The Death of Nature: Women, Ecology and the Scientific Revolution*. New York: HarperCollins, 1980.

Merrim, Stephanie. *Early Modern Women's Writing and Sor Juana Inés de la Cruz*. Nashville: Vanderbilt University Press, 1999.

Messbarger, Rebecca. *The Century of Women: The Representations of Women in Eighteenth-Century Italian Public Discourse*. Toronto: University of Toronto Press, 2002.

Miller, Nancy K. *The Heroine's Text: Readings in the French and English Novel, 1722–1782*. New York: Columbia University Press, 1980.

Miller, Naomi J. *Changing the Subject: Mary Wroth and Figurations of Gender in Early Modern England*. Lexington: University Press of Kentucky, 1996.

——— and Gary Waller, eds. *Reading Mary Wroth: Representing Alternatives in Early Modern England*. Knoxville: University of Tennessee Press, 1991.

Monson, Craig A. *Disembodied Voices: Music and Culture in an Early Modern Italian Convent*. Berkeley: University of California Press, 1995.

———., ed. *The Crannied Wall: Women, Religion, and the Arts in Early Modern Europe*. Ann Arbor: University of Michigan Press, 1992.

Moore, Cornelia Niekus. *The Maiden's Mirror: Reading Material for German Girls in the Sixteenth and Seventeenth Centuries*. Wiesbaden: Otto Harrassowitz, 1987.

Moore, Mary B. *Desiring Voices: Women Sonneteers and Petrarchism*. Carbondale: Southern Illinois University Press, 2000.

Mujica, Bárbara. *Women Writers of Early Modern Spain*. New Haven: Yale University Press, 2004.

Musacchio, Jacqueline Marie. *The Art and Ritual of Childbirth in Renaissance Italy*. New Haven: Yale University Press, 1999.

Nevitt, Marcus. *Women and the Pamphlet Culture of Revolutionary England, 1640–1660*. Women and Gender in the Early Modern World. Aldershot: Ashgate Publishing Co., 2006.

Newman, Barbara. *God and the Goddesses: Vision, Poetry, and Belief in the Middle Ages*. Philadelphia: University of Pennsylvania Press, 2003.

Newman, Karen. *Fashioning Femininity and English Renaissance Drama*. Chicago: University of Chicago Press, 1991.

O'Donnell, Mary Ann. *Aphra Behn: An Annotated Bibliography of Primary and Secondary Sources*. Aldershot: Ashgate Publishing Co., 2nd ed., 2004.

Okin, Susan Moller. *Women in Western Political Thought*. Princeton: Princeton University Press, 1979.

Ozment, Steven. *The Bürgermeister's Daughter: Scandal in a Sixteenth-Century German Town*. New York: St. Martin's Press, 1995.

———. *Flesh and Spirit: Private Life in Early Modern Germany*. New York: Penguin Putnam, 1999.

———. *When Fathers Ruled: Family Life in Reformation Europe*. Cambridge: Harvard University Press, 1983.

Pacheco, Anita, ed. *Early [English] Women Writers: 1600–1720*. New York: Longman, 1998.

Pagels, Elaine. *Adam, Eve, and the Serpent*. New York: Harper Collins, 1988.

Panizza, Letizia and Sharon Wood, eds. *A History of Women's Writing in Italy*. Cambridge: University Press, 2000.

Panizza, Letizia, ed. *Women in Italian Renaissance Culture and Society*. Oxford: European Humanities Research Centre, 2000.

Parker, Patricia. *Literary Fat Ladies: Rhetoric, Gender and Property*. London: Methuen, 1987.

Pernoud, Regine and Marie-Veronique Clin. *Joan of Arc: Her Story*. Rev. and trans. Jeremy DuQuesnay Adams. New York: St. Martin's Press, 1998 (French original, 1986).

Perry, Mary Elizabeth. *Crime and Society in Early Modern Seville*. Hanover: University Press of New England, 1980.

———. *Gender and Disorder in Early Modern Seville*. Princeton: Princeton University Press, 1990.

———. *The Handless Maiden: Moriscos and the Politics of Religion in Early Modern Spain*. Princeton: Princeton University Press, 2005.

Petroff, Elizabeth A., ed. *Medieval Women's Visionary Literature*. New York: Oxford University Press, 1986.

Perry, Ruth. *The Celebrated Mary Astell: An Early English Feminist*. Chicago: University of Chicago Press, 1986.

The Practice and Representation of Reading in England. Ed. James Raven, Helen Small, and Naomi Tadmor. Cambridge: University Press, 1996.

Quilligan, Maureen. *The Allegory of Female Authoreity: Christine de Pizan's "Cité des Dames"*. Ithaca: Cornell University Press, 1991.

———. *Incest and Agency in Elizabeth's England*. Philadelphia: University of Pennsylvania Press, 2005.

Rabil, Albert. *Laura Cereta: Quattrocento Humanist*. Binghamton: MRTS, 1981.

Ranft, Patricia. *Women in Western Intellectual Culture, 600–1500*. New York: Palgrave, 2002.

Rapley, Elizabeth. *A Social History of the Cloister: Daily Life in the Teaching Monasteries of the Old Regime*. Montreal: McGill-Queen's University Press, 2001.

———. *The Devotés: Women and Church in Seventeenth-Century France*. Kingston: McGill-Queen's University Press, 1989.

Raven, James, Helen Small and Naomi Tadmor, eds. *The Practice and Representation of Reading in England*. Cambridge: University Press, 1996.

Reading Mary Wroth: Representing Alternatives in Early Modern England. Ed. Naomi Miller and Gary Waller. Knoxville: University of Tennessee Press, 1991.

Reardon, Colleen. *Holy Concord within Sacred Walls: Nuns and Music in Siena, 1575–1700*. Oxford: Oxford University Press, 2001.

Recovering Spain's Feminist Tradition. Ed. Lisa Vollendorf. New York: MLA, 2001.

Reid, Jonathan Andrew. "King's Sister—Queen of Dissent: Marguerite of Navarre (1492–1549) and Her Evangelical Network." Ph.D. diss., University of Arizona, 2001.

Reiss, Sheryl E. and David G. Wilkins, eds. *Beyond Isabella: Secular Women Patrons of Art in Renaissance Italy*. Kirksville: Turman State University Press, 2001.

The Renaissance Englishwoman in Print: Counterbalancing the Canon. Ed. Anne M. Haselkorn and Betty Travitsky. Amherst: University of Massachusetts Press, 1990.

Renaissance Women Writers: French Texts/American Contexts. Ed. Anne R. Larsen and Colette H. Winn. Detroit: Wayne State University Press, 1994.

Rereading Aphra Behn: History, Theory, and Criticism. Ed. Heidi Hutner. Charlottesville: University Press of Virginia, 1993.

Rheubottom, David. *Age, Marriage, and Politics in Fifteenth-Century Ragusa*. Oxford: Oxford University Press, 2000.

Richardson, Brian. *Printing, Writers and Readers in Renaissance Italy*. Cambridge: University Press, 1999.

Riddle, John M. *Contraception and Abortion from the Ancient World to the Renaissance.* Cambridge: Harvard University Press, 1992.

———. *Eve's Herbs: A History of Contraception and Abortion in the West.* Cambridge: Harvard University Press, 1997.

Roper, Lyndal. *The Holy Household: Women and Morals in Reformation Augsburg.* New York: Oxford University Press, 1989.

Rose, Mary Beth. *The Expense of Spirit: Love and Sexuality in English Renaissance Drama.* Ithaca: Cornell University Press, 1988.

———. *Gender and Heroism in Early Modern English Literature.* Chicago: University of Chicago Press, 2002.

———, ed. *Women in the Middle Ages and the Renaissance: Literary and Historical Perspectives.* Syracuse: Syracuse University Press, 1986.

Rosenthal, Margaret F. *The Honest Courtesan: Veronica Franco, Citizen and Writer in Sixteenth-Century Venice.* Foreword by Catharine R. Stimpson. Chicago: University of Chicago Press, 1992.

Rublack, Ulinka, ed. *Gender in Early Modern German History.* Cambridge: Cambridge University Press, 2002.

Russell, Rinaldina, ed. *Feminist Encyclopedia of Italian Literature.* Westport: Greenwood Press, 1997.

———. *Italian Women Writers: A Bio-Bibliographical Sourcebook.* Westport: Greenwood Press, 1994.

Sackville-West, Vita. *Daughter of France: The Life of La Grande Mademoiselle.* Garden City: Doubleday, 1959.

Sage, Lorna, ed. *Cambridge Guide to Women's Writing in English.* Cambridge: University Press, 1999.

Sánchez, Magdalena S. *The Empress, the Queen, and the Nun: Women and Power at the Court of Philip III of Spain.* Baltimore: Johns Hopkins University Press, 1998.

Sartori, Eva Martin and Dorothy Wynne Zimmerman, eds. *French Women Writers: A Bio-Bibliographical Source Book.* Westport: Greenwood Press, 1991.

Scaraffia, Lucetta and Gabriella Zarri. *Women and Faith: Catholic Religious Life in Italy from Late Antiquity to the Present.* Cambridge: Harvard University Press, 1999.

Scheepsma, Wybren. *Medieval Religious Women in the Low Countries: The 'Modern Devotion', the Canonesses of Windesheim, and Their Writings.* Rochester: Boydell Press, 2004.

Schiebinger, Londa. *The Mind Has No Sex?: Women in the Origins of Modern Science.* Cambridge: Harvard University Press, 1991.

———. *Nature's Body: Gender in the Making of Modern Science.* Boston: Beacon Press, 1993.

Schutte, Anne Jacobson, Thomas Kuehn, and Silvana Seidel Menchi, eds. *Time, Space, and Women's Lives in Early Modern Europe.* Kirksville: Truman State University Press, 2001.

Schofield, Mary Anne and Cecilia Macheski, eds. *Fetter'd or Free? British Women Novelists, 1670–1815.* Athens: Ohio University Press, 1986.

Schutte, Anne Jacobson. *Aspiring Saints: pretense of Holiness, Inquisition, and Gender in the Republic of Venice, 1618–1750.* Baltimore: Johns Hopkins University Press, 2001.

———, Thomas Kuehn, and Silvana Seidel Menchi, eds. *Time, Space, and Women's Lives in Early Modern Europe.* Kirksville: Truman State University Press, 2001.

Seelig, Sharon Cadman. *Autobiography and Gender in Early Modern Literature: Reading Women's Lives, 1600–1680.* Cambridge: Cambridge University Press, 2006.

Seifert, Lewis C. *Fairy Tales, Sexuality and Gender in France 1690–1715: Nostalgic Utopias*. Cambridge: Cambridge University Press, 1996.

Shannon, Laurie. *Sovereign Amity: Figures of Friendship in Shakespearean Contexts*. Chicago: University of Chicago Press, 2002.

Shemek, Deanna. *Ladies Errant: Wayward Women and Social Order in Early Modern Italy*. Durham: Duke University Press, 1998.

Sibling Relations and Gender in the Early Modern World: Sisters, Brothers and Others. Ed. Naomi Miller and Naomi Yavneh. Women and Gender in the Early Modern World. Aldershot: Ashgate Publishing Co., 2006.

Silent But for the Word. Ed. Margaret Hannay. Kent: Kent State University Press, 1985.

The Single Woman in Medieval and Early Modern England: Her Life and Representation. Ed. Dorothea Kehler and Laurel Amtower. Tempe: MRTS, 2002.

Smarr, Janet L. *Joining the Conversation: Dialogues by Renaissance Women*. Ann Arbor: University of Michigan Press, 2005.

Smith, Hilda L. *Reason's Disciples: Seventeenth-Century English Feminists*. Urbana: University of Illinois Press, 1982.

———. *Women Writers and the Early Modern British Political Tradition*. Cambridge: Cambridge University Press, 1998.

Snook, Edith. *Women, Reading, and the Cultural Politics of Early Modern England*. Aldershot: Ashgate Publishing Co., 2005.

Sobel, Dava. *Galileo's Daughter: A Historical Memoir of Science, Faith, and Love*. New York: Penguin Books, 2000.

Sommerville, Margaret R. *Sex and Subjection: Attitudes to Women in Early-Modern Society*. London: Arnold, 1995.

Soufas, Teresa Scott. *Dramas of Distinction: A Study of Plays by Golden Age Women*. Lexington: The University Press of Kentucky, 1997.

Spencer, Jane. *The Rise of the Woman Novelist: From Aphra Behn to Jane Austen*. Oxford: Basil Blackwell, 1986.

Spender, Dale. *Mothers of the Novel: 100 Good Women Writers Before Jane Austen*. London: Routledge, 1986.

Sperling, Jutta Gisela. *Convents and the Body Politic in Late Renaissance Venice*. Foreword by Catharine R. Stimpson. Chicago: University of Chicago Press, 1999.

Steinbrügge, Lieselotte. *The Moral Sex: Woman's Nature in the French Enlightenment*. Trans. Pamela E. Selwyn. New York: Oxford University Press, 1995.

Stephens, Sonya, ed. *A History of Women's Writing in France*. Cambridge: Cambridge University Press, 2000.

Stephenson, Barbara. *The Power and Patronage of Marguerite de Navarre*. Aldershot: Ashgate Publishing Co., 2004.

Stocker, Margarita. *Judith, Sexual Warrior: Women and Power in Western Culture*. New Haven: Yale University Press, 1998.

Straznacky, Marta. *Privacy, Playreading, and Women's Closet Drama, 1550–1700*. Cambridge: Cambridge University Press, 2004.

Stretton, Timothy. *Women Waging Law in Elizabethan England*. Cambridge: Cambridge University Press, 1998.

Strong Voices, Weak History: Early Women Writers and Canons in England, France, and Italy. Ed. Pamela J. Benson and Victoria Kirkham. Ann Arbor: University of Michigan Press, 2005.

Stuard, Susan M. "The Dominion of Gender: Women's Fortunes in the High Middle Ages." In Renate Bridenthal, Claudia Koonz, and Susan M. Stuard, eds. *Becoming Visible: Women in European History.* Third edition. Boston: Houghton Mifflin, 1998.

Summit, Jennifer. *Lost Property: The Woman Writer and English Literary History, 1380–1589.* Chicago: University of Chicago Press, 2000.

Surtz, Ronald E. *The Guitar of God: Gender, Power, and Authority in the Visionary World of Mother Juana de la Cruz (1481–1534).* Philadelphia: University of Pennsylvania Press, 1991.

———. *Writing Women in Late Medieval and Early Modern Spain: The Mothers of Saint Teresa of Avila.* Philadelphia: University of Pennsylvania Press, 1995.

Suzuki, Mihoko. *Subordinate Subjects: Gender, the Political Nation, and Literary Form in England, 1588–1688.* Aldershot: Ashgate Publishing Co., 2003.

Tatlock, Lynne and Christiane Bohnert, eds. *The Graph of Sex* (q.v.).

Teaching Tudor and Stuart Women Writers. Ed. Susanne Woods and Margaret P. Hannay. New York: MLA, 2000.

Teague, Frances. *Bathsua Makin, Woman of Learning.* Lewisburg: Bucknell University Press, 1999.

Thomas, Anabel. *Art and Piety in the Female Religious Communities of Renaissance Italy: Iconography, Space, and the Religious Woman's Perspective.* New York: Cambridge University Press, 2003.

Tinagli, Paola. *Women in Italian Renaissance Art: Gender, Representation, Identity.* Manchester: Manchester University Press, 1997.

Todd, Janet. *The Secret Life of Aphra Behn.* London: Pandora, 2000.

———. *The Sign of Angelica: Women, Writing and Fiction, 1660–1800.* New York: Columbia University Press, 1989.

Tomas, Natalie R. *The Medici Women: Gender and Power in Renaissance Florence.* Aldershot: Ashgate Publishing Co., 2004.

Traub, Valerie. *The Renaissance of Lesbianism in Early Modern England.* Cambridge: Cambridge University Press, 2002.

Valenze, Deborah. *The First Industrial Woman.* New York: Oxford University Press, 1995.

Van Dijk, Susan, Lia van Gemert, and Sheila Ottway, eds. *Writing the History of Women's Writing: Toward an International Approach.* Proceedings of the Colloquium, Amsterdam, 9–11 September. Amsterdam: Royal Netherlands Academy of Arts and Sciences, 2001.

Vickery, Amanda. *The Gentleman's Daughter: Women's Lives in Georgian England.* New Haven: Yale University Press, 1998.

Vollendorf, Lisa. *The Lives of Women: A New History of Inquisitional Spain.* Nashville: Vanderbilt University Press, 2005.

Walker, Claire. *Gender and Politics in Early Modern Europe: English Convents in France and the Low Countries.* New York: Palgrave, 2003.

Wall, Wendy. *The Imprint of Gender: Authorship and Publication in the English Renaissance.* Ithaca: Cornell University Press, 1993.

Walsh, William T. *St. Teresa of Avila: A Biography.* Rockford: TAN Books and Publications, 1987.

Warner, Marina. *Alone of All Her Sex: The Myth and Cult of the Virgin Mary.* New York: Knopf, 1976.

Warnicke, Retha M. *The Marrying of Anne of Cleves: Royal Protocol in Tudor England*. Cambridge: Cambridge University Press, 2000.

Watt, Diane. *Secretaries of God: Women Prophets in Late Medieval and Early Modern England*. Cambridge, England: D. S. Brewer, 1997.

Weaver, Elissa B. *Convent Theatre in Early Modern Italy: Spiritual Fun and Learning for Women*. New York: Cambridge University Press, 2002.

———, ed. *Arcangela Tarabotti: A Literary Nun in Baroque Venice*. Ravenna: Longo Editore, 2006.

Weber, Alison. Teresa of Avila and the Rhetoric of Femininity. Princeton: Princeton University Press, 1990.

Welles, Marcia L. *Persephone's Girdle: Narratives of Rape in Seventeenth-Century Spanish Literature*. Nashville: Vanderbilt University Press, 2000.

Whitehead, Barbara J., ed. *Women's Education in Early Modern Europe: A History, 1500–1800*. New York: Garland Publishing Co., 1999.

Widowhood and Visual Culture in Early Modern Europe. Ed. Allison Levy. Aldershot: Ashgate Publishing Co., 2003.

Widowhood in Medieval and Early Modern Europe. Ed. Sandra Cavallo and Lydan Warner. New York: Longman, 1999.

Wiesner, Merry E. *Working Women in Renaissance Germany*. New Brunswick: Rutgers University Press, 1986.

Wiesner-Hanks, Merry E. *Christianity and Sexuality in the Early Modern World: Regulating Desire, Reforming Practice*. New York: Routledge, 2000.

———. *Gender, Church, and State in Early Modern Germany: Essays*. New York: Longman, 1998.

———. *Gender in History*. Malden: Blackwell, 2001.

———. *Women and Gender in Early Modern Europe*. Cambridge: Cambridge University Press, 1993.

———. *Working Women in Renaissance Germany*. New Brunswick: Rutgers University Press, 1986.

Willard, Charity Cannon. *Christine de Pizan: Her Life and Works*. New York: Persea Books, 1984.

Wilson, Katharina, ed. *Encyclopedia of Continental Women Writers*. 2 vols. New York: Garland, 1991.

Winn, Colette and Donna Kuizenga, eds. *Women Writers in Pre-Revolutionary France*. New York: Garland Publishing, 1997.

Winston-Allen, Anne. *Convent Chronicles: Women Writing about Women and Reform in the Late Middle Ages*. University Park: Pennsylvania State University Press, 2004.

Women and Monasticism in Medieval Europe: Sisters and Patrons of the Cistercian Reform, ed. Constance H. Berman. Kalamazoo: Western Michigan University Press, 2002.

Women, Crime and the Courts in Early Modern England. Ed. Jenny Kermode and Garthine Walker. Chapel Hill: University of North Carolina Press, 1994.

Women in Italian Renaissance Culture and Society. Ed. Letizia Panizza. Oxford: European Humanities Research Centre, 2000.

Women in Reformation and Counter-Reformation Europe: Public and Private Worlds. Ed. Sherrin Marshall. Bloomington: Indiana University Press, 1989.

Women in Renaissance and Early Modern Europe. Ed. Christine Meek. Dublin-Portland: Four Courts Press, 2000.

Women in the Inquisition: Spain and the New World. Ed. Mary E. Giles. Baltimore: Johns Hopkins University Press, 1999.

Women in the Middle Ages and the Renaissance: Literary and Historical Perspectives. Ed. Mary Beth Rose. Syracuse: Syracuse University Press, 1986.

Women Players in England, 1500–1660: Beyond the All-Male Stage. Ed. Pamela Allen Brown and Peter Parolin. Aldershot: Ashgate Publishing Co., 2005.

Women, "Race," and Writing in the Early Modern Period. Ed. Margo Hendricks and Patricia Parker. London: Routledge, 1994.

Women's Letters Across Europe, 1400–1700: Form and Persuasion. Ed. Jane Couchman and Ann Crabb. Women and Gender in the Early Modern World. Aldershot: Ashgate Publishing Co., 2005.

Woodbridge, Linda. *Women and the English Renaissance: Literature and the Nature of Womankind, 1540–1620.* Urbana: University of Illinois Press, 1984.

Woodford, Charlotte. *Nuns as Historians in Early Modern Germany.* Oxford: Clarendon Press, 2002.

Woods, Susanne. *Lanyer: A Renaissance Woman Poet.* New York: Oxford University Press, 1999.

——— and Margaret P. Hannay, eds. *Teaching Tudor and Stuart Women Writers.* New York: MLA, 2000.

Writing the Female Voice. Ed. Elizabeth C. Goldsmith. Boston: Northeastern University Press, 1989.

Writing the History of Women's Writing: Toward an International Approach. Ed. Susan Van Dijk, Lia van Gemert, and Sheila Ottway Proceedings of the Colloquium, Amsterdam, 9–11 September. Amsterdam: Royal Netherlands Academy of Arts and Sciences, 2001.

INDEX